SPLIT SCREEN

Home Entertainment and the New Technologies

by DAVID ELLIS

In Collaboration with Julia Johnston

Prepared for the Friends of Canadian Broadcasting

Canadian Cataloguing in Publication Data

Ellis, David, 1945-
Split Screen: home entertainment and the new technologies

Includes bibliographical references and index.
ISBN 0-9695660-1-8

1. Television — Technological innovations.
2. Television — Canada.
3. Television broadcasting — Social aspects — Canada.
4. Digital communications.

I. Johnston, Julia.
II. Friends of Canadian Broadcasting.
III. Title.

TK6643.E44 1992 621.388 C92-095722-6

Friends of Canadian Broadcasting
29 Prince Arthur Avenue
Toronto, Ontario M5R 1B2
Telephone: (416) 964-0559
Fax: (416) 964-9226

Friends of Canadian Broadcasting is a voluntary organization of 33,000 concerned Canadians who share a commitment to expanding the quality and quantity of Canadian programming on our nation's airwaves.

Friends relies entirely upon donations from its supporters to finance its public policy initiatives, public opinion leadership and research activities.

Foreword by the Friends of Canadian Broadcasting ix

Preface xiii

Chapter 1

INTRODUCTION: EYE ON THE SPLIT SCREEN 1

Audiences: a watching brief 5

Active and passive viewing 9

Predicting levels of viewer activity 10

Viewer benefits 11

Choice 12

Control 14

Quality 14

Interactivity 17

The changing face of TV entertainment 18

New suppliers 18

User-pays 21

Standards 21

Technology & the viewer 22

Visible vs invisible technologies 24

Broadcasting & national sovereignty 27

Chapter 2

BACK TO THE FUTURE 31

Established technologies 1 & 2: Cable TV & communications satellites 32

In the beginning 34

Established technology 3: the VCR 37

A little history 38

Format wars 39

Making friends with your VCR 41

Contents

What do viewers want? 45

Established technology 4: the remote control 48

Videoway: the next stage 51

Chapter 3

FROM BOOB TUBE TO SMART-TV: THE DIGITAL REVOLUTION HITS BROADCASTING 55

A message in search of a storage medium 57

The CD arrives 59

Interacting with a disc: the CD grows up 62

Digital broadcasting 66

Who benefits? 68

HDTV 69

Background 71

The standards mess 72

The costs to consumers 73

Delivery channels 74

Broadcasters: little to gain, lots to lose 75

Smart-TV 77

Chapter 4

TV & THE MOVIES: HOLLYWOOD HEADS FOR THE LIVING ROOM 83

A marriage made in heaven? 83

The 1975 watershed 85

Video comes home to roost — and stays 87

Windows & bucks 90

Hollywood commits, Canada committees 92

Bad news, good news 93

The Canadian film industry: not a pretty picture 95

Integrated we conquer 96

Invidious comparisons 98
Bucking trends 103
The rise of the living room 106
The home theatre 107
Technology & the in-home "cascade" 110
Pay-per-view: the next bonanza? 112
Market base & economics 114
Viewer's Choice Canada (VCC) 117
Curtains for theatres? 119

Chapter 5

CANADIAN PRODUCERS, CANADIAN CONTENT 125
The growth of independent production 127
International co-production 128
Content rules & the "Top Cops" syndrome 132
Market fragmentation & niche audiences 137
New services: good news for producers? 140
The supply-side view of Canadian content 142

Chapter 6

TECHNOLOGY: THE ULTIMATE DEREGULATOR? 147
Rationales for the established regulatory framework 149
Spectrum scarcity 149
Intrusiveness & potential for harm 150
Intangible cultural benefits 151
Advertiser sovereignty 153
Merit goods 154
New technologies, new rules 155
Who's afraid of Deathstars? 160
What's wrong with this picture? 163

Legal battle lines drawn 164
Regulation & the quid pro quo 171
Broadcasters & Cancon 172
Consumer protection & cable rates 177
The myth of the basic tier 179
S.12: regulating cable American style 183
Regulation vs competition 187

Chapter 7
CAUTION — MERGING TRAFFIC 189
Broadcasting vs telecommunications 191
The regulator's dilemma 194
Dealing with competition after Unitel 199
From TV viewer to information consumer: the "protection" issues 202
The media multinationals & corporate convergence 206
The Time Warner colossus 207
TV's new global village 210

Appendix: Some Broadcasting Basics 215
Broadcasting as an analog technology 216
The screen display 218
Spectrum & bandwidth 223

Bells, Whistles & Black Boxes 227
A GLOSSARY FOR THE MODERN VIEWER

Bibliography 251

Endnotes 257

SPLIT|SCREEN
VOLUME

Foreword

Split Screen *describes the end of television broadcasting as we have come to know it. It is being published at a time of strong concern for Canada's cultural survival, and also at a time of great frustration with the mystification of technology.*

Friends of Canadian Broadcasting has sponsored Split Screen *to enhance public understanding of the future of television, and to promote public scrutiny of the behaviour and decisions of major players in this field — such as the cable monopolies. Through* Split Screen, *Friends also intends to assemble and make accessible a wide variety of information, to stimulate debate, and to raise the visibility of issues which arise from the text — among them:*

→ *Information is becoming a strategic national resource, and therefore has cultural implications.*

→ *News, current affairs, entertainment and enlightenment are elements in a no longer free flow of information within Canada and the world.*

→ *Information marketing is concerned with market shares in a global information market — and promotion of choice between sources of information is a part of information marketing strategies.*

→ *The American film industry is a policy actor in all countries, seeking a dominant market share. Nowhere has it achieved more success than in Canada.*

Friends foresees consequences for public policy in Canada:

→ *Regulation has worked well for business — it's time to make it work for the public, and for content providers.*

→ *Because of the trend to transactions across national frontiers, Canadian cultural policies for the mass media must be matched by Canadian consumer protection policies.*

→ *'Policy' is more than 'regulation' — and will require coordination among more than one government agency, and between federal and provincial governments. Protecting the interests of Canadian information consumers involves not just the Department of Communications, but also External Affairs, the Treasury Board, Finance, Consumer Affairs, Justice, and Industry Science and Technology (for FTA and GATT matters), as well as a number of provincial ministries.*

→ *Because of the transactional nature of information creation and exchange, policies in the Canadian public interest will increasingly involve economic motivations and sanctions not just through chosen instruments of communication, but across a full range of public and private institutions which form the Canadian broadcasting* system *— as well as Canadian cultural and electronic industries.*

→ *Despite the end of spectrum scarcity, the public interest will increasingly require that government manage access to electronic networks of all kinds, whether based on established or emerging technologies.*

→ *Because of the prominence of feature motion pictures in information creation and marketing, and the links with American policy, national film policies assume new and added importance. Canadian weakness in this area is a weakness not just in cultural policy, but also in broadcasting and industrial policy.*

The author of Split Screen *is David Ellis, a communications consultant who spends much of his time writing about the state of television in Canada. Specializing in audience research and regulatory affairs, he acts as Director of Research for the Friends of Canadian Broadcasting. In 1990, Friends commissioned him to write* Networking: How Are Canada's English TV Networks Performing? Split Screen, *Friends' second major research study, expands upon a number of themes introduced in* Networking.

David Ellis is also author of Evolution of the Canadian Broadcasting System, *a historical monograph used widely in college courses, and the article on television in the* Canadian Encyclopedia. *He holds a doctorate in communication theory from the Sorbonne Nouvelle.*

David Ellis undertook the research for Split Screen *at arms-length from the Steering Committee of Friends of Canadian Broadcasting. Consequently, the opinions and conclusions in* Split Screen *are his own, and not those of Friends' Steering Committee.*

Friends of Canadian Broadcasting is a citizens' organization concerned to improve the quality and quantity of Canadian programming on Canadian airwaves. Friends draws support from some 33,000 Canadian families from all parts of the country who have invested voluntary contributions towards this goal. The research leading to the publication of Split Screen *has been financed entirely through these contributions.*

Readers are invited to associate with Friends of Canadian Broadcasting in order to support its program of research, advocacy and policy interventions. Friends' priorities in 1993 will focus on the CRTC's structural hearings on the future of television, and on raising the public visibility of the citizen consumer's interest in broadcasting questions in the period leading up to the forthcoming federal general election.

Ian Morrison
on behalf of the Steering Committee
Friends of Canadian Broadcasting

Preface

For many years, watching TV has been our dominant leisure activity. Canada's policymakers also consider it to be our most important cultural institution.

This book is about a new era in television that promises to change some heartfelt assumptions about both leisure and culture.

Our subject — new communications technologies — is not exactly obscure any more. Over the last year or so, most major newspapers and weekly magazines have carried features on Deathstar satellites, video compression, multimedia computers, the spread of CD-ROMs, the encroachment of cable into telephone services and telephone into cable services, and how the whole world is going digital.

A number of best-sellers have also been written about the changing face of television, including Ken Auletta's *Three Blind Mice*, which documents the decline and fall of network television in the United States. Meanwhile, we've had more than the usual share of consulting reports on the subject of new technologies.

So why another run at these same themes? Well, the author and sponsors of *Split Screen* would like to think that these other publications, however helpful to some readers, have left a few stones unturned.

Rather than take all the technical background for granted, we have tried to describe and explain the new media in a way that doesn't require an engineering degree. Both the first half of the text and the glossary at the end are devoted to this educational purpose. We're all so used to hearing routine discussions on digital technology, for example, we may not have stopped to think about what a binary digit actually is and does, and how it may change activities like watching TV.

Not everyone, of course, feels the need to understand how such things work. For those readers, *Split Screen* treats technology — and understanding technology — as a means to an end, not as an end in itself. Our real preoccupation is the changing relationship between TV set and TV viewers, especially Canadian viewers. We've therefore tried to create a context for this discussion that encompasses viewer needs and behaviours, as well as social issues such as the use of television as an instrument of nation-building.

Another perspective we've adopted here concerns public policy — a topic some may consider even less inviting than engineering favourites like digital video compression. We've looked at a number of issues that affect how TV is regulated and publicly financed in Canada. And we have not shied away from making editorial and prescriptive comments where appropriate.

Everyone is well aware of the pervasive influence of the electronic media, especially TV. What is less well known is the degree to which conventional television, purveyor of sitcoms and game shows, is merging with other electronic media, like the computer and the telephone, to form what commentator George Gilder calls the new "digital computerscape". This is the relatively recent phenomenon of "convergence" — the blurring of lines between TV shows, data transmission and phone calls, among other things.

The message? The future holds a lot more in store for your TV set than just old-fashioned broadcasting. Thus, you may find other reasons, apart from what's on tonight, for being curious about how technology is turning the TV screen into a meeting ground for broadcast and non-broadcast forms of TV.

If you watch TV, this book is for you. Even if you don't watch TV, it may be for you anyway.

We hope you will find the style of presentation to be clear and straightforward. In order to achieve this, we've deliberately cut some corners. For example, we've elected not to include a full battery of footnotes or citations from all available sources for every tendentious point. While the reader is not expected to take everything on faith, an attempt has been made to keep the pace moving by avoiding technical minutiae.

In keeping with the mission of the Friends of Canadian Broadcasting, *Split Screen* has been written with the goal of serving the public interest. Like its predecessor, *Networking*, released in 1991, it has been entirely funded through voluntary contributions to the Friends from concerned individual Canadians. The views expressed here have not been influenced by financial support from either government or industry. This is therefore in some ways a citizen's guide, even though we'd be pleased to have specialist readers pay heed as well.

Organization

The book is organized into seven chapters. The first three are primarily descriptive, intended to provide the reader with a context for our discussion, as well as some background on the new technologies themselves. The latter four chapters are more editorial in their approach, and are particularly concerned with how business and policy issues are affecting Canadian viewers.

Chapter One • **Introduction: Eye on the Split Screen** provides several interpretations for the concept of the "split screen" and the fragmentary nature of the new television. With our focus on the changing relationship between viewers and TV set, we review some ideas about what and how people watch when they watch TV. After establishing a number of basic distinctions, such as that between visible and invisible technologies, we move on to the benefits that supposedly matter to viewers: choice, control, quality and interactivity. We end with a brief look at the ways in which broadcasting can and cannot be expected to promote national sovereignty.

Chapter Two • **Back to the Future** is a look back at several established TV technologies. The idea is to look for lessons about consumer acceptance, convenience, pricing and other factors, that may give us clues about what to expect from newly emerging technologies. We review the role and functions of cable TV, communications satellites, the VCR and the remote control.

Chapter Three • **From Boob Tube to Smart-TV: The Digital Revolution Hits Broadcasting** is our review of the most influential and highly publicized new technologies. Two major themes emerge. One is that digital processing will have a profound effect on the types and uses of TV we have at our disposal in the future. The other is that broadcast types of TV, the "intrusive" ones like over-the-air, cable and satellite, will be competing for screen time in the future with non-broadcast or "non-intrusive" types of TV, such as those provided on optical discs — CD-ROM, laserdisc, Compact Disc Interactive and so on. Detailed material is included on the latest developments in High Definition Television (HDTV) and so-called "smart-TVs".

Chapter Four • **TV & the Movies: Hollywood Heads for the Living Room** opens the issues-oriented discussion, particularly in the Canadian context. The main topic of this chapter is the gradual shift of movie consumption from theatres to living rooms and the methods Hollywood has used, in its strange partnership with TV, to shift the box office to the living room. The unhappy fate of Canadian theatrical distribution and exhibition is examined in the light of emerging distribution vehicles like pay-per-view. Doubts are raised about the wisdom of pursuing aggressive policy support for theatrical film-making when all the evidence suggests Canadian creators and producers will have better access to viewers in the future through broadcast and non-broadcast forms of TV.

Chapter Five • **Canadian Producers, Canadian Content** returns to the central theme of how technology and related factors are changing the rules by which programs get made for Canadian television. Here the two most important developments are the continuing internationalization of TV production and the continuing fragmentation of TV markets and audiences. We discuss the strategies employed by Canada's leading independent producers and suggest that it may be time to look at changes in how the Canadian content rules are applied.

Chapter Six • **Technology: The Ultimate Deregulator?** takes a long look at how and why television is regulated in Canada. After explaining the main legal and technical rationales for regulation, we show how technology is undermining each and every one of these to at least some degree. We take "Deathstar" satellites as a case study in what Canadians might expect from an unconventional multichannel distribution technology. Rather than focus on its alleged potential for "damage" to the broadcasting system, however, we look at how the vested interests in broadcasting and cable are using the prospect of Deathstars to protect their market power. We raise the idea that regulation will need to be preserved, but in a form that better serves the interests of program-makers and viewers.

Chapter Seven • **Caution — Merging Traffic** takes a broad view of TV regulation in Canada and the TV and video business in the international marketplace. The theme that ties this all together is the convergence of technologies and technology companies. Convergence means that broadcasting can no longer be regulated and subsidized in isolation from other communications media, and that the regulator must start to take account of new social issues such as fair and equitable access to networks for both video suppliers and end-users. Convergence also means that conventional entertainment media are merging into huge multinational information companies, such as Time Warner. Our conclusion is that Canadians must learn to thrive in the international arena by offering the best possible conditions at home for creative endeavour in the new media.

With the main narrative at a close, the book provides a good deal of additional information and reference material, including an appendix entitled **Some Broadcasting Basics.**

Bells, Whistles & Black Boxes offers an extensive glossary of technical terms used in the main text. The glossary can be read independently or in conjunction with the text. Every effort has been made to provide clear, authoritative and interesting definitions, while keeping the length of most items to a few sentences. Readers with an interest in the technical side but little technical background are invited to consult the glossary freely.

Acknowledgements

The research for this book was carried out in a fairly traditional way, combining analysis of primary data, published books and documents, as well as interviews with experts and decision-makers.

In addition to interviews and meetings conducted in Canada, the Friends supported two research trips to the United States — the first to Los Angeles, the second to New York and Washington. These trips proved to be valuable, since they enabled me to meet with a number of influential people working actively in consumer entertainment, new areas of technological research, regulatory affairs and so forth.

Many of the opinions expressed in interviews did not reflect the policies or positions of employers. For this reason we decided it would be more prudent not to include affiliations in the list that follows. In the preparation of the book itself, I have naturally taken further liberties with the raw material in developing my arguments and reaching conclusions. All opinions and conclusions expressed here are my own — as are any errors or misstatements of fact. The reader should not assume that the use of a quotation or company name reflects agreement or approval, unless otherwise indicated.

Those who consented to take time out of busy schedules to participate as interviewees or resource persons were part of a large group that helped get this book written and published. It gives me great pleasure to acknowledge their support and pass along my personal thanks. May you be content to see your name here even *after* reading what follows:

Fritz Attaway, Berg Avayzian, Paul Brown, Cynthia Brumfield,

Jeffrey Chester, Suzette Couture, Stan Cornyn, Carol Darling, Mark Dillon, Donald Dulchinos, David Ellis (still no relation), Charles Firestone, Glenna Forbes, Stephen Godfrey, Peter Grant, Gordon Harris, Debra Henderson, Hank Intven, John Jacobi, Hudson Janisch, Sudhir Joshi, Barry Kiefl, Ann Kronen, Jonathan Levy, Michael MacMillan, Roy Martin, David McKendry, John McManus, Steve Mendelson, Rockley Miller, Paul Mills, Kathryn Montgomery, Len Muscarella, Michael Nash, Harriet Novet, Lewis Ostrover, Robert Pepper, Dorothy Phillips, Bruce Read, Alan Richter, Pierre Sarrazin, Robert Schaulis, Florence Setzer, Kevin Shea, Juris Silkans, Jon Slan, Richard Stursberg, Israel Switzer, Stephen Tapp, Thomas Whalen.

In creating a finished product from all the raw material I was fortunate to have worked with talented and devoted collaborators. I relied heavily on Peter Bloch of Interactive Arts in Santa Monica for advice, files and personal contacts in learning about the leading edge in new media. Sarah Anson-Cartwright ensured we had an up-to-date understanding of the Canadian production business. Besides supplying extensive draft material for Chapter 5, she kept a watchful and experienced eye on revisions of that material.

If this book reads well and looks good, credit for that goes to two people in particular — my editor, Sue Elo, and the book's designer, Barb Woolley, of Hambly & Woolley Inc. Aside from their professional skills, they showed patience and care through all the trials, mishaps and delays that seem to attend projects of this kind. Thanks as well to Barb's partner Bob Hambly and technical wizard Gord Woolley for their contributions.

This book was prepared in collaboration with Julia Johnston. Julia came to the project under the auspices of the Summer Fellowship Program in Public Interest Advocacy, administered by the Faculty of Law of the University of Toronto. Credit for making this happen goes to Bonnie Croll and her colleagues at the Faculty of Law, as well as to McCarthy Tétrault, which engaged Julia as a 1992 summer intern. The firm was not only gracious enough to let us benefit from Julia's services, but also paid her salary for a full two-month period, no strings attached. Needless to say, the views expressed on any legal or regulatory matters are entirely the responsibility of the author.

This arrangement proved to be a revelation. Julia attacked her assignment with a sense of confidence and professionalism that is reflected in this book in many ways. In the best educational tradition, I might offer thanks by noting that the supervisor learned as much from the experience as the intern.

In TV circles, somebody has to "exec-produce" — manage the talent, the budget, the schedule, make sure the product gets realized in the way envisaged. For *Split Screen*, that person was Ian Morrison, spokesperson for the Friends and executive director of the Canadian Association for Adult Education. They and I were ably assisted at many stages of the project by Jim Thompson and Tim Woods, who found ways to communicate the message.

Ian and his colleagues on the Friends Steering Committee deserve credit and gratitude for the unusual opportunity they created with this project. They provided me and the rest of the team with generous support, sound advice and a remarkable degree of creative freedom. I hope they and others will find this a model to be emulated in the future. *D.E. November 1992*

Split Screen

Chapter 7

INTRODUCTION:
EYE ON THE SPLIT SCREEN

"Forget about TV sets. In three years there won't be any."

Andrew Lippman, MIT Media Lab, 1991

Our story starts in a typical Canadian living room… The centre of attention is the TV set. As a piece of technology this set has undergone a lot of changes in a few short years, with plenty more to come.

Split Screen is about the effects of the new technologies, as well as the technologies themselves. Let's get a feel for our subject by suggesting what the image of the split screen might tell us about the new world of television.

Picture in a picture. First, the title is literal: if you buy the right set, you can now split your screen and watch two or more programs at once. The manufacturers that offer this feature call it "Picture in (a) Picture", or PIP. TV sets, like many electronic durables, are getting smarter or having intelligence built into them. PIP is the precursor of many such special effects or features that embedded computer chips make possible. They speak the language known as "digital" — those streams of zeroes and ones sometimes referred to loosely as "computer language".

Split feed. The screen splits; so does the signal feeding into the set, whether from cable or a source like direct-to-home satellite. For the new technologies won't stop at offering multiple images on the screen. As just about everybody knows by now, the one thing we can be sure of in the technological future is that the number of images arriving on the screen will be greatly increased.

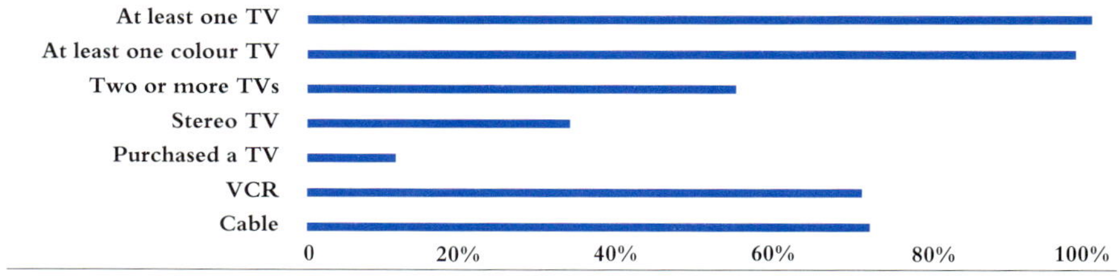

Canadian TV Households in 1991
Sources: CBC Research, Market Facts, Statistics Canada

The 200-channel universe is coming not because of creative ferment among the production community, but because of the ingenuity of the engineering community — thanks to a process known as "digital video compression". This is a process that takes redundancy out of a video signal, compresses it into a narrower electronic space and allows broadcasters and program distributors to transmit many more video signals without a corresponding increase in the number of channels. Much more TV at much less cost.

Result: a splitting of the electronic pathway into the TV set, from cable, satellites, wireless providers, even the phone company. The big question: will this in turn produce an increase in the much-touted viewer choice? That depends on what you mean by "choice".

Multiple screens. The screen splits and begets other screens. In the traditional Canadian living room, the whole family was huddled around the one TV set. Along with fewer viewing options, it was likely that if the family watched anything, they did so together.

No longer. Now over half of all Canadian households have more than one TV set. The number of households with three TV sets continues to grow. Older sets are being replaced by sets with much higher image quality and the ability to reproduce stereo sound.

Not much is known about the distribution of viewing in multi-set households.

It can be safely assumed, however, that family members are splitting up to watch different programs on different sets in many of these households.

Broadcasting plus. The TV screen is splitting in functional terms. No longer will the TV be used for the sole purpose of watching TV programs. After digitization, the second most important technological trend is convergence — the linking of video with computer technology and telecommunications. In addition to bringing you sitcoms, your TV will read your meters and make your phone calls.

It is digitization that is making this marriage possible, as more and more devices learn to communicate with one another using binary digits, or "bits" as computer folks say. The convergence of TV with other devices and functions means a new division of labour on the screen. The "smart" TV sets referred to earlier will act more and more like computers: that's because they will *be* computers or at least will have computers embedded in them. They will also have companion devices hooked up to them, the way VCRs are now, which will make available to viewers vast non-entertainment resources in the form of databases like encyclopedias.

In addition to their traditional role as purveyor of entertainment, TV sets will act as all-purpose monitors for household security and mechanical functions; they will also be used to communicate with outside agencies unconnected with broadcasting, like banks and department stores. TV broadcasting may be undermined by this degree of competition for screen attention, though as we've seen, the proliferation of screens in Canadian households will provide more turf for the turf wars to be fought on. And they will be fought not just by and among broadcasters, but will expand to include telephone companies and publishers.

Fragmentation. The new technologies are having a fragmenting effect — splitting audiences by giving us more of everything. Some service providers, notably the cable companies, and some policy-makers, have been trying to convince Canadians that more is better. This makes good consumer doctrine, especially since the advent of more hardware, more channels, more choices and so on, is pretty much inevitable.

The "split screen" reflects a pervasive fragmentation not just among those who watch, but also among those who make and deliver television. In the 1980s, the term "audience fragmentation" came into vogue: it meant then, as it does now, that more broadcasters were competing for roughly the same number of viewers or viewing hours, and therefore having to be satisfied with a static or shrinking market share.

For almost four decades home entertainment meant nothing more or less than network TV. The decline of mainstream network television, the major victim of market fragmentation, has been well documented. Technology certainly played a role in its demise, particularly in the form of the communications satellite, which made national, cable-delivered specialty and pay channels a possibility, starting in the 1970s.

In the 1990s, the new technologies will break up television into even smaller and less recognizable pieces:

→ video service providers won't necessarily be broadcasters;
→ "networks" will tend to be superstations, not aggregations of local stations;
→ and far more program content will be directed at small, homogeneous audiences, and far less to mass audiences.

Rugged individualism. As the screen splits, so shall the audience. Multi-set households find different family members spending time apart using different sets for different purposes.

While we don't suggest that multiple TV sets will hasten the decline of the nuclear family, we can assume that more services and more sets will spell the decline of shared viewing experiences among the national audience as a whole. Three kinds of television events will continue to attract large numbers of simultaneous viewers:

→ major sports finals, like the Stanley Cup
→ movies and entertainment specials featuring bankable stars
→ important breaking news stories, like disasters and civil wars

But gone are the days when millions of viewers will spend their evenings watching the same half-dozen programs from a handful of network broadcasters.

These shared viewing experiences, however valued by some, may now be a thing of the past.

Audiences: a watching brief

The technological changes discussed in this study will profoundly affect the relationship between the viewer and the television. The most important question to be answered by this study concerns the effects the new technologies will have on audiences, whether they are considered as consumers, with certain interests to protect in the commercial marketplace, or as citizens of a sovereign state, with certain values that distinguish it from others.

As noted at many points in this study, our aim is not merely to understand how new entertainment devices work in a technical way. It is primarily to understand how they work in relation to viewers, and especially how they work in the viewer's home setting. That presupposes some prior understanding of how people use TV, what expectations they have of TV and what lessons we've learned from the introduction of devices like VCRs.

So what do we watch when we watch TV? A large, powerful and profitable industry grew up in the 1940s and 50s to provide broadcasters with the answers to this question. The corporate name that has become synonymous with TV audience research and ratings is A.C. Nielsen, which first started estimating audience size in 1942 with the "Audimeter". Indeed, according to one commentator, "Nielsen *is* television" because of its "influence over the culture, content and business of television" (Larson, p.66).

There are two main methods of audience measurement in use today. The first of these is the "diary method", which requires participants to keep track of their viewing habits in a written diary provided by the audience measurement company. This method has met with considerable criticism. Douglas Newell of media buying agency Harrison, Young, Pesonen and Newell in Toronto maintains that most respondents complete their diary entries from memory, not while they're watching television (Chilton, p.2).

This problem has been addressed in recent years by the introduction of electronic meters to record TV tuning habits automatically. Meters are installed in sample homes by audience measurement firms. The meter consists of a microprocessor that monitors which channel each set is tuned to and for how long, as well as a modem that sends the accumulated data over the telephone line to a computer at a central collection point.

While they monitor activity in the set itself far more accurately, meters have always presented the problem of how to measure the people watching as well as the channels tuned. Over the last few years, various methods have been devised to do so. Most of these, including so-called "people meters", have depended on the initiative of the participating viewers (see accompanying box).

Regardless of how television has changed over the years, it is first and foremost a device for distraction and relaxation. That doesn't mean merely that most viewers prefer sitcoms to political documentaries. It also means that many "viewers" use TV as a backdrop to some foreground activity like housework and pay no attention at all to what's on the screen.[1]

Even among viewers who are making a conscious effort to watch the screen, any old program might do. In that sense, our viewer really is watching "programming", or as we say, just watching TV. (At some time or other, of course, this hypothetical viewer can be almost any of us.) It

Counting Eyeballs

A.C. Nielsen's "People Meter" consists of three parts: the home unit, the keypad and the remote control. Family members are assigned buttons on the remote control, which they are expected to push when they start and stop viewing. The home unit tracks which channels are being watched and the information is downloaded to a central computer which tabulates ratings.

People meters have met with criticism from industry personnel. Rodger Hone, senior vice-president at Global Television, maintains that up to 35% of respondents do not push their personal buttons to indicate that they actually viewed a particular program (Chilton, p.2).

Now "passive" people meters are on the horizon. They correct for the problem of "button fatigue", since they do not require the viewer to do anything. Nielsen's newly developed box scans the room every two seconds looking for signs of life. It is even able to detect whether a person's head is turned to or away from the television set.

may seem like mere semantics to differentiate watching "programming" from watching "programs"... to suggest that the random viewing of the least objectionable programming is not the same as watching a particular program or programs. But this is no trivial difference to the broadcaster who has gone to great lengths to reach an audience by careful marketing and scheduling, and wishes to capture viewers by conscious decision rather than the happenstance of channel surfing.

Another of the mysteries of audience research arises from the fragmentation of viewing choices. When viewers in the U.S. and Canada had only three or four viewing choices (and no remote control), they pretty much knew not only what program they were watching, but which network as well. One of the great anxieties for broadcasters in the multi-channel marketplace is an alleged loss of viewer loyalty to particular stations and networks. People, the claim goes, watch programs not networks.

In *Television and its Audience*, Barwise and Ehrenberg note (p.6) that "we usually choose to watch programs, not channels and we are not always well aware of which channel we are watching. We are not glued to one channel if there is choice." While the evidence for this observation is uncertain, it appears that many cable subscribers are confused by the way channels are allocated, packaged and identified. Thus, in assessing problems

Even if some researchers succeed in measuring with greater accuracy who is actually watching TV, other researchers and TV executives are still worrying about who's paying attention and who isn't — not to mention how much viewers are enjoying what they are watching. This is what TV people call qualitative research, because its goal is to assess the quality of the TV viewing experience.

One such scheme is the "Q Rating", a measure of the familiarity and popularity of television shows and their stars. A sample of viewers are mailed questionnaires that ask "have you heard of the program" and if so, "how do you rate it"? A "Q" rating is then calculated by dividing the percentage of respondents who describe the show as "one of my favorites" by the percentage who recognize the show at all. The American comedy series In Living Color *had the highest Q rating for 1991 (source:* New York Times).

with diary-based research, Keirstead and Keirstead observe in *The World of Telecommunication* (p.195) that

> viewers and listeners do not understand how stations are identified. They will report Z-103 instead of WOOF radio or say they are watching channel 6, except that they are watching cable and channel 6 on the cable system happens to be the channel 13 on-air station! Viewers and listeners are confused partially because the stations develop logos or ways to be identified that are not tied to either their legal ID or the frequency or channel on which they actually broadcast.

Meanwhile, the advent of specialty channels and narrowcasting has added a new wrinkle. Certain viewing experiences can now be much more readily identified with a particular broadcaster. Thus, the sports fan can turn to TSN in the conscious desire to be entertained by sports or sports news. As for a service like MuchMusic, it not only caters wholeheartedly to fans of rock music and its variants, but it also has helped to dissolve the boundaries around distinct programs — if it has not eradicated the idea of "programs" altogether.

This development has led to talk of TV services as "brands". Not surprisingly, the talk has come primarily from those broadcasters who are most threatened by market fragmentation — the conventional networks. The problem for CTV, not to mention CBC and the American networks, is how to stand out from the crowd in the ever more crowded marketplace that television has become in North America. One of the great champions of branding and marketing the network itself as forcefully as the network's programs is CTV president John Cassaday. Writing in the *Globe and Mail* in late 1991, John Partridge described Cassaday and his strategy in the following terms:

> John Cassaday, the former cigarette and soup super-salesman who took over as president of CTV almost two years ago, spent much of his pre-CTV business career as a marketer, buying commercial time on TV in an attempt to create and increase brand loyalty among consumers. Now he is trying to bring the same

A.C. Nielsen's "People Meter"

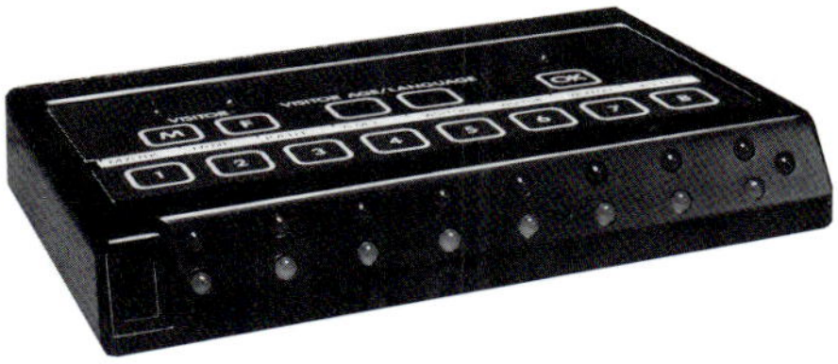

approach to marketing CTV to both advertisers and viewers. In doing so, he is out to disprove the notion that people generally watch particular TV programs rather than particular stations. "I believe in the power of branding", he says.

All of these research and marketing issues raise one big question for conventional broadcasters facing drastic changes in their operating environment — what are viewers looking for in the multichannel marketplace? Programs? Specialty channels? Network "brands"? Or just any old TV?

Active and passive viewing

Traditional audience research is not very helpful in answering questions of this nature. One way to approach the problem is to examine not merely *what* people watch on TV but *how* they watch it. One factor we need to pay particularly close attention to is the level of viewer activity or passivity in relation to the TV set. This is significant for our purposes because many of the new broadcast and non-broadcast technologies presuppose a much higher level of viewer involvement than has been typical in the past.

Virtually every time someone watches TV, they engage in some minimal level of activity — turning the set on, changing channels, adjusting volume and picture. "Active" can also be understood in an intellectual rather than physical sense. We will therefore take "active" to refer to the mechanical storage or mental retention of program content for some instrumental purpose other than passive viewing. Thus, while timeshifting a broadcast program on a VCR is an active function, viewing it from start to finish as one would on TV would qualify as passive. Definitions like this are not cut and dried: for example, is a timeshifted movie viewed without its commercials by zipping with a remote control an active or passive viewing experience? The answer might be: more active than without the zipping, but much less active than playing a video game...

Moreover, viewers can't all be put neatly into active and passive psychological profiles. Particular individuals use TV differently at different times, depending on mood, setting, program material and so on.

Thus, at one end of the continuum, we have viewers who do not want to be faced with complicated controls to achieve any task beyond finding and watching a program. These are passive users, or users behaving passively. At the other end, "viewers" using video technology for work-related tasks want enough controls and functions to get things done quickly and enhance their productivity. These are active users, or users behaving actively.

From the programming perspective, *passive entertainment* is the dominant form of conventional broadcasting. It is one type of "escapist" leisure pursuit, comparable to reading a novel, the point of which is to become engrossed and surrender choices to the creator (sometimes including the choice of turning off the set and going to sleep). The typical program material, like a movie, is no longer the exclusive domain of conventional broadcast television.

Active entertainment is wide-ranging, comprising both established and emerging technologies. Among the established group would count both the VCR and video games. The emerging technologies constitute a more complex set, partly because they include various optical platforms like Compact Disc Interactive, which also operate as standalone TV peripherals, as well as an expanding group of networked interactive technologies.

Predicting levels of viewer activity

It is hard not to be struck by how conservative North Americans seem to be in their reactions to new entertainment products and services. The apparent reluctance to take a more active role, along with the steadfast attachment to ease-of-use, suggest that the traditional patterns of television use are not about to be swept away by new discoveries fresh from the lab. Couch potatoes don't necessarily want to leap off the couch any more than they have to — even if it's only an intellectual leap.

The traditional habit we're alluding to is the passive consumption of the entertainment programming TV has become famous for — sitcoms, action adventures, movies, sports, talk and game shows. Some radical departures from these TV conventions are already on the market, such as interactive fiction packaged on optical discs, allowing the user to alter the narrative in much the way that video games do. But common sense and some empirical evidence indicate that many of the story-tellers who work as script-writers, producers and directors, along with many viewers who come home tired from work, are going to keep passive entertainment alive on TV for some time to come.

Scepticism about a more active kind of TV viewer-consumer is being voiced even by representatives of the consumer electronics industry, which in Japan alone is devoting hundreds of millions of dollars to research on new TV peripherals and hybrid devices that will be both multimedia and far more interactive than conventional TV. Consider, for example, the views expressed by Koje Hase, a senior executive of Toshiba, who was a featured speaker at the 1992 Digital World Conference in Los Angeles.

In a published report on his remarks in *Digital Media*, Hase notes that "fully *one-third* of the support calls that Toshiba receives are resolved by having the customer plug the device into an electrical socket" (Caruso, p.17).

Hase went on to draw a sharp distinction between "storytelling", passive entertainment, and "game-playing", active entertainment: "I want to sit down and really absorb myself into the dreamy world of some producer, not interact with what those producers brilliantly executed [...]. Do we want, when we watch *Lethal Weapon*, to interact with them? I don't think so. If we interact, Batman may not return."

The history of the VCR provides good reason to be sceptical about how much a new technology, even one in wide use, actually changes how people behave. While the VCR did have a significant impact on patterns of expenditures, its introduction did not dramatically alter either the total level of TV viewing or the content of that viewing. This seems to be the overall conclusion of one of the few widely available scientific studies on VCR use — *The VCR Age: Home Video and Mass Communication* (Levy 1989).

Viewer benefits

How should we go about assessing the effects of the new technologies on the individual viewer? Out of all the claims and counter-claims, which are credible and point to measurable benefits? We believe four leading attributes of these developments need to be singled out. These are: *choice, control, technical quality and interactivity*.

Taking the viewer as the focal point for the analysis presents some risks. For one, there's no such thing as a typical viewer, and averages tend to conceal the truth as much as reveal it. For another, the viewer's interests are not necessarily coincident with those of other citizens that deserve to benefit from new technologies and services, such as independent producers and creative talent.

The idea of "quality" is particularly tricky. While the new technologies will do wonders for technical quality, they are likely to have little impact on aesthetic quality, except in their ability to make the production values of TV programs and movies all the more spectacular and engrossing — better special effects, better stunts, better blends of live action and computer-generated action, and so on. Nevertheless...

Fast forward into the 150-channel future. Choice, control, quality and interactivity. But the greatest of these is choice.

Choice

For a few thousand Americans in the borough of Queens, New York, the 150-channel future arrived in 1991 thanks to Time Warner, the local cable operator — and the world's largest entertainment company. Canadians will have to be more patient, thanks to the CRTC's timetable for licensing new services, which places the launch of a significant number of Canadian specialty services in 1994 or even 1995.

"Choice" on the grand scale does not, of course, mean getting to choose from among 150 different entertainment or broadcast services, let alone 150 different programs at any given moment. Viewers who live in large urban centres will already be familiar with the phenomenon of program duplication: lots more channels than there are programs, since the same programs often run on different stations.

Choice has long been treated in Canada as one of the central goals of broadcasting policy, usually in the form of program diversity. The idea is enshrined in section 3(1)(d)(ii) of the 1991 *Broadcasting Act*, which mandates that the broadcasting system should provide "a wide range of programming". Choice is also one of the central planks in the cable industry's strategy for dealing with the new technologies — and the new consumer of the 90s.

In the document describing this strategy, *A Clear Vision*, the Canadian Cable Television Association (CCTA) says (p.7) the following:

> In Canada, a recent CCTA study of consumers suggested that, after reasonable cost, the "freedom to choose" the optional channels and packages that suit different consumer needs and interests was one of the changes in cable services that they found most appealing. Offering services that consumers were aware of but couldn't yet obtain on cable and providing a greater range of services at different price levels also had high consumer priority. The central thrust linking each of the things which they said were appealing was the desire for more ability to exercise choice.

As can be seen from the schedules of pay and pay-per-view movie services, what the new technologies promise to bring us is not necessarily more diversity of content. What they do promise is to liberate our schedules by providing a greater choice of times at which we can watch the programs we want to watch. This is the kind of service alluded to in the concept of video on demand or near video on demand. Canadians have now got an approximation of this in the pay-per-view service Viewer's Choice Canada (VCC).

This ambiguity between diversity of content and diversity of scheduling is not a new issue. In fact, part of the rationale for licensing pay and specialty services in Canada was to allow broadcasters to use repeats as a scheduling strategy for the convenience of viewers who, because of work or preferences, are not available at peak viewing hours.

So choice involves content, channels or services, and exhibition times. But it involves something else that will be increasingly important to Canadian viewers and policymakers alike in the future, and that is choice of service providers. This raises a number of issues affecting viewer welfare, not the least of which is cost. We have to ask, therefore, not only what choices will technology bring to our screens, but also who will provide those choices and how will prices be set.[2]

Control

Many of the new video technologies share the attribute of giving more control of the viewing experience to the viewers themselves. This control takes a number of different forms, including: the ability to program smart-TVs and other end-user devices; controlling what ends up on the screen and paying only for what you want; by implication, controlling the price you pay for entertainment services; and by extension, using integrated home electronics to control many other household functions.

We leave aside the question of whether viewers will wish to make the effort to program their TVs. Once speech recognition becomes widely available in home electronics, user-friendliness will have become an issue of the past for most people. Speech recognition will allow you to talk to your electronic equipment and have it respond to many different kinds of commands. The microchips that will make this happen are already well into development by Apple Computer and other manufacturers.

In our final two chapters, we will question whether the current regulatory framework, which presupposes that cable will continue to control access to Canadian homes, will allow technology to put more control in the hands of subscribers.

Quality

In this discussion, we have to distinguish among three different kinds of quality, all of which have a bearing on the consumption of television.

Production quality refers to attributes of a TV program or movie as it was produced. These attributes are sometimes referred to as production values, which describe the creative and technical polish of a movie or TV program. They include the calibre and drawing power of the actors, the novelty and complexity of special effects, the quality of the cinematography and music or sound track, the use of stunts and so on. Production values are mostly about execution and have little to do with aesthetic considerations, such as the quality of the writing in a script or screenplay (though many actors and directors would probably take issue with this interpretation).

Technical quality as we define it refers to the clarity and fidelity of sounds and images delivered and reproduced by technologies or devices like cable, TV sets and VCRs. Significant improvements in quality have already come to television, and many more are on the way.

Artistic quality is a term used by many commentators to refer to the artistic merits of TV programs. The notion is notoriously elusive and subjective, and also very important. While the present study is mainly concerned with the other kinds of quality, especially technical quality, a comment is in order on the distinction between the quality of individual programs and the quality of channels or services or entire broadcasting systems.

The distinction is nicely expressed in one of the few documents published on this subject, *Quality in Television: Programmes, Programme-makers, Systems*, a compendium of expert comment issued in 1989 by the Broadcasting Research Unit, based in London, England. Many trenchant comments on "quality programming" are offered. On the first page, for example, we read that quality programming

> ... seeks constantly to renew, not to repeat formulae; it explores, takes risks, pushes the boat out, extends the frontiers, takes itself and us by surprise as to what is possible in good television.

Many other attributes of quality programming are noted by the contributors: respect for the audience, exercise of the imagination, doing the unexpected, broadening perceptions and so on. But the point is also made in no uncertain terms that programming standards "matter not just at the atomised level of the individual programme, but to the overall output of a series or a channel..." (p.2).

The next passage on the same page takes an even wider view:

> The argument about what constitutes "good" radio and television is, or should be, only partly about what constitutes good individual programs. A service that offered only Shakespeare, wildlife documentaries and penetrating interviews with Mrs Thatcher would not be a "good" service, even if each programme were of prize-winning quality. Range and variety matter, too. The problem is not that *Dallas, Neighbours* and quiz shows exist, but that unless broadcasting is sensibly organised, variety will diminish. Broadcasting must be so organised as to grant all kinds of endeavour access to all kinds of audience.

The inclusive notion of quality in programming — pointing up the virtues of appeal to different audience tastes — is reminiscent of our earlier discussion of choice. Analysis of the artistic merits of individual programs is not only contentious, but beyond the mandate of this study. The technologies of interest to us have little or no impact on artistic merit.

What is part of our mandate, however, is to question whether, by bringing us programs in far greater numbers, the new technologies will also bring us more choice — in the sense of diversity, variety and range of program type.

Interactivity

If technical quality is the least controversial of the supposed benefits of the new technologies, then interactivity — talking back to your TV — is undoubtedly the most misunderstood and overrated.

Interactivity in its ideal form means two-way communication between parties that can switch sender and receiver roles, change the format or structure of the communication on the fly, and effect unanticipated changes at both ends. TV has a long way to go before this kind of interactivity will become commonplace.

In the meantime, some limited forms of "upstream" communication have become fixtures in the TV landscape. Two notable examples are the phone-in show and, on an even more infrequent basis, vote-in shows that allow viewers to vote for a particular movie preference or musical recording artist by dialing a certain phone number.

Here are some other issues that need to be noted in this area:

Interactivity vs selectivity. These days, what we mostly mean by interactivity is in fact nothing more than selectivity. This is a feature of some services that simply allows the viewer to select one or more options from a pre-established menu of choices. This is what the 150-channel Time Warner cable systems offer in their Quantum package of pay-per-view services: on-screen menus listing movie titles and times, which can then be selected by means of a remote control device.

The upstream connection. Viewer's Choice Canada now offers a similar pay-per-view movie service on cable. But there are two differences. One is that Quantum has a far greater selection of times and movies, largely because of its much greater channel capacity. The other lies in the upstream connection: Quantum's interactivity (or selectivity) operates entirely within the cable network, moving signals both downstream to the viewer and upstream to the cable headend within the same wires. In virtually all other systems, however, including VCC, the upstream capability is external to the cable system and must resort to the public telephone network.

Broadcasting & non-broadcasting. Conventional, advertiser-supported television may be on the wane, but that doesn't mean interactivity — the viewer talking back — is going to make sales pitches disappear from the screen. On the contrary, the new technologies are being exploited already to make home shopping an even more instantaneous and gratifying process. Viewers will soon be able to order what's being promoted on the screen by pressing the buttons on a keypad linked to the TV set.

Videotex. During the 1980s, many large companies like AT&T, IBM, Sears, CBS, Knight Ridder and others lost millions of dollars on interactive services known as videotex. The distinguishing feature of videotex services is they require a computer or other proprietary device to provide the two-way link with the service provider. After many spectacular failures, only a few such services are still showing any signs of life, most notably the Prodigy service in the United States owned by Sears and IBM. The many videotex failures should be a warning to those who believe that the viewers of the nation are prepared to throw off the mantle of the couch potato and become active participants in the selection and arrangement of what comes to their screens.

On a more general level, all of these attributes — choice, control, quality, interactivity — must be tested against the experience of individual Canadian viewers in their evolving relationship with the TV set — already becoming a Home Entertainment Centre. What real choices, what real costs, who benefits?

The changing face of TV entertainment

Passive entertainment is not going to disappear in the near future. However, it would be a mistake to assume that the survival of passive TV entertainment will go hand in hand with the survival of broadcasting as we know it today. Conventional movies and sitcoms, and conventional ways of viewing them, will not disappear in a technological revolution. But many crucial factors in the new context will be different and cannot be ignored. Chief among these factors are new suppliers, the "user-pays" model and standards.

New suppliers

Passive entertainment has ceased to be the exclusive domain of over-the-air network television. It is a well known fact that the networks have lost a huge proportion of their audience over the last decade. In the U.S., the big three networks — ABC, CBS and NBC — "which fifteen years ago claimed more than nine out of ten viewers nightly, have lost a third of their audience — nearly ten million viewers" (Auletta, p.3). The single most important technology that has hastened this decline is cable.

In Canada, cable-delivered services are divided between specialty channels like YTV, TSN and Chinavision; pay movie services, like First Choice and the Family Channel; and a number of approved American imports that include both specialty services like CNN and several superstations like WTBS Atlanta and WGN Chicago. Many but not all of these services offer programming that fits the traditional mold, though it is of course packaged and marketed on a very different basis. It is important to note that Canadian specialty services are not general interest broadcasters, but rather narrowcasters. Viewers must normally pay for them, whether as part of a basic cable subscriber fee or as a separate discretionary service.

American cable services, known generically as "cable networks", began much earlier than their Canadian counterparts and were allowed by the FCC to develop across a much wider range of programming formats, including advertiser-supported and general interest formats that have competed with conventional broadcasters — a situation that the CRTC could not allow in the much smaller, more fragile Canadian market. At least half a dozen of the current top 20 cable video networks (as ranked by subscriber numbers) can be described as general interest entertainment programmers, or at least not specialty programmers. These include the USA Network, TBS, TNT, The Family Channel[3] and WGN (TBS and WGN being classified as superstations).

What is more, financial success for American cable channels is not based upon niche or specialty programming, as might be assumed from the rationale for the original development of cable networks, which was to offer an alternative to conventional television. According to *Variety* (March 9, 1992, p.31), "the presumption that niche networks are the key to cable's future success may be unfounded: The USA Network, with its mix of original movies and series, boxing and wrestling, and off-network shows has, for the first time, vaulted to No. 1 among all basic cable networks".

Other, newer technologies are also entering the picture, many of them to compete in this same entertainment arena. Three are worth mentioning here: pay-per-view (PPV), direct-to-home (DTH) satellite services and a family of wireless transmission technologies that includes multipoint distribution services (MDS).[4]

PPV is a delivery vehicle that represents a significant change in how programs are marketed, although the existing services — including Viewer's Choice Canada — depend exclusively on cable to reach purchasers. Most of the programming they offer is movies and sports events, especially wrestling and boxing, with a certain number of other events like rock concerts.

The *DTH* services that will become available over the next few years will offer a mix of "basic" services like superstations and PPV services, not unlike their terrestrial counterparts the cable systems. These services will bypass the conventional and cable-delivered broadcasting systems to reach viewers directly in their homes. While it is too early to predict how well these services will do in taking market share away from other suppliers, there is no doubt that they will be competing using much of the same types of popular entertainment programming fare.

MDS is a wireless distribution technology whose basic function is similar to that of cable distribution — to package a number of channels and services and distribute them to local subscribers for a fee, only using microwave transmission instead of cables.

A number of such systems are operating in the United States in competition with established cable systems. MDS has certain constraints, such as the need for proprietary antenna and receivers and line-of-sight transmission. But it has the corresponding advantage of doing away with the need to build a cable network linking subscriber homes to the operator's headend, a lengthy and expensive process.

What we conclude is that the new television environment, while offering much of the fare we are used to — i.e. passive entertainment — will differ in terms of who delivers it.

User-pays

In contrast to free TV, cable, cable PPV, DTH and MDS all involve the viewer in a financial transaction: this is the concept that lends its name to what we are calling the "transactional" or "user-pays" model of television, as distinct from conventional, "free", over-the-air television. Some American basic cable networks are promoted as being made available "free" to subscribers. A distinction is made in Canadian cable between foundation channels, like local CBC affiliates, which carry no extra charge and specialty channels, like CBC Newsworld, which carry a so-called pass-through fee.

The distinction is largely academic because no cable operator offers access to any over-the-air signals free of charge. As we note in numerous other places, three-quarters of Canadian homes now subscribe to cable and thus pay something for all their television viewing. CBC and CTV are theoretically available to many Canadians over the air. But that doesn't change the fact that the broadcasting system in Canada is now transactional and can only become more so.

Transactional television will change the nature of the programming we see, and the way government supervises the relationship between program suppliers and viewer-subscribers.

"Transactional" decisions also have implications for viewer convenience. Some people prefer to order a movie over the phone from their pay-per-view provider, even though they then have to watch it at the scheduled time (unless they record it for later viewing). Others find it more convenient to get a tape of the movie from a video store, even though it means leaving home twice (once to get it, once to take it back), because then they have complete control over when and how they watch, as well as how many times they watch.

Standards

In the short term, what ends up on the screen may be tied to a particular technology. Now we can watch an ordinary movie by means of several different delivery systems, none of which makes a difference to the actual viewing experience. In the future, however, some kinds of TV watching will be dependent on new technologies: a leading example would be so-called "interactive" TV.

As new technologies and home entertainment services proliferate, we will experience a long transition period when many different standards and platforms will be cluttering the marketplace and confusing consumers. At last count, for example, there were over 20 different proprietary audio and video systems using the five-inch compact disc or CD. Furthermore, half a dozen proprietary interactive TV standards are being developed in the United States.

In other words, if you haven't got the right equipment, you won't be able to get the service. This also applies to well established, run-of-the-mill technologies. For example, some Canadian TV households are still without a converter or converter equivalent, which means those households can't tune in any of the programming services distributed by cable on the channels above 13. In the near future, radio broadcasters will be introducing digital audio broadcasting (DAB), which will be incompatible with existing radio receivers.

Technology & the viewer

What all this means is that viewers will likely be paying more attention in future to how programs get to their screens, as well as to the programs themselves. While we too are primarily concerned with what gets on the screen and how the viewer relates to it, we also have to be concerned with the technologies that deliver the content.

That doesn't mean, of course, that viewers will automatically become any more interested in or knowledgeable about the technologies themselves. Nevertheless, engineers, bureaucrats and others responsible for the creation and regulation of TV technologies are usually unwilling or unable to take the mystery out of what they do for a living. You don't have to know how a car works to be able to drive it. But if you do, you're likely to get more out of it, keep it running better and most of all, you're a lot less likely to get taken to the cleaners when you take it to the garage.

Laserdisc

Discussions about new entertainment and communications technologies often get polarized. One camp sees utopia, the other sees the world turning into a vast video arcade.

The trouble with the first — the benevolent or whiz-bang view — is that it treats technology as though it were neutral. A machine gets invented by inspiration and goes to market because it's a good idea. This overlooks the power relationships in the business world that determine which technologies will get promoted and which won't. The trouble with the second, apocalyptic view is that it treats technology as though it were the determinant of *all* relationships with end-users, content and other technologies.

Technological determinism holds technology alone responsible for both its successes and failures. A prominent example from the 1980s is the spectacular failure of Telidon, a good idea in the lab that fell on its face in the marketplace. Currently we are witnessing an entire broadcasting industry scrambling frantically to figure out how to create program content to fill the vast amount of channel space being created by engineers through the development of digital video compression.

The perspective adopted in this study does not assume that technical things come first and then set the ground rules for everything else. Examples of what we might call reverse technological determinism:

Content pushes technology. Videocassettes didn't take off in the late 1970s and early 1980s just because the VCR was an efficient and affordable piece of consumer engineering. They took off at least in part because of the demand for X-rated movies, which could now be procured and viewed in a much more private and convenient manner.

Profit margins push technology. More recently, we've been witnessing the spread of the set-top boxes from the cable company called "addressable descramblers", which can be individually addressed from the cable operator's headend computer and decode scrambled channels like movie services. This technology makes pay-per-view services possible. But what is likely to give pay-per-view releases of new movies their big push is not just the presence of the technology, but the fact that the major Hollywood studios and other producers stand to make more money from this delivery method than from others, like home video.[5]

Visible vs invisible technologies

Very few people come home tired from work and sit down to stare at their descrambler or choose a program purely because of the technology that made it available. The vast majority of viewers want to be entertained and distracted by programming. The last thing they want to think about is the jumble of wires that brought it there.

Moreover, people don't buy technology for what it is but for what it can do. This isn't always the case for what marketers call "early adopters" — consumers enamored of new technologies who purchase them even when prices are still high and the advantages of ownership uncertain. But these are the exceptions. Most North Americans are notoriously unwilling to buy and use home entertainment devices that require programming, physical effort or technical skill.[6]

The maxim that people watch programming not technology should be heeded by business people — as well as pundits who write reports about technology and try to make predictions about how it may influence behavior.

But let's be clear about something. None of this is an argument for *not* studying technology, new or otherwise. Naturally we need to avoid naive ideas — such as the belief that technology shapes its own destiny. Our main job is to size up what we believe the effects of technology are likely to be. In order to do so, we have to understand some basic technological distinctions. One of these is the distinction between technologies TV viewers see and manipulate, and those they don't — visible and invisible technologies.

The VCR is an example of the first category. Just how the viewer interacts with it, how much it costs, what functions it performs, how easy or difficult it is for the ordinary person to operate… these are all important questions in sizing up the response to a new piece of consumer electronics.

In years to come, few people will know or care that their ability to receive

hundreds of channels of video will have been made possible in large measure by digital video compression algorithms. Despite their undeniable importance in revolutionizing television delivery, these and other engineering triumphs are of no direct concern to the end user. The end user certainly sees the *results* of video compression, but compression itself (and the algorithms that make it possible) belong in the second category of technologies.

The distinction between visible and invisible technologies is not hard and fast. For one thing, every living room entertainment device is ultimately a black box that conceals more technical secrets than it reveals. The owner of a VCR or video game or CD player is also enjoying the benefits of technological effects and not of the technologies themselves, which are mostly out of sight and out of mind, buried in invisible microchips and circuit boards.

For another, some technologies straddle the two categories. This is true of delivery technologies like cable and direct-to-home or DTH satellite services.

Most of the cable and satellite equipment that picks up, transmits and processes TV signals is located far from the living room. Nevertheless, both cable and DTH services require that some reception equipment be located on the viewer's premises. This may be nothing more than a few feet of coaxial cable, or it may be an elaborate system comprising a satellite dish antenna, receiver-decoder and other paraphernalia.

What's important here is the fit between what is visible to the end user and what we can describe as "non-broadcast" or "standalone" TV technologies — devices like VCRs, laserdisc players and video games, which, despite their connection to the TV set, operate independently of any outside link to a broadcaster. Under conventional arrangements, TV viewers were passive participants in a one-way process terminating at the set. Short of a technical mishap, nothing was visible to viewers or under their control except which of three or four stations to tune in. All the other decision-making "intelligence" was kept strictly under the control of the broadcasters themselves.

The trend among broadcast and non-broadcast technologies alike is a shift of control — or potential control — to the viewer. This includes control over image quality, service provider, scheduling, program version and other attributes which will eventually involve two-way interactivity between viewer and TV set. Greater control implies an emphasis on the interface between viewer and TV set, along with the flood of peripheral devices expected on the market during the 1990s. In other words, what's in the living room will come to have an increasing influence over the nature and quality of the viewing experience.

We need to be aware of the contrast between broadcast and non-broadcast technologies for two reasons.

→ First, discussions about the future of broadcasting tend to overlook the standalones, like the VCR. That may be in part because those with a vested interest in conventional broadcasting would rather not think of standalone technologies as competitors for time on the small screen.

→ Second, we need to be aware of the contrast precisely because the contrast is going to become less and less meaningful as home entertainment moves towards

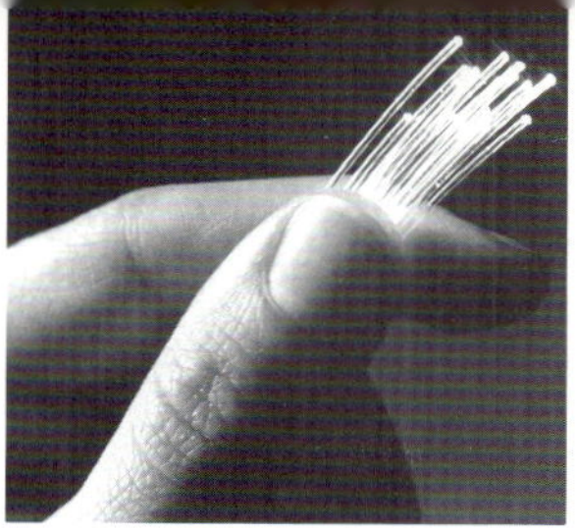
Fibre optic "wires"

video on demand, free television gradually disappears and competition opens up to new and untried service providers, like the telephone companies.

Broadcasting & national sovereignty

Broadcasting is a responsibility of the federal government, which is charged with ensuring that the system is managed in the public interest. How then have politicians and regulators tried to keep abreast of new developments in technology?

Until the introduction of the new *Broadcasting Act* in 1991, "broadcasting" was defined in section 2(1) of the 1968 *Act* as "any radiocommunication in which the transmissions are intended for direct reception by the general public". The accompanying definition of "radiocommunication", which referred to electromagnetic waves "propagated in space without artificial guide", was clearly and deliberately based on conventional over-the-air broadcasting.

By 1991, cable TV and satellite communication had become fixtures in Canada's broadcasting landscape. The advent of these and other distribution technologies, and in particular the notion of payment for a signal, made it necessary to provide a more inclusive definition of "broadcasting" than one based on a fixed transmitter beaming a "free" signal from the local TV station to local rabbit ears or outdoor antennas. Thus, the new *Act* defines broadcasting as

> any transmission of programs, whether or not encrypted, by radio waves or other means of telecommunication for reception by the public by means of broadcasting receiving apparatus...[7]

What this means is that broadcasting in Canada now officially covers virtually all forms of both wired and wireless transmission by means of coaxial or other types of cable, such as fibre optic lines or copper wire, as well as microwave, satellite and other similar technologies, whether or not they are land- or space-based, and regardless of whether they are scrambled electronically to restrict access. The chief incentive for rewriting the legislation was to strengthen the government's hand in regulating broadcasting in Canada by keeping ahead of new technological developments.

Unlike the new technical definitions, however, the cultural goals enshrined in the legislation have remained largely intact. Broadcasting regulation in Canada has always been concerned with ensuring that the system is "predominantly Canadian" and serves to "safeguard, enrich and strengthen the cultural, political and economic fabric of Canada".

The Canadian broadcasting system is seen as "a public service essential to the maintenance and enhancement of national identity and cultural sovereignty". The *Act* provides that:

> The Canadian broadcasting system should
> (i) serve to safeguard, enrich and strengthen the cultural, political, social and economic fabric of Canada
> (ii) encourage the development of Canadian expression by providing a wide range of programming that reflects Canadian attitudes, opinions, ideas, values and artistic creativity, by displaying Canadian talent in entertainment programming and by offering information and analysis concerning Canada and other countries from a Canadian point of view...

Regulation of the broadcasting industry has sought to meet these goals primarily by three different methods:

→ Canadian content quotas and conditions of licence on program expenditures, types, scheduling, etc.;

→ a high degree of protectionism to exclude unapproved U.S. services and enhance Canadian broadcaster revenues;

→ public subsidies to CBC, educational broadcasters, and to producers through government funding programs, such as the one administered by Telefilm Canada (the Canadian Broadcast Program Development Fund).

We have entered an era in which all of these measures will be undermined. It's important to understand that the threat to these policy measures and thus to

national cultural expression won't come exclusively or directly from the new technologies themselves, though technology will do its share to make national borders less meaningful. Canada will face two other kinds of problems stemming indirectly from technological convergence: scarce resources for "Canadian" production and the phenomenon of globalization.

Our ultimate purpose is to help the readers of this book understand and deal with these broader issues on their own. For now we delve into the subject of the technologies themselves.

Split Screen

Chapter 2

BACK TO THE FUTURE

"No one ever bought a ticket to watch technology."

Syd Silverman, Former Publisher of Variety, *1983*

The way you watch TV can be affected by many environmental factors that have nothing to do with technological innovation. Some of these, like family status, place of residence and income, are important determinants of viewing patterns and taste in programming. For example, the way you watch TV might be radically transformed by the arrival of a new husband who loves to watch sports. But we will treat these as secondary considerations.

Notice, furthermore, that we haven't referred to "TV" or "broadcasting" technologies. There's good reason for that. One of our central themes is that new technologies like digital video compression and computerized TV sets will completely undermine the established ways of making, financing, distributing and watching TV. They will also make concepts like "broadcasting" and "TV program" largely meaningless. At the very least, we have to start thinking in terms of broadcast TV and non-broadcast TV.

So, what do we count as a new technology and what do we leave out? Our organizing principle is this: all technologies affecting what can be viewed on home TV screens — *regardless of the source* — are considered grist for our mill. "Information" may arrive as a conventional TV broadcast, whether over-the-air, by cable or satellite; from a standalone device or peripheral, like a laserdisc player or

Nintendo machine; or from a separate processor that monitors household functions like heating.

Furthermore, the devices of interest to us do more than handle what we have always thought of as TV "programs". Some of these will resemble computer programs more than TV programs; indeed some of them will *be* computer programs, or take the form of text or data rather than moving images or talking heads. As we'll see, the question remains as to whether the TV screen should encompass the monitors that accompany personal desktop computers in the home.

One practical reason for proceeding this way is that all of these sources are competing for space on the screen, as well as for the viewer's time and attention. To some degree, the screen is becoming less of an issue. That's because many Canadian homes now have more than one TV. But viewers still have only 24 hours in the day. Even those who timeshift programs using their VCR still have to find the available time in which to play the material back.

The way we watch TV has changed in many ways since TV came to Canada in the 1950s. Our assumption in this chapter is that to understand the emerging new technologies we need to understand the established technologies that were new in their day. To establish a framework for our discussion, we'll now look at four aspects of video technology: *coaxial cable, communications satellites, the VCR and the remote control.*

Here and elsewhere, we're interested in the effects of technology on both cultural goals and the viewing experience.

Established technologies 1 & 2: Cable TV & communications satellites

Until the 1970s, the TV industry was structured along rigid lines. Local stations were either network-owned, network-affiliated or independent, though the vast majority were affiliates. Each and every station provided local service and, as affiliates, acted as an outlet for the network's national programming, usually reserved for the evening period. This was a marriage made in heaven. Hundreds of local stations gave the networks ready-made geographic coverage, in exchange for

Ted Turner

compensation payments and advertising time. What the stations got was highly attractive but expensive entertainment programming, licensed by the networks and amortized over dozens or hundreds of local markets.

We can get some perspective on how much the landscape has changed by recalling what happened to Ted Turner's WTBS. Mr Turner is best known around the world now as the founder of CNN.

Back in 1970, Turner purchased an almost bankrupt UHF station in Atlanta, then designated WJRJ. Communications satellites were just coming into routine use by broadcasters. Cable was struggling to make a name for itself. Then Turner did the unthinkable. Instead of trying to turn around the property as just another local UHF station, he created North America's first superstation. He did so by sending his signal up to an RCA communications satellite, Satcom III-R, then bargained with cable operators across the country to take down the signal and make it available to their local subscribers.

The superstation idea flew in the face of industry logic which said TV stations had to look after local interests, while offering network-quality programs to broaden their appeal. For another thing, the market for specialty channels was unproven.

While non-conventional television of this kind has not been an unqualified success, the story has unfolded happily for WTBS. Its programming offerings are limited but undeniably popular. They include reruns of old series, lots of movies and lots of sports. Despite competition from several other national superstations, and countless other cable and pay networks, WTBS is now in 58 million American homes. That represents 63% of American TV households. And as of the fall of 1991, WTBS had been picked up by nearly half a million Canadian cable subscribers.

No single superstation, including WTBS, accounts for a significant proportion of total viewing time in a given period. The experience in Canada has been analogous. Services like Newsworld, First Choice and TSN do not enjoy individual audience shares on anything like the scale of the conventional national networks. But the cumulative effect of specialty and pay-TV has been to erode the market share and revenues of conventional network television.

The effects of fragmentation on the big three American networks is illustrated

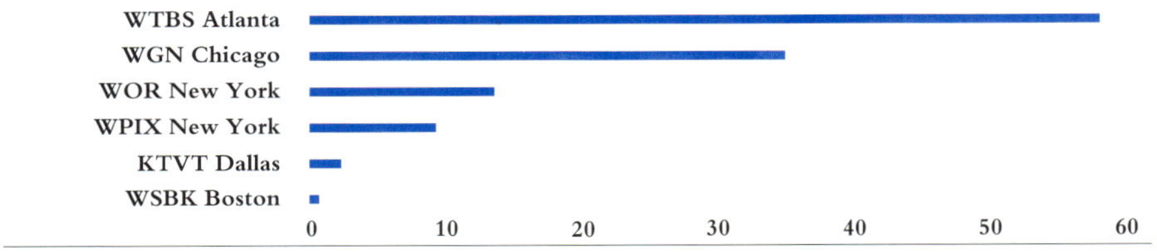

U.S. Superstations Authorized for Distribution in Canada
(U.S. subscriber base in millions — 1991)
Source: Variety

by Ken Auletta, who notes (p.3) that cumulative profits for the three American networks fell from $800 million in 1984 to $400 million in 1988.

We now take cable and satellites for granted. And yet there was a time when they too were new technologies.

In the beginning

As far as Canada is concerned, cable began inconspicuously and with little fanfare in 1952 in London, Ontario. The first so-called Community Antenna Television (CATV) systems in the U.S. were established in Mahoney City, PA and Astoria, OR in 1948. Cable's original purpose was simply to improve the quality of signal reception from local and regional TV stations.

For their part, satellites were the subject of a stunningly accurate prediction made by science fiction writer Arthur C. Clarke. Clarke wrote in 1945 that communications satellites could be used for TV transmissions by being placed in a stationary orbit relative to the Earth's surface (which is why they are known as "geostationary"). He even calculated that to work effectively they would have to be placed some 36,000 kilometres over the equator. That was more than 15 years before the first active communications satellite was launched.

What neither Clarke nor anyone else did was predict the effects satellites would have on the structure of the broadcasting industry or on the viewing habits of the North American audience. As we'll see below, satellites and their potential effects on TV have become a hot topic of debate in the 1990s, in the guise of so-called "Deathstars" or direct-to-home satellites. New video technologies have unpredictable and disruptive effects on the established order of things.

As a corollary, we can also observe that their effects are greatly multiplied when two or more technologies are brought together to work in tandem. One kind of unpredictability was described by presidential science advisor Vannevar Bush when he said that "we always overestimate the impact of a new technology in the short term and underestimate its impact in the long term" (as quoted in the Report of the Task Force on Broadcasting Policy, p.59).

Cable illustrates one version of this phenomenon. As cable spread slowly through Canada in the 1960s and early 1970s, it was hailed as a harbinger of what was then referred to as the "wired world". Cable and the wired world became associated with two other ideas, plant integration and switched broadband networks. Essentially, plant integration foretold of the day when cable networks and telephone networks would be integrated. Together they would be able to offer many more complex services than just voice, such as video, which requires a broad electronic pathway, on a switchable basis: the best of cable TV (video services, which weren't switchable), with the best of telephony (switching, which was limited to voice and data).

Twenty years later plant integration as originally envisaged is unlikely ever to take place. Similarly, switched broadband services may still be several years and many billions of dollars away. Even though the short-term glory of the wired world never came to pass, that didn't mean a bleak future for cable. On the contrary, by the 1980s, two developments made it the cornerstone of the Canadian broadcasting system.

→ One, the CRTC, bowing to public pressure, finally allowed cable systems operating at a distance from the U.S. border, as in Edmonton and Ottawa, to do more than just erect a modest antenna to capture and redistribute locally available signals. They could now combine their coaxial technology with microwave distribution technology, a well-established means for getting TV signals across long distances, in order to bring in the broadcast signals of American border stations.

The CRTC recognized the potential negative consequences of allowing the importation of a greater number of American signals. In its public announcement ("The improvement and development of Canadian broadcasting and the extension of U.S. television coverage in Canada by CATV", 3 December, 1969), the Commission predicted that "acceleration of the present trend of extending coverage of U.S. networks and stations in Canada and importing programs wholesale from the U.S. networks and stations by using microwave or other techniques will, in a relatively short time, risk disrupting the Canadian broadcasting system".[8]

→ Two, cable TV came to be regarded as the "chosen instrument of public policy". The regulation of the broadcasting system would be carried out through careful control of cable operations, in the form of priority carriage for Canadian signals and other measures. This policy made more sense as cable penetration continued to grow: by 1977, the number of Canadian households subscribing to cable had passed the 50% mark (source: CCTA).

Cable TV in Canada has now grown to the point where three-quarters of Canadians watch all their TV, including free TV, on cable. The power and influence of cable are also evident from the financial results it has enjoyed in the last few years. Profit margins for cable companies have far outperformed those of Canadian broadcasters, especially in the period since 1990, when the effects of declining market share were being compounded by the onset of recession. The rise of cable technology to the position of chosen instrument provides an important object lesson. Technology is not merely unpredictable in its effects; it can also have effects that run entirely against the grain of what policy-makers intend.[9]

In addition to provoking audience fragmentation, the introduction of cable and satellites has challenged regulation. National responses to disruption of the status quo have differed sharply. In Canada, the regulator has tried, through tight control of program distribution, to make the cable and satellite tandem work for the system. In the United States, the Federal Communications Commission (FCC) has tried to improve the financial health of their system by doing just the

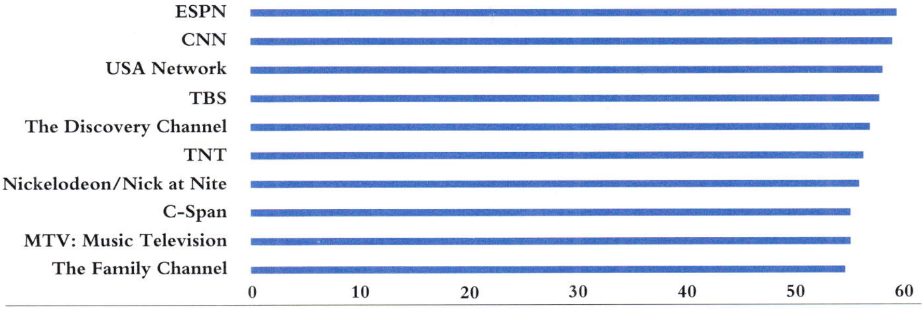

Top 10 U.S. Cable Networks — A Close Contest
(Ranked by number of subscribers in millions)
Source: NCTA

opposite — loosening the reins and encouraging competition. It gives some indication of the policy gulf between the two countries to learn that all U.S. satellite-delivered specialty and pay services, like HBO and MTV, operate without any form of programmer licensing by the FCC.

Established technology 3: the VCR

So far we've been talking about how the TV landscape has been changed by the advent of two particular technologies, cable and satellites. The TV set took another giant step away from conventional broadcasting — and away from the reaches of the regulator — with the arrival of the VCR.

Understanding the VCR and its place in the home is vital to our purpose. That's because the VCR is the first TV "peripheral" or attachment to gain wide acceptance among consumers. The VCR is our introduction to a whole family of standalone, home entertainment technologies which share two important attributes: they are competitors for time on the TV screen and viewer "share of mind", while at the same time they operate entirely unregulated, outside the structure of the broadcasting system as we know it today.

VCRs perform several distinct functions. These are timeshifting (recording a program for playback at a later time) and playing back prerecorded cassettes, whether commercially released (as in rented movies) or personally recorded (as in "home" movies). Each of these functions has different implications for the viewer's relationship with the TV and for the welfare of Canadian broadcasting.

A little history

The VCR was the pioneering non-broadcast home entertainment technology and remains one of the great success stories of consumer electronics. It's a story that involves a couple of unlikely twists in the plot, and some useful lessons for technology pundits.

What we now know as the videocassette recorder, the VCR, was not invented as a consumer product and it was not invented by the Japanese. The VCR actually began life as an industrial product known as the VTR, or video tape recorder. Generally speaking, the video machines used by professionals are still referred to as VTRs, while the consumer product is referred to as a VCR. Apart from that, no careful distinction is maintained, even by those who manufacture them. Sony's consumer literature refers to some popular models as both a VCR and a VTR. The VTR revolutionized television production. Prior to its introduction, the three main methods of television presentation (live, film and kinescope) all had significant drawbacks.

The precursor to the consumer VCR was actually developed for commercial production in April, 1956 by the Ampex Corporation of California. By 1966, various manufacturers were working on developing open-reel VTRs for consumers. Ampex itself had reportedly sold 500 VTRs for home use by 1967. All of these machines were not only expensive but difficult to use. As well, they all utilized open-reel video tape. It was not until 1972 that Sony introduced a cassette recorder for home use.

Sony's 3/4" U-Matic sold for $1,600. Then, in 1975, Sony introduced its SL-6300, a 1/2" Betamax VCR, to the U.S. This system, with one-hour recording capability, included a built-in 19-inch Trinitron colour TV and was priced at $2,295. The following year Sony finally brought out a standalone Betamax. The consumer product they launched in 1976 had two big advantages. First, it was relatively easy to operate. Second, it was relatively cheap: the first models cost about $1,300. The machines quickly became popular.

The rest, however, was not exactly history. Rather it was a lesson in what really counts to consumers, as well as a lesson in technological unpredictability. The VCR story also illustrates nicely the pitfalls of formats and platforms.

Format wars

Most readers with any interest in video will know that the Betamax format for the videocassette has taken years to die a slow, lingering death in the marketplace. Betamax is the textbook illustration of the marketing maxim *that nobody buys technology for what it is but for what it can do.* In the case of home entertainment and VCRs in particular, that means being able to play back the most popular and profitable product of all — movies. As Beta-compatible titles have gradually dried up at video rental stores, Beta has ceased to be a viable standard and the machines themselves have all but disappeared from store shelves.

In 1976, JVC introduced the "Video Home System" (VHS) VCR, which was incompatible with Sony's format. It was cheaper (under $1,000), recorded longer and took only two years to control 57% of the American VCR market. *Videoweek* reported that Beta's market share had dropped to 17% in 1984, 10% in 1985 and 5% in 1986 (August 25, 1986). Sony announced in 1988 that it would begin manufacturing VHS VCRs.

The irony is that VHS did not win the format wars because of superior quality. On the whole, the Beta format, at least in its earlier incarnations, produced a higher quality image than did its VHS counterparts. (Controversy exists over whether later Beta models produced superior images than VHS.) And back in the late 1970s, it was an even contest as far as titles are concerned, since none of the movie studios had moved into what would become the home video market.

Sony's fatal mistake was to let its concern for quality blind it to the fact that the original Beta tape standard of one hour's playing time effectively cut it out of

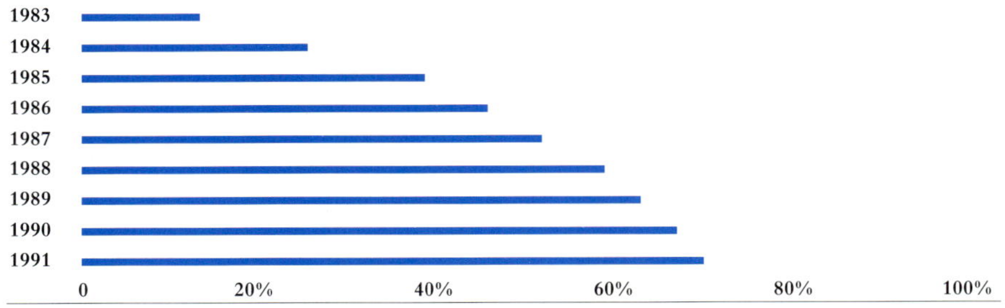

VCR Penetration in Canada
(Percentage of households)
Source: CBC Research (BBM)

any chance at growing into this market. The first VHS tapes, by contrast, could record up to two hours of programming. In 1988, Beta tapes had a maximum recording time of 5½ hours, while VHS had a maximum of 8 hours. VHS also maintained a price advantage over Beta.

Even as Sony's competitors were developing VHS, and cross-licensing its development to other companies, another format was being touted as the home entertainment standard of the future — the *videodisc*. It had first been introduced with much technical fanfare by RCA at about the same time as Sony's first VCR. MCA's DiscoVision, introduced in 1978, offered high quality pictures, stereo sound, random access and freeze frame. Two systems attempted to crack the videodisc market in the early 1980s — one from RCA, the other from Philips. But the VCR manufacturers, seeing videodisc players as a potential threat, lowered the price of their VCRs to predatory levels. A decade and a half of hindsight tells us just how far the laserdisc has fallen short of expectations.[10]

Like the Beta/VHS war, the poor acceptance of disc-based video technology demonstrates how much more important convenience is to consumers than the quality of sound and image. Laserdiscs offer reproduction superior to the best that tape formats can muster. As well, because they use a rigid, unbreakable metal core that can't stretch or wear out, they are far more durable than their tape counterparts. But tape offers a convenience feature that outweighs the quality factor for at least some consumers: tape can record and then be erased and record again. The Hollywood studios, in fact, enthusiastically endorsed the videodisc platform over the videocassette for this very reason: videodiscs, because they could not record, would preclude copyright infringement.

Two ingredients were needed to make VCRs overperform by comparison with what sales in the early 80s would have indicated. The first, convenience, was a given, despite the format wars and despite a number of features which to this day have not made VCRs entirely user-friendly.

The second ingredient was "software", i.e. movie titles. When the VCR was first introduced, its only real selling feature was that, unlike laserdiscs, it could be used for timeshifting broadcast programming. Thus, all television programs were potential software sources. Renting prerecorded tapes was not an option, since they were virtually non-existent.

The industry was caught in a classic standoff: consumers didn't want to buy machines until they had ready-made product for viewing, preferably of the entertainment variety, while the owners of the major movie titles, the Hollywood studios, didn't want to commit resources in a market where only a tiny proportion of households owned a machine.

The home video industry can thank X-rated movies for breaking the logjam. In 1979, approximately 75% of all prerecorded tapes sold were X-rated. Some dispute exists over whether the existence of X-rated movies actually fuelled sales of VCRs, given that they were promoted almost exclusively during the first few years for their ability to record broadcast programming, not to play back prerecorded material. In any case, the proportion of "adult" movies found in typical video store inventories was only some 7% as of 1991 (see accompanying chart).

Making friends with your VCR

One of the remarkable things about the VCR success story is how consumers have adjusted to the "interface" — the functions that have to be mastered to make a VCR perform. The fact that VCRs are now in almost three-quarters of Canadian

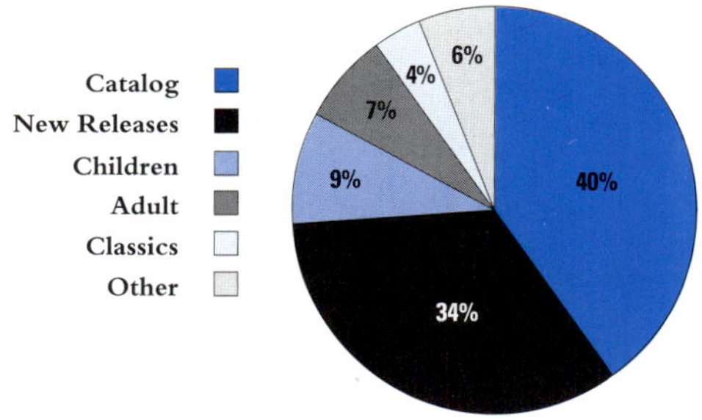

Average Video Store Inventory by Genre
Source: 1991 Video Store Magazine U.S. Retailer Survey

homes, about the same number of homes as have cable TV, is testament to their convenience as a home entertainment device. Or is it?

It's important to remember that the mere purchase of consumer products, especially electronic ones, is not a reliable indicator of regular, long-term use. Examples are legion: fitness equipment, food processors, cameras and so on. The picture's even more complicated with VCRs since they have more than one use, and measuring those uses is difficult. Industry analysts have been at loggerheads on just how VCRs are used ever since consumers began buying them in large numbers.

With few exceptions, you can't simply connect your VCR to a jack in the TV set, plug it into a wall socket and make it perform. The exceptional cases concern viewers who do not subscribe to cable or do not wish to record programs, or both. Complications arise because most Canadian households do subscribe to cable. Some non-cable households still use a form of external antenna, while a significant number of cable households subscribe to extra-cost services that require a descrambler, a special converter box from the cable company that can descramble the cable delivery of First Choice/Superchannel, American superstations and others.

The result? Well, to illustrate, let's take a current, medium-priced VCR offered by Sony, the SLV-595HF. This is a popular VHS model that features hi-fi

Sony's SLV–595HF

stereo capability and retails for between $500 and $600. The 74-page owner's manual provides 11 pages of information merely on getting this unit properly hooked up to the owner's other equipment.

Because of the many different equipment configurations just noted, the manual in question outlines five separate hookup alternatives: the audio/video hookup, antenna hookup, simple cable hookup, alternate cable hookup and advanced cable hookup. And that's not all, because the first two offer a total of six sub-alternatives. One configuration comprising this VCR, a cable descrambler and a stereo TV requires about 18 different back panel connections, not counting all AC power cords and optional outputs to an external stereo system.

Getting hooked up is only half the battle. It's the easy half for most people, because a dealer or other helper can always intervene, and once the hookup is complete, it usually doesn't need to be fiddled with again.

Operating the VCR is another story. Now our hapless viewer is faced with that familiar litany of problems: juggling two or even three remote control devices; figuring out the correspondence between broadcast and cable channel allocations; and worst of all, uncovering the secrets to programming the VCR to record a broadcast in the viewer's absence… or to record a program, period.

Some help is on the way:

→ Many remote control devices will now operate more than one component, in some cases even equipment made by different manufacturers.

→ *TV Guide* is collaborating with cable operators to make their channel numbers identical, so that channel "7" on cable is also "7" in *TV Guide*. The broadcast designation remains different, so that in Toronto channel "7" still happens to be "57" for official purposes (and used to be "79", until cellular telephones came along and took some of the TV spectrum away).

→ An invention called VCR Plus + Instant Programmer™ is being built into VCRs, like the Sony model here. Individual TV programs are assigned numerical codes recognized by suitably equipped VCRs, so that these programs (whose codes are published in *TV Guide*) can be recorded simply by punching in the code from the remote keypad.

→ Most VCRs can now be set up and programmed by means of on-screen menus, much like those used in computer interfaces like Windows.

Does this mean we're winning the battle of VCR user-friendliness? The question is important because we believe the way viewers interact with the VCR holds valuable clues for understanding emerging technologies, both broadcast and non-broadcast. Indeed, the VCR itself occupies a strategic position as a cross-over or hybrid technology, part standalone, part extension of the TV as a broadcasting receiver.

In answer to the question, consider these other factors:

→ Some manufacturers have tried to improve the VCR interface and the design of their remote controls. In March of 1992, *Consumer Reports* stated (p.160) that:

CONVERTER GUIDE

VCR Plus+™ owners are advised to verify their cable company's channel lineup to ensure successful taping of programs on VCRs.
VCR Plus+™ is a trademark of Gemstar Development Corporation.

20	22	24	25	26	27	30	31	32	33	38	39	40	43	44	45	50	51	52	53	54
3	29	V	YTV	NW	MM	TSN	A&E	TNN	CNN	FC1	FC2	FC3	SBK	FAM	FC4	13	12	TBS	WGN	SE
44	22	24	23	25	30	28	33	27	31	37	38	39	50	40		46	45	49	51	52
21	20	27	26	29	30	23	34	33	35	24/48	49	50		25		18	19	36	37	44
32	36	30	29	25	16	15	17	50	14	24	51	53		37		34	33	44	45	
20	36	23	21	22	29	26	24		25	14				35		38	37	44	45	

years ago, you had to learn to use an assortment of buttons on the VCR console. Today, VCRs feature easier on-screen programming that you perform with a remote control. Still, what's utterly lucid to a product engineer can remain a dubious murk to someone trying to record *Masterpiece Theatre* for the second time this year.

Witness the remote control for the Sony SLV-595HF, a high quality but strictly mass market machine, which comprises no less than 51 keys and controls.

→ Though the channel guide is helpful, every issue of *TV Guide* (in this case the Rogers Cable edition) requires a double page spread that identifies channels, provides a cable converter guide and explains VCR Plus +.

→ The Sony VCR manual noted above requires nearly four pages of text and diagrams to explain how to set up VCR Plus + and then use it, each of which is a seven-step process.

→ Like VCR Plus +, on-screen menu systems are designed for viewers who are reluctant to read lengthy manuals and need simple, linear instructions. Many of these menus can only be understood by first consulting the owner's manual. Many of them require setup decisions, such as whether preset channels are to be designated as "NORM" or "CATV".

→ Most contemporary VCRs are promoted as "cable-ready". That means they have a built-in converter, which is why separate, set-top converter units are gradually disappearing... except of course for the cable company converter box that also descrambles scrambled signals. What that means in turn, now that pay-TV services are widely available, is that these sophisticated VCRs aren't cable-ready at all, even if they can tune 125 channels or more. Not only can they not decode or descramble; they are also incapable of being individually "addressed" by the cable headend or signal source.

What do viewers want?

On the surface, it would appear that given the apparent degree of confusion involved in installing and operating a VCR, it's a minor miracle that VCRs have been purchased by virtually three-quarters of Canadian households. As we noted above, however, the acid test is not mere ownership but extent and types of use.

Let's recall that VCRs have a kind of split personality. They are an extension of the broadcasting infrastructure when they are used to record and playback broadcast programs. (Of course they're also a broadcasting device when used to tune programs for viewing in what technical folks like to call "real time", i.e. simultaneously.) But they are non-broadcast, peripheral entertainment devices when used to play back prerecorded videocassettes, such as those rented or purchased from a video store.

One of the major assumptions of this study is that non-broadcast forms of TV will continue to erode the market share of broadcast TV. Our further conviction is that technology will reach a point, certainly within this decade, at which it will no longer make any sense to distinguish between broadcast and non-broadcast TV for purposes of regulation. The question as to whether viewers prefer VCRs for timeshifting or playing rental cassettes has a significant bearing on this assumption.

The question has been addressed by industry analysts by examining the effects of VCRs on broadcast viewing levels. In an audience survey entitled *How People Use Television*, released in 1991, CBC Research notes (p.61) that "the jury is still out on whether VCR's increase or decrease the audience to programs offered by conventional broadcasters". While the CBC study leaves this a more or less open question, it does go on to make a firm judgment about preferred use (p.61):

> Time-shifting [...] is the major use of VCR's in Canadian homes. Indeed, according to initial research done by CBC Research in 1986, the longer the VCR is in the home the more attention shifts from renting tapes to recording from TV.

Although hard evidence to the contrary is lacking, a number of historical and anecdotal factors can be adduced that suggest renting tapes is more important to viewers than timeshifting:

→ First and foremost, we have the blinking "12:00", which has become an international metaphor for the average person's frustration with programmable

technology. For years the non-functioning VCR clock was a staple of the Johnny Carson monologue. This and other anecdotal evidence must cast doubt on the widespread practice of timeshifting, not only because several other programming steps are required to record on many VCRs, but also because all other programmable functions depend on having the clock and date set correctly.

→ The CBC study itself suggests that even though VCR penetration has increased dramatically over the last several years, the amount of time people have spent watching TV has not increased. Timeshifting would seem to provide a "bonus" audience, but of course every minute that bonus audience is reviewing a timeshifted broadcast, it is not available to watch whatever is being broadcast in "real" time. If the same number of viewing hours are being devoted to an increasing amount of program material, then audience fragmentation — and a decrease in individual broadcaster audience shares — would seem to be the inevitable outcome.

→ We also read in the study under "VCR Reach and Share" that VCR viewing has increased significantly though not dramatically since 1986: reach (defined as spending at least 15 minutes a week with some form of VCR programming) has gone up from 15% of all viewers two years or older to 20% in the last couple of years. VCR viewing share has also increased, from 2.6% of all TV viewing in 1986, to 3.4%, where it too has levelled off: this includes both rentals and timeshifting. In the fall of 1991, CBC research found that 22% of all persons over two years of age spent at least 15 minutes each week viewing some form of VCR playback and this VCR viewing accounted for 3.9% of all TV viewing.

→ But the real story here is the spectacular increase in videocassette rentals and sales over this same period of time. American data indicate that the home video market has grown steadily in the last five years, in both rentals and sell-through.

On the basis of all these developments, including the growth in annual home video rentals, it is difficult to concur with the idea that timeshifting is the major use of VCRs in Canadian homes. While the trends reported in the 1986 research may have held true for some transition period in the industry, all the evidence suggests that at least in the first half of the 1990s, home video sales and rentals will be the predominant VCR-related activity among Canadian viewers. If this observation is true, then it would lend support to our view that VCRs, far from adding a bonus audience to broadcast programming, will continue to draw viewers away to the home video market.

The VCR has helped create a huge and profitable home video market that not only changed the way we watch TV, but also changed the way Hollywood does business. Despite continuing problems of user-unfriendliness, the VCR has reached a position of dominance in home entertainment thanks to four compelling features:

→ relative ease-of-use for simple playback of recorded tapes
→ complete control of the timing and pace of playback
→ a huge inventory of inexpensive prerecorded material to draw from
→ the ability to erase and record

Although VCRs are not about to disappear from the marketplace, they are gradually getting caught in a pincer movement between two competing technologies. One of these is a family of standalone technologies based on the optical disc, the other is pay-per-view TV. These are discussed in Chapters 3 and 4 respectively.

Established technology 4: the remote control

TV remote controls began life in two different forms, hard-wired and wireless, the latter based on infra-red technology. They were designed for use with at least three different appliances: the TV set itself, VCRs and cable converter boxes.

The remote control is a prominent example of a technology created for the convenience of consumers which has worked against the interests of broadcasters and program producers. This situation has much in common with the struggles surrounding development by the major Japanese firms of dual-cassette "dubbing" machines, digital audio tape (DAT) machines and even the VCR itself. All of these tape-based technologies were and are viewed by the major recording labels and movie studios as a threat to their livelihood and to their ownership of songs, albums, movies and other entertainment properties.

"Simple" cable hookup for VCR

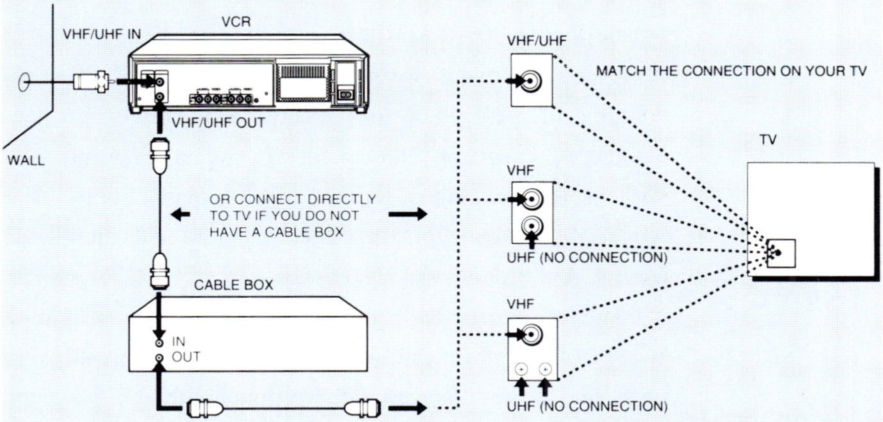

The threat perceived by broadcasters in the form of the remote control is based on a somewhat different problem — "zapping", the practice of using the remote to change channels in rapid succession, typically in order to avoid commercials or other program material. CBC survey data indicate that as of 1991, some 91% of English-Canadian TV households were equipped with a remote control.

Twenty-five or 30 years ago, viewers had a lot less incentive to change channels than they do today. The growth of the marketplace to 20, 30 or more channels in large cities is a mixed blessing. Conventional broadcasters have been the victims of the resulting audience fragmentation — too many broadcasters chasing too few viewers. For commercial broadcasters, the problem of shrinking audiences is particularly acute, since their revenues depend on the size of the audiences their programs attract.

Needless to say, audience fragmentation wasn't caused by the remote control. While it's pretty clear also that remotes have changed the way we watch TV, it's much less clear whether they've changed TV itself. In the last several years, advertising agencies and their clients have altered the way they make commercials, as well as their length and their placement in programs, in order to retain viewer interest or catch viewers with the same ad on several different channels.

Since the late 1980s, the TV advertising business has developed into a buyer's market, the inevitable consequence of fragmenting audiences and a much larger pool of TV placement options. These developments have helped undermine broadcaster revenues. Have remote zapping and zipping actually done material damage to broadcaster ad revenues?

We can narrow the issue down to whether large numbers of viewers actually began at some measurable point to use remotes to avoid commercials. Despite the mythology surrounding the zapping phenomenon, the empirical evidence is less than convincing. For example, Barry Kiefl, CBC's Director of Research, has analyzed detailed viewing patterns from people meter data and found little support for the idea that zapping has caused a wholesale disaffection from commercial messages ("Zapping concerns downplayed", p.18):

> Detailed analysis of minute-by-minute recorded TV viewing shows that zapping is not a threat to audience levels during commercials as consumers either do not zap, or, as many zap in as zap out so the audience level remains the same.

So what's all the fuss about? Why have broadcasters and advertisers reacted with such trepidation over zapping, to the point of changing how commercials are made? Part of the reason may have more to do with the TV programs themselves than with commercial messages; and part may have to do with the rocky transition from mass-appeal to more targeted television, from broadcasting to narrowcasting.

Even if large numbers of remote-equipped viewers aren't choosing to avoid commercials, there's plenty of anecdotal evidence to suggest that they are choosing to skip right past programs that don't hold their interest, or to use the remote as a browsing device — the phenomenon known as channel surfing.

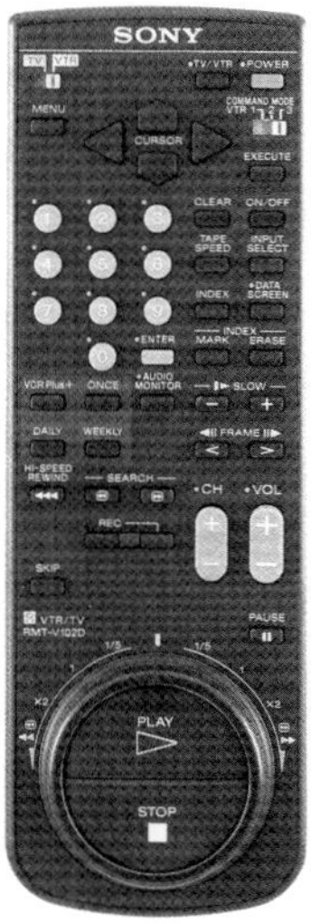

It's a little like taking readers who've had only a few worn volumes on the shelf at home and suddenly dropping them into a huge bookstore for the first time. Will they pick a favourite and stick with it? The fear among observers who care about the dramatic and technical quality of entertainment programming is that in a world of electronic publishing, we're all going to turn into full-time browsers.

But something else is going on: a massive industry anxiety attack over old habits dying hard. The remote control is helping push TV culture out of the era of passivity and into the era of interactivity. But for the time being, we seem to be stuck somewhere in the middle, where even the metaphors are all mixed up. Who wants to go channel surfing? Couch potatoes.

Videoway: the next stage

The best example of just how far the remote control has come in 1992 is Canadian and that's the so-called interactive TV service called Videoway, developed and operated by Quebec's largest cable multiple systems operator (MSO), Vidéotron.

Videoway is apparently a hit. According to a 1992 study carried out by the University of Montreal's Research Laboratory on New Technologies, subscribers who take the Videoway service are watching more TV, considerably more TV, than those who don't. The researchers contend (Caron et al., p.70) that:

> On average, VW subscribers spend a little over 13 hours a week on various Videoway components. They also watch a little over 18 hours of traditional television. The total weekly viewing time for VW subscribers is, therefore, a little over 31 hours or approximately 7 hours more than the average viewing time of Montrealers.[11]

What the Videoway service does is "multiplex" the signals originating with a particular broadcaster, so that instead of one feed, the cable system delivers, say, four different camera angles from a sports event. Those four signals are delivered to a special decoder box supplied by Vidéotron, which allows the viewer to select from among the four feeds or signals. This device does not allow for any upstream communication from viewer to cable headend, let alone to the originating broadcaster.

Videoway offers its subscribers a predetermined and limited choice of alternative signals, all of which are present in the box in the living room. For technical purposes, there's no real difference between pressing the remote to change channels and pressing it to change camera angles.

Remote controls and a lot of channel selections became the enemy of conventional television in the 1980s. Now, in an ironic twist to the remote control story, we can see just how adaptable television really is.

The problem is that while viewers have had plenty of channels to choose from and plenty of opportunity to exercise their options, they've had no such luck with commercial messages. Videoway may have finally put commercial monotony to rest by offering not only a selection of camera angles, news items and so on, but a selection of commercials as well. In recent experiments with national advertisers, Vidéotron has extended the idea of greater control over program content to include advertising content. By placing four or five different ads for the same product in front of viewers and asking interested viewers to select the one that appeals most to them, the advertiser is getting these viewers to form their own demographic segments — limited of course by the range of tastes and values reflected in the commercials on offer.

Once again, we've seen in our glance at the evolution of the remote control and selectivity that new TV technologies are highly unpredictable. After helping to accelerate the decline of ad-supported TV, the remote control may now turn out to be part of its salvation. Although a clear shift has taken place in the last couple of years from ad-supported to user-pays video services, it is likely that many specialized products and services will find a niche on "interactive" television. As the evolution of specialty television in Canada has demonstrated, many services are well suited to enjoying the dual stream of revenue from subscriber fees on the one hand and advertising on the other.

Even though many of the emerging technologies we've been alluding to represent a gradual transition from some earlier technical stage, most will still upset the status quo and in particular the regulation and financing of conventional broadcast television. We've tried to show how the relatively innocuous changes anticipated with the advent of cable TV and the VCR have in fact led to significant and largely unpredictable changes in the structure of the TV industry.

We're now ready to look at the single most important technological change to affect broadcasting in this decade. It will almost certainly create disruptions, not only for the changes it will bring directly to broadcasting, like HDTV, but also because it is paving the way for non-broadcast forms of entertainment based on the optical disc. The culprit is digital technology.

Chapter 3

FROM BOOB TUBE TO SMART-TV: THE DIGITAL REVOLUTION HITS BROADCASTING

"Many technologies, for all their marvellous potential, fall short of universal acceptance or are only partially exploited by those who use them."

Ervin S. Duggan, FCC Commissioner, 1992

So what is digital anyway? Why is it such a breakthrough? And why won't people stop talking about it?

We know a digit is a number, in particular the 10 whole numbers 0 through 9 introduced to the West by the Arabs (and therefore referred to as Arabic numbers or numerals). "Digit" also refers to the fingers and toes, but that's another story. For our purposes, "digital" refers to something numerical, using numbers... but to do what?

First of all, we need to understand that television has always been a so-called "analog" electronic medium. Analog signals are called analog because as they travel through a circuit or device, they only approximate the encoded information as it's transferred from one component to another.[12] Almost everything electronic has always worked this way, including that very rare animal, the analog computer. (Please refer to the Appendix and the Glossary for more details.)

To appreciate what happened to computers, we have to think of information as all-encompassing — images, colours, motion, voices, text, numbers, graphics.

Originally, computing devices registered changes in information by means of an analog technique, such as the movement of a mechanical part or a change in the voltage of an electrical current.

At around the time that television was being introduced in North America, however, the science of computing was revolutionized by the invention of the digital or binary computer. Computer scientists needed a way to process information that was both extremely accurate and extremely fast. Fortunately what they had to work with in most business and scientific applications was discrete units of information, like letters and numbers. So a common language was invented based on binary digits, or "bits" for short.

What this binary code allows programmers and users to do is express all the information they have to work with in two simple numbers: zeroes and ones (that's where the binary comes in). While it may be hard to believe and even harder to explain, most of the vastly complicated things computers can do boil down to strings of zeroes and ones zipping around circuits at the speed of light. In fact, the use of zeroes and ones is just a convenient shorthand for an even more general two-way state of affairs, which can be represented as a positive or negative charge, an on or off signal, or an open or closed gate.

These binary digits or bits are the building blocks of a larger coding unit called a "byte". This is a string of eight bits that signify something common sense can relate to, such as the letters of the alphabet, punctuation marks or whole numbers. Two crucial things make it possible for many computers and computer programs to talk to each other: standard codes that share the same string of bits for the letter "A" or the number "1"; and that well-known and intimidating property of computers, their ruthless lack of ambiguity.

Computers don't approximate the letter "M" or the number "8": what they give you either is or is not that symbol. No matter how many times you process that letter "M", it's still going to be that letter "M" until you decide to change it. Nor are there any half-measures with binary digits: you can't have some "zero" and some "one", or a half positive, half negative charge. In the digital world, it's an all or nothing game.[13]

A MESSAGE IN SEARCH OF A STORAGE MEDIUM

Back in the 1970s, research scientists at Philips and Sony wanted to develop a better way to record and play back music. Before we delve into the complexities of the digital revolution in pictures, it makes both historical and logical sense to pick up the musical story first.

All the major music systems on the market at that time were analog. That included both tape formats and the vinyl LP.

And all of these systems presented two serious kinds of quality limitations. One had to do with the mechanics of how musical sounds are approximated and how they degenerate quickly when copied. The other had to do with the physical medium used to convey recordings to the public. Tape stretches, wears and tangles. Vinyl also wears out, especially if not handled and cleaned with great care. Both of these media are also highly prone to extraneous noise, like tape hiss and the pops and worn grooves that attack LPs.

We won't be spoiling the punchline of the story by revealing that the ultimate solution was the audio compact disc or CD. The CD was an innovation in two ways: how it stores musical information and how that information is retrieved. The CD was the first digital breakthrough in consumer electronics. To appreciate what was accomplished, we need to return briefly to our basic description of information types.

Electronic devices allow us to handle two different kinds of information — one that's discrete and static, like alphanumeric text, and the other, which is time-based and continuous, like music and motion video. Digital computers and processors have a relatively easy time with information like numbers in a database, because they are separate entities that can be coded and manipulated individually. There's little doubt where one codable piece of information ends and another begins. That discrete quality helps enhance the ability of digital computers to sort and modify data with great speed and accuracy.

But with music, there's a problem. Musical information is neither generated nor perceived by the human ear in discrete units. Be it the swell of a heavy metal band or the swell of a string quartet, the sounds come in continuous streams. Enter digitization.

To imagine how continuous sounds get digitized — turned into discrete digits — a visual metaphor may help. A wave form representing a musical passage moves up and down and left to right. (In reality, of course, this is no metaphor, since musical and other sounds display like this on an oscilloscope). In order to digitize musical passages, engineers had to devise a way to divide that wave into thousands of slices, each capturing one codable piece of information. How many "slices" you take from each second of music makes an enormous difference to what you hear when the music is reassembled during playback.

This process is termed "sampling" and it's called that because the digital device samples the signal carrying the musical information in on-and-off pulses rather than continuously. Then it assigns a digital code to each and every sample, just like the code used to represent discrete information in a computer. As you'd expect, sampling has its own elaborate rules. Generally speaking, music must be sampled at a rate of 44,100 times *a second* in order for a CD to reproduce it in an acceptable fashion.

This sampling rate is the musical equivalent of picture resolution in video, the ability of a TV screen to resolve fine visual detail. Think of one part of the curve in the wave form, magnified many times, like a letter in display type. If the curve in the wave or letter is constructed of just a few coarse "slices", then the curve won't be smooth — it'll have what designers call the "jaggies". The finer the slices and the more of them, the smoother the look, or the sound, as the case may be.

Now each one of these coded digital slices or samples of music takes on a life of its own. *And this is where the big break with analog signal processing comes in.*

When those samples are captured on tape, copied to a master for commercial recording or processed in any other way, digital equipment doesn't simply approximate those coded digital slices. It reads them as a discrete, unambiguous string of digits and passes on all and only those digits — no more, no less. And in theory, no matter how many times this digital music is copied, absolutely no degradation will take place.

The difference in quality, especially when repeated processing or copying takes place, is like the difference between successive photocopies of an original

Compact Disc Surface

document and a series of original printouts. The copies will look more and more like copies, the originals will keep on looking like originals. A digital string like "1-0-0-1-1-0-1-0" does not change its form the way light and electrical energy change form in analog processing. The significance of this digital consistency lies not only in the ability to preserve musical fidelity, but also in the ability to interoperate with other kinds of computing equipment, whose primary functions may have nothing at all to do with music. Therein lies the key to convergence.[14]

The CD arrives

Digitizing sound was half the battle; the other half was putting it onto a medium that could do justice to the fidelity of the music, as well as be convenient for the consumer. The CD itself was an ingenious invention for several different reasons, not the least of which is that it has turned out to have many other applications besides music recording.

The hard, shiny disc that most people now recognize as an audio CD propelled digital music onto the world stage and in a few short years practically wiped out its predecessor, the vinyl LP. The digitized information is recorded on a CD in the form of microscopic pits. The CD player reads this information not by direct mechanical contact, as in older recording technologies. Instead, a highly focused and extremely accurate laser beam is directed onto the pitted surface and interprets the pits as the disc spins in the player.

Because CD technology uses beams of light to read information, rather than heads rubbing against magnetic tape (or a stylus over vinyl), such systems are known as "optical" technologies. (We'll see in a moment how this applies to video disc formats.) The CD itself, which is made of polycarbonate, is very durable. Its lifespan is vastly increased as a result of the fact that there is virtually no wear and tear from use, because no direct mechanical contact is made with a stylus or tape head.

So-called "CD-quality" sound has become the standard of excellence in musical reproduction. And compared to most vinyl and tape-based systems, the digital audio CD represents a huge leap forward in sound quality, especially for home sound systems.

When CDs first began appearing on the market, however, some audiophiles were heard to complain that they (the CDs) had a somewhat shrill or unnatural

Why all information isn't created equal...

CD players and other digital devices have feedback circuitry that enables the equipment to keep checking for problems like tracking error by monitoring the position of the laser, comparing that position with a reference standard and compensating for any mistracking by making instantaneous and imperceptible adjustments. A new generation of disc players can actually compensate for problems by calling on a few seconds of music stored redundantly in a memory chip and constantly updated as the recording is played back.

Note that this capability — detecting errors of reproduction — is a feature entirely absent from analog technologies like record turntables. Analog stereo equipment is equipped with features to help minimize extraneous noise, such as filters and tone controls. High-end turntables are also designed to minimize the tracking error induced by the movement of the stylus from the quality, depending on the type of music in question. While some of the debate between purists and others is buried in subjectivity, it's important to realize that the very strength of digital recording is also a weakness. A digital sample will reproduce exactly what it has sampled... but by definition the sampler can't sample everything. It's a lot like sampling in public opinion research. If the sample is large enough and drawn carefully, the questions are posed properly, and so on, opinion research can provide a fairly accurate picture of what the whole population thinks. But the picture can't ever be *perfectly* accurate, since every exercise in sampling has an unavoidable margin of error.

Digital gives near-perfect reproduction as far as it goes, but like any representation of a real-life process, it's still only a copy, not the real thing. One area in which musical purists say this shortcoming is obvious to sensitive ears is in the digital reproduction of strings, woodwinds and other non-electronic instruments which produce rich harmonics and overtones when played. Ironically, better reproduction can often be achieved for some types of music through the use of analog equipment, especially expensive turntables and loudspeakers.

But in the mass market, the trade-off is clear. For those without thousands of dollars to spend on a sound system, the CD offers a better cost-quality ratio. Convenience is also a force to be reckoned with.

outside to the inside of the record surface. Unfortunately, none of these features is "intelligent": that is, they are incapable of detecting a problem at random and making some change to the playback parameters on the fly. Analog filters, noise reduction and sophisticated tone arms exercise their quality control in a completely non-discriminating way and can only deal with problems in a predetermined way.

When a CD player detects a scratch or imperfection on the surface of a disc, it doesn't attempt to repair the damage in any physical way — it can't. What it does do once the damaged portion is detected is activate a suppression circuit that helps to mask unwanted noise or a memory circuit that fills in for missing musical information. As soon as the recording returns to normal, the error correction circuitry goes back to standby, waiting for any other potential problems.

It's safe to assume that, outside of early adopters and audiophiles, most consumers find great utility in not having to fret about cleaning or wear and tear.

Interacting with a disc: the CD grows up

Stereo music is only the beginning of what the entertainment and consumer electronics industries have in store for the 5-inch digital compact disc.

The big news lies in one of the greatest challenges yet to engineering ingenuity — putting moving pictures on a CD. All of the problems associated with digitizing the massive amounts of information in moving video are compounded by squeezing it into the space on a 5-inch disc. And then putting it in a package that will capture the hearts and minds of jaded consumers, who are still busy trying to figure out how their VCR works. They are the successors to the larger format laserdisc, but with several new wrinkles.

To make things just a little more complicated, engineers and designers at the world's biggest electronics firms have set themselves the task of making the CD not only multimedia but also interactive. The products and platforms at issue belong to the category of "non-broadcast" or "standalone" technologies. They have much in common with the VCR in that they are TV peripherals: they plug into the TV set and play back a product you've bought or rented from a local retailer, not received over the air or the cable from a broadcaster.

That's about where the similarity ends, however. The new disc-based technologies are like a combination of VCR convenience, CD quality and video game interactivity. The result — often referred to as interactive multimedia — has been a long time in the making. "Multimedia" generally refers to the communication of messages or information through the combined use of text, graphics, animation, audio and motion video.

Of course all of these "media" can be utilized by ordinary TV sets. Rock concerts and boardroom presentations could also lay claim to providing a multimedia experience. In the narrower modern sense, however, multimedia goes hand in hand with that other basic concept of the new technologies — interactivity.

That's where computers enter the picture. Multimedia has come to mean

more than just the convergence of voice, music, alphanumeric text and so on. It also implies that the user has some degree of interactive control over these elements, instead of being merely a passive viewer, as with broadcast TV. The elements had all been in place for years, but not in *one* place: TVs and home entertainment systems were certainly multimedia and getting more so. Meanwhile, computers were certainly interactive: they basically won't do anything until you tell them what to do.

Then engineers began figuring out how to take advantage of the soaring increase in the power of desktop computers to process and reproduce the sights and sounds normally associated with home entertainment products. The most difficult hurdle to overcome was (and in 1992 still is) how to handle full-motion, full-screen, colour video, so that the image looks like what we're used to from TV.

Both the established laserdisc format and the emerging CD video formats offer much higher technical quality than any other current method of getting a movie or comparable program material to the home TV screen. They also offer something else. Tape formats of all kinds are restricted to linear access by the end-user. That means you can't get to a certain scene in the middle of a movie without fast winding through everything else first.

What optical discs allow is random access, the ability to move almost instantaneously to any selected point in the movie or program (in just the way an audio CD makes it possible to move to a particular track or passage). Many of the new disc formats are taking advantage of this feature to make the TV experience interactive rather than passive and one-way.

The marriage, or at least engagement, of the computer and the TV has given rise to a whole new industry devoted to interactive multimedia. In some ways the grandaddy of them all has never met a real TV set and that's a technology that goes by the glamorous name of "Compact Disc Read Only Memory" or CD-ROM for short. The CD-ROM disc looks exactly like its cousin the audio CD. The difference is that a CD-ROM, used with a suitable drive or player, can reproduce multimedia sounds and images. The immense storage capacity of CD-ROM discs — up to 650 megabytes — makes data-intensive, interactive programs possible. That, by the way, is enough storage capacity to hold some 900 copies of this book!

Interactive multimedia discs are just starting to infiltrate the home environment. In 1991, a number of disc-based multimedia technologies designed to be easy to use and to offer both the gloss of television and the processing power of a computer were introduced to the market. As *Fortune* described it (Alpert 1992), the breakthrough came with CD-ROM:

> The compact disc was one of the great success stories of the 1980s, revolutionizing the recorded music business in less than five years. Now something similar is happening in the personal computer industry: After years of anticipation, the CD-ROM — which stands for compact disc, read only memory — is becoming an essential piece of business software and making its way into the home as well. Corporate managers are using the shiny silver platters to store voluminous reports and manuals. Publishers are creating multimedia CD-ROM discs that combine reference works like encyclopedias with music, photographs, and flashy video. And software companies are writing CD-ROM games that are way cooler than anything available on a floppy disk.

Products for non-broadcast media are being developed by:

A phone company: *ImagiTrek, a wholly owned subsidiary of GTE, the huge American telephone company that controls Canada's BCTel, has more than 40 producers, designers and engineers working on title development for the consumer market.*

A consumer electronics company: *Philips NV, the Dutch conglomerate that developed the compact disc, expanded from the hardware into the software business when it founded Philips Interactive Media and spent hundreds of millions of dollars developing Compact Disc Interactive and scores of CD-I titles.*

A niche software company: *The Voyager Co. of Santa Monica, California, a relatively tiny and eccentric production house, has released movie and educational titles for both TV applications, like laserdisc, and non-TV applications, like CD-ROM.*

The Imagination Machine

But the real excitement — and the big money — are in the consumer market, where several of the big multinationals are trying very hard to capture share of mind and share of screen time for their new products, which connect directly to the television instead of the computer.

One of the first and most costly to develop was Philip's CD-I (Compact Disc Interactive). It is being marketed in the United States as the "The Imagination Machine" and retails now for approximately $700. It allows the user to browse through material on a CD-I disc and interact using a simple remote control. By Christmas of 1992, Philips promises to have models available capable of running full-motion video from their proprietary 5-inch disc. Current CD-I titles, retailing at between $20 and $50, include, for example, "Treasures of the Smithsonian", which gives the viewer a private audio-video tour that can be customized to suit individual tastes and pacing.

A long battle lies ahead before such products will make a big dent in the world of consumer electronics. Several hurdles have to be overcome. First of all, because the long-term market is seen as so lucrative, companies like Philips now face competition from a host of other companies with good ideas and deep pockets. These include Commodore, with its "CDTV", which can be expanded into a home computer system, NEC's Turbo Graphix and Tandy's VIS multimedia player. One obvious problem for the consumer is that most of these products are mutually incompatible — which makes the Beta-VHS wars look pretty tame by comparison.

The other two problems are also familiar ones. These concern the importance to consumers of attractive titles, whether educational, entertainment or reference. The slow market penetration of CD-I, for example, has been attributed to the relatively small number of titles available on its launch in the fall of 1991 — about 50 altogether. And finally, there's the whole issue of whether and to what degree consumers will want to interact with their TV, determine their own pace, even make up their own endings to interactive fiction titles, when it's late, they're tired and there's a ball game on.

One optimistic sign for this whole family of non-broadcast technologies however, is the remarkable range of companies that are developing titles for CD-I and other platforms (see accompanying box).

Digital broadcasting

Digital technology has progressed through several stages in the electronics industries. Broadcasting will be one of the last areas in which digital technology will be widely implemented. That's mostly because the vast amounts of information that must be encoded when moving video images are digitized has required the development of powerful new processing and compression techniques. And this is to say nothing of the dislocation that the adoption of a new digital television standard will create among both broadcasters and consumers.

Engineers and research scientists spent years developing digital tools for use in computer applications. Applications in many related fields, however, had to wait on progress in the development of technologies like microchips, fibre optics and the laser, to mention but three examples. Two of the most significant uses of digital that are now well developed are the use of digital transmission techniques by telephone companies and the introduction of the digital audio CD.

Back in the 1970s, long-distance telephone transmission started to move

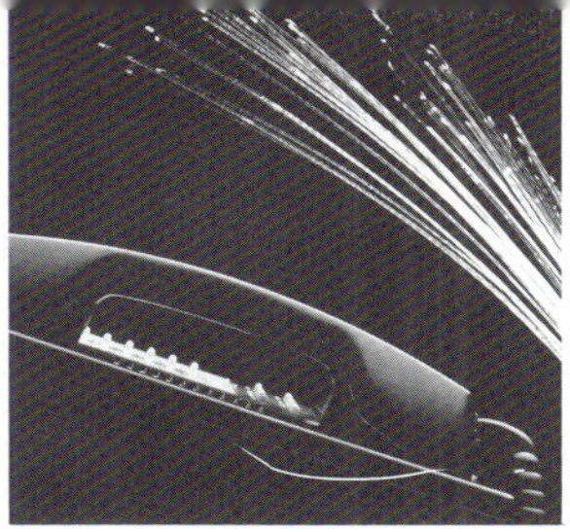

away from analog transmission and mechanical switching to digital techniques — quite a few years, in other words, before the arrival of the digital CD in North American homes.

The use of digital telephone transmission in telephony began over ordinary copper lines. But the real advantages of digital only came to the fore when the major carriers like Bell Canada and AT&T began to deploy fibre optic lines for both public and private transmission facilities. What fibre added to digital's computer-like accuracy was computer-like speed, because of the vast increase in bandwidth (carrying capacity) afforded by fibre.

Why is it only recently that broadcasting has begun to incorporate digital technology?

It turns out that the *production* end of broadcast television has already been heavily infiltrated by digital technology. In June of 1992, *Video Innovations* noted (p.3) that

> what the word processor did for writing, digital editing is rapidly doing for video production. Through the marvels of digital editing, editors can now insert, delete and move scenes on a computer monitor like a writer can move words, sentences and paragraphs.

Television transmission and reception, however, have remained resolutely analog. There are three reasons why over-the-air television transmission and reception have been so long getting around to digitization:

→ the huge amounts of information in full-motion, colour video, compared to voice and music;

→ the cost of converting from established TV standards;

→ the regulatory complexities of managing the spectrum under a new standard.

Digitization as applied to the reproduction of artistic creations like music and movies has great potential for enhancing the listening or viewing experience. This can of course be credited to digital's ability to reproduce sounds and images in a much more accurate and comprehensive way than comparable analog methods.

Thus, there is a trade-off in virtually all broadcasting technologies between efficient transmission and high quality reception and reproduction. Everything else being equal, technical and thus aesthetic quality increases with the amount of information being conveyed. More information in this sense can be considered a positive attribute. But more information in any transmission channel increases the load on that channel, and increased load means higher costs for capacity, maintenance, access, signal separation, switching, etc. This is not just an issue of costs to the carrier or customer; it is also an issue of scarcity of capacity even within closed systems like cable or fibre optic networks.

From the viewer or end-user perspective, what this trade-off comes down to is service choice versus technical quality.

TV buyers have been replacing their colour sets at a brisk pace in Canada. Meanwhile, the quality and versatility of TV sets made by the major manufacturers have increased significantly. Large-format TVs have made the 27- or 28-inch screen a de facto market standard; sets with screens larger than this jump sharply in price because of high rejection rates in the quality control process.[15] Circuitry and speakers for stereo sound have become common. Resolution has also become a selling feature: high and low resolution models now give consumers an option. Microprocessor and digital control features like picture-in-a-picture have come into the high end of the market and, like all such things, will drop steadily in price and percolate down to less expensive models.[16]

Who benefits?

Viewers have certainly derived some benefit from these increases in both service choice and technical quality over the last several years. As far as choice is concerned, however, we must remain sceptical towards the claims made by both industry and government about the degree to which more and more channels actually translate into improved viewing experiences. As we've seen, a vast increase in available services will only make the going tougher for broadcasters, especially the conventional networks.

What about technical improvements and new technologies? Herein lies a bitter irony for the conventional broadcaster. It's pretty obvious that the real beneficiaries of sales of new and improved TV sets are the manufacturers — not all of whom are Japanese, by the way, the world's largest actually being the European-owned Philips and Thomson. The consumers who are buying these sets are obviously finding some utility in their improved features and quality, although they are also highly sensitive to prices: markups on video equipment are among the lowest in any retail sector and competition is fierce.

It would be good news for broadcasters if the ability to see and hear their programming in exquisite clarity and fidelity translated into more revenue, but there's no evidence that it does.

In fact, improvements can have negative effects on broadcasters. When improvements like stereo broadcasting come along, viewers get used to them quickly. Those broadcasters who are late adopters of a new technology may actually lose audience share if they don't make the investment necessary to upgrade. In other words, there's no competitive edge to be gained by adopting the technology, but there may be something to lose if a broadcaster doesn't. The one measurable difference between adopting early and adopting late is that many technologies cost less at a later date. Therefore, improvements like stereo sound produce negative fallout for broadcasters, rather than a sales advantage.

Subtle, incremental changes like the shift to stereo TV broadcasting may not have much of an effect on large segments of the audience. Many still do not have stereo sets and, while no research is readily available on audience reactions, it seems highly unlikely that even viewers equipped with stereo would not watch a program they wanted to watch because it wasn't in stereo. The same cannot be said of far more sweeping and visible changes like the move to colour.

As we'll now see, a change is coming to TV technology that has been compared to the change to colour in the 1960s in the scope of its impact on broadcasters, producers and consumers. It's called HDTV.

HDTV

HDTV stands for High Definition Television. It is one of the most hotly debated "new" technologies in the television and video industries. HDTV has been under development for over a decade, has enormous implications for broadcasters and consumers, and yet may still be 10 to 15 years away from full implementation in North America.

A vast improvement in picture quality has always been the avowed objective of HDTV research and development. It is not at all certain, however, that picture quality alone will lead to wide consumer acceptance of this controversial technology. HDTV will also have a different aspect ratio than traditional television. The aspect ratio of a screen or image is the ratio of its width to its height.

We can say two things about the proposed HDTV aspect ratio of 16-to-9 (as opposed to the conventional ratio of 4-to-3). First, a number of manufacturers are already bringing wide-screen sets to the market that contain decoders making them adaptable to the existing analog NTSC system. Marketing managers at Philips and elsewhere probably took little time to see the wide screen as a distinctive and historic change in the standard set configuration that they could leverage into a marketing advantage. And while it needs some adapting, the wide screen has the added benefit of not being dependent on high definition protocols, digital or otherwise. By December 1992, Thomson Consumer Electronics will start selling its first TV sets with 16:9 aspect ratios.

Second, the new aspect ratio does not simply represent a distinctive selling point, one that defines a whole new generation of TV sets (before the set is even turned on!). It brings the home entertainment environment a giant step closer to being at the movies. The wide TV screen will make modern movies easier to watch because of the ratio and better to watch because of the enhanced picture quality.

This may have one important result: it could make many viewers feel less obliged to go to the cinema for technically authentic and arousing viewing experiences. If video entertainment for the home becomes truly competitive, and the prices of rentals and pay-per-view remain low while cinema admissions keep rising, the advent of HDTV will make people even more reluctant to leave the home for entertainment. As we will argue below, this scenario also casts doubt on the wisdom of spending a large proportion of our federal cultural dollars on the

production and promotion of Canadian movies for theatrical release, rather than concentrating on niche markets in the new home media.

HDTV will require an entirely new broadcasting standard for television. The current standard for North America is NTSC. What is therefore being proposed with the introduction of HDTV is a complete change in the TV broadcasting standards that have been in place in North America since the 1940s.

Background

Although HDTV is being compared to the change-over in TV from black-and-white to colour, that revolution was accomplished without having to do away with the NTSC standard. What's comparable is the Catch-22 situation it puts everybody in. Broadcasters can't broadcast on a standard incompatible with all the TV sets in the land. TV viewers don't want to go out and buy new sets until there's programming available to receive in the new standard. Who makes the first move?

HDTV has been under development for years in several parts of the world, mainly Japan, the U.S., Canada and Europe. Japan has the world's first and only functioning consumer HDTV system. It was developed under a standard known as MUSE by Japan's public broadcaster, Nippon Hoso Kyokai (NHK) and launched in November 1991. "Launched" is the operative term here, because this is not a terrestrial system, but one operating from a direct broadcast satellite.

In the U.S., HDTV is taking longer to get off the ground. The FCC appointed a special working group to study HDTV at the Advanced Television Test Center in Alexandria, Virginia. It is due to complete its research in 1993, at which time the FCC will mandate a new standard that will eventually replace NTSC.[17]

Even in Canada, HDTV has been on the broadcasting agenda, not only at the inevitable conferences but in the studio. A CBC mini-series called *Chasing Rainbows* was in fact one of the first, if not the first, TV program of its kind to be shot entirely on Sony HDTV equipment. Although that was in 1987, it may be several more years before anyone will ever get to see it sitting in front of an HDTV receiver in their living room.[18]

The standards mess

Despite the FCC's hands-off doctrine on many industry issues, like AM stereo (it refused to impose a standard), the American regulator has taken an interventionist approach to HDTV. In addition to appointing an expert working group to recommend a standard, it called for an open competition among all interested parties.

The standards issues to be solved are daunting.

Transition. As with colour, the FCC requires that the transition from one system to another be accomplished with the least amount of disruption. Some proposals have suggested that the new standard be compatible with NTSC, but the FCC announced in 1990 that broadcasters will be required to simulcast an NTSC transmission of their signal on one frequency allocation while they transmit on another frequency in HDTV.

Bandwidth. HDTV entails the transmission of far more electronic information than NTSC: the 6 MHz of bandwidth required by the latter would increase by a factor of five, to 30 MHz, under some proposals. Without the application of other technological innovations to reduce the requirement, particularly compression, this amount of spectrum would put television broadcasters on a collision course with other spectrum users, like cellular phone companies.[19]

International rivalry. All hope of agreement on an international consumer transmission standard seems to be irretrievably lost. For reasons of both national pride and international trade, the Europeans seem determined to stick by their MAC standard. While the Japanese have made a huge financial commitment to the development of their MUSE system, it is possible that the MUSE system may eventually be altered or replaced. Some compromise may be made possible by the separation of the HDTV monitor and the decoder required to process the incoming HD signal.

Digital vs analog. What's behind the standards tug-of-war is another analog-digital story. It's important to understand that HDTV is not necessarily one or the other. As it happens, both MAC and MUSE have been implemented as analog systems. For at least a year or two after its original call for proposals, the FCC was considering both analog and digital systems. One of the original analog proponents withdrew and it is now a foregone conclusion that the system chosen will be digital. This will have enormous — and probably positive — repercussions for most consumers and video suppliers in the future.

The costs to consumers

Converting to HDTV will not be cheap. The research and development costs committed for the FCC study alone, which may amount to hundreds of millions of dollars, will be recouped in part by the successful bidder (and it's conceivable they may join forces at a later date with one or more of the unsuccessful ones).

In April 1991, *Video Technology News* reported that several Japanese and European manufacturers had announced prices for a range of consumer-oriented HDTV monitors. By way of example, a 36-inch MUSE-based model from Sony was priced at $18,000, while a Thomson model with the same screen size but operating on the D2-MAC system was priced at $6,000.

Price announcements have fluctuated up and down for monitors based on these two analog systems, because of developments like a simplified version of the MUSE monitor. But compared to the retail prices for current high-end, large-screen monitors in Canada and the U.S., these prices are still in a rarefied climate. Advanced Broadcasting Systems of Canada (ABSOC) estimates that by the time HDTV is implemented in Canada, starting as early as 1996, HD receivers will be priced in the same bracket as the most expensive current NTSC models, i.e. at well over $2,000.

Delivery channels

HDTV does not exactly spell paradise for over-the-air broadcasters. In fact, several factors point to a situation in which other programming distributors may be handed a competitive advantage by the advent of HDTV.

First and foremost among these is cable, followed by direct broadcast satellite services and video services that may eventually be delivered by the telephone companies both here and in the United States.

The potential advantage for these other three interested parties lies in the delivery channels that would be used by each. Broadcasters who use over-the-air spectrum face a protracted and expensive conversion process, as mandated by the FCC and described above. They are also limited to one NTSC channel and one additional HDTV channel for implementation of the FCC simulcast scheme.

By contrast, the other distribution systems are not faced with either major mandated plant conversions or with the limitations imposed by single-channel operation. Cable operators, the only established alternative as of 1992, already have a broadband path into subscriber homes, which could be used for HDTV applications, or one of the hybrid or compromise "enhanced" TV delivery systems. One or more HDTV channels could be devoted to optional special services like pay-per-view, which would carry an extra charge.

DTH service providers would likely follow the same strategy, using selected channels for HDTV from among the 60 to 80 comprising their total service offering. Because of both regulatory and technical constraints, the phone companies are probably several years away from being in a position to offer competitive video services, whether in HDTV or otherwise. One industry expectation, however, is that allowing the telcos into the information and video businesses will provide the incentive to bring fibre optic cable much closer to homes, perhaps as far as the local loop. Whether that comes to pass or not (and debate continues to rage about the cost and benefits of an extensive fibre replacement of copper lines), the telcos will have the networks, the switching capability, the lines into subscriber homes and billing infrastructure to make HDTV and companion video services a possible alternative to the traditional providers.

As just noted in the reference to billing, cable, DTH and phone company providers have or will have the means to recoup user or subscriber fees and make any investment in HDTV programming a paying proposition. As things now stand, this is impossible for ad-supported over-the-air broadcasters. In an era that seems to be encouraging strange bedfellows, however, two or more of these potential providers could find themselves in strategic alliances or joint ventures to sell HDTV.

All of this leaves one small problem unresolved: HDTV services from any provider won't do anything for a viewer or subscriber who doesn't own an HDTV receiver or decoder. Keeping its watching brief on the whole situation, ABSOC reports that "no scenario has the market penetration of HD receivers at more than 2% in the U.S. and less in Canada by the turn of the century".

Broadcasters: little to gain, lots to lose

Let's be optimistic and assume that consumer uptake of HDTV runs ahead of predictions. Let's also assume that at least some conventional broadcasters strike up partnerships with cable operators to make their market entry more effective. Even under such hopeful conditions, it is difficult to see what broadcasters have to gain from HDTV in the long run, at least compared to rival service providers who enjoy fewer technical constraints and much better operating margins.

American broadcasters have had few kind words for the FCC's vision of how

HDTV will be implemented. The trade magazine *Broadcasting* (April 13, 1992) reported industry reactions in the following terms:

> Broadcasters blasted the FCC's decision last week to give TV stations only five years to broadcast in HDTV once the agency green lights a standard [...]. One irate group owner said the FCC's action "puts enormous capital demand on the industry without new revenue sources. They have taken one giant step backward." [...] Reaction from the broadcasting industry ranged from scepticism to anger.

HDTV will be costly for broadcasters to implement. For broadcasters the price tag will look like this. As reported by ABSOC in 1991, early adopter stations in large U.S. markets might pay as much as $11.5 million (U.S.) for total conversion of their studio and transmission facilities from NTSC to HDTV over a five-year period. Late adopters would pay about 50% less than that, over a period of about nine years.

Broadcasting magazine revealed in April of 1992 that "the big three [networks] had a combined operating margin of under 6%, the worst in at least 20 years". Thus, the huge capital outlay that broadcasters will have to make to convert to HDTV could not have come at a worse time.

If the situation is tough for American broadcasters, it's worse for their Canadian counterparts. For in addition to the no-win business prospect — no return on a hefty investment — Canadian industry people have to stand on the sidelines while the Americans decide the timetable and the manner of the most important technical change to our broadcasting system in its entire history.

The reasons for this have to do with Canada's long tradition of having to do broadcasting things the American way. Geographical proximity and market size are only the most obvious of the reasons explaining why Canada was obliged to adopt technical standards such as NTSC transmission and to compromise with the Americans on the sharing of radio spectrum.

Canada now finds itself in the unenviable position of having a lot at stake in the HDTV decision-making process but little say in the matter. Unlike the Japanese, the Europeans and (depending on how events unfold) the Americans,

Canadian industry has little to gain from long-term TV receiver replacement purchases, since we have no indigenous design or manufacturing capacity (except in a few small niche hardware areas).

Canadian broadcasters will, however, be deeply affected by the long-term costs and timing of HDTV implementation. The FCC has invited Canadian representation to its HDTV committee, but Canadians will have little or no influence over its policy recommendations on bandwidth, compression ratios and simulcasting with NTSC.

The introduction of HDTV is likely to give an even greater marketing boost to cable in Canada than in the United States. The reasons for this lie in Canadian cable's protected monopoly position and its role as cultural gatekeeper in current public policy.

It is difficult at this time to estimate how much more costly it will be for broadcasters in Canada to prepare for HDTV than it will for cable operators. In its published strategy document, *A Clear Vision*, the CCTA has spoken of an expenditure of six to ten billion dollars by the whole industry in the next decade to modernize Canadian systems completely, by upgrading capacity, implementing fibre optics, introducing addressability and so on (p.27). Although detailed estimates are not available, it would seem highly improbable that the net investment by cable operators in HDTV conversion would be anything like as great as that for broadcasters. Whatever the discrepancies, cable has recoupment possibilities, i.e. a return on its investment, that is unlikely to materialize for broadcasters outside of a joint venture with non-traditional carriers.

If they are required to invest a great deal of capital in technical upgrades, broadcasters will have less money to invest in Canadian programming; however, cable operators will see new revenue streams open up through avenues such as HDTV pay-per-view. This development in the industry raises serious questions about how responsibility for making and subsidizing Canadian programs should be divided.[20]

The much heralded advent of HDTV, while holding great promise, is only a small part of the home entertainment revolution.

Smart-TV

Digital high-def TV — some call it a smart-TV or telecomputer, others just a massive computer masquerading as a TV. If things go according to expectation in Washington, we'll end up with TV sets that will make the passive reception of fixed broadcast signals look like a bad joke.

As we've seen, high definition can go either way, analog or digital. We've also seen that the debate over standards has little to do with the apparently central issue of picture quality. In the long run, what's really going to count with HDTV is not just a few lines of scanning more or less, because proposal X goes ahead instead of proposal Y. *What's going to count is whether or not it's digital.* One of the biggest boosters of a digital standard over analog is FCC chairman Alfred Sikes, who with his colleagues will decide what kind of television system we have for the next couple of decades or more.

What a digital high-def standard will do is sanction the convergence between the computer and the television. A handy way to look at the home electronics marketplace is to divide products between those that started life as computers and are becoming more like TV sets, and TV sets that are becoming more like computers. The important point is that a digital high-definition television standard will finally turn this modest home appliance into a computing, manipulating monster.

One of the best known prophets of what we might call the school of radical digital convergence is George Gilder, author of *Microcosm*. (Gilder himself likes to talk about something he calls a "digital computerscape".) In a 1991 article written for *Forbes*, Gilder described the death of analog TV and its digital rebirth (p.188):

> Crammed with memory chips, mass storage devices and special microprocessors that add and multiply, TV sets will change from passive receivers of preformed pictures into digital broadcast stations. While receiving and displaying images better than existing TVs, the new machines will also process, store, create and even transmit the images in computerized form. This smart-TV, or telecomputer, will eventually be linked to the world by telephone-style networks that will switch video as readily as they do voice today.

Here's what "watching" television be like on this non-TV set, according to Gilder (p.198):

> Every home in a neighborhood is connected, whether by cable or powerful wireless systems, to a high-capacity fiber-optic network. A viewer could dial up a month's worth of selected movies or Harvard Business School courses and receive them in a five-minute burst of scrambled bits. With a meter in his set, the viewer gets billed only for the items he decides to descramble. Politics could, of course, slow the transition to a competitive, digital information system; but the technology is there.

This story has been followed with considerable interest by the business press. The reason, as explained by Gilder and others, is that the American lead over the Japanese in some digital technologies might allow American industry to capture some market share back from Japan in home electronics, over which the Sonys and Matsushitas now have a stranglehold. (We might recall, by the way, that in another twist on the convergence theme, Sony and Matsushita are the two Japanese firms that stunned Hollywood in 1989 and 1990 when they bought Columbia Pictures and MCA Universal respectively.) The development that could turn the tide is a digital high-def standard and aggressive investment in the new technology by American interests like IBM and Time Warner.

In the spring of 1992, the *Wall Street Journal* and other publications began reporting on talks about a strategic alliance allegedly taking place between IBM and Time Warner. If some marriage between the world's largest computer maker and the world's largest entertainment conglomerate were to transpire, it would represent the ultimate convergence between the thinking machine and the boob tube. The WSJ's reporters published a lengthy article in the issue of May 21, 1992 on the subject of the rumoured alliance and how such developments will affect the development of smart-TV sets.

Despite some talk of "cautionary history" and uncertainties, the article makes a strong case for how smart sets will finally turn our old-fashioned selectivity into real interactivity. That fits the vision of future TV outlined by Trip Hawkins of Electronic Arts, one of America's most successful distributors of interactive video games:

> One day cable companies will build "intelligent filters" into viewers' homes, tracking what people watch and tailoring things to their tastes [...]. A filter, watching someone pick rock videos on 100 channels devoted to MTV [the American model for MuchMusic], would see a pattern: "He's watching the Beastie Boys, now Madonna." Pretty soon, Mr. Hawkins says, "it will be sending you videos of groups you've never heard of that are somehow related to what you've watched. Then maybe the TV would say, "Hey, these guys are going to be in town next Thursday. Would you like to see them? If you would, just hit the button and we'll send the tickets to you, because we know who you are and where you live and what your credit card number is." Yikes.

As the article goes on to point out, this kind of interactivity and addressability will be pounced on by advertisers and their clients. All the signs indicate that a large number of the hundreds of future TV channels we're promised will be bigger and better versions of the Home Shopping Network.

The predictions we've just quoted will probably come to pass — some day. They'll take longer than many pundits think and many manufacturers want. And they won't emerge out of an epiphany in regulatory offices, when the FCC and their counterparts decide it's time to open the digital floodgates.

Smart-TV will happen slowly and incrementally, and probably in four stages, though not necessarily in this order:

→ High-end analog NTSC TV sets already have a lot of chips and digital features. It's digital processing that allows a viewer with such a set to see a picture-in-a-picture or grab and store a single frame from a cable or broadcast signal. This stage is well underway. As Gilder points out (p.189), some of the consumer TV sets now made by Sony and Matsushita "contain more microchips than low-end computers do".

→ At a later stage, which may have to wait until HDTV or some transitional technology is implemented, TV sets will have built-in decoders and decompression chips, which will allow them to handle scrambled and compressed signals from a variety of sources — cable, satellites, MDS and so on. In a perfect world, these chips would be standardized and universal, so that mere mortals can throw away the boxes sitting on their TVs and just plug in a wire. That kind of perfection may prove to be elusive.

→ Recognizing a barrage of differently coded instruction sets from incoming signals, peripheral devices and viewers presents a problem for receivers. Devices that make either sets or networks more intelligent will become "trainable". They will take programmability to a new level at which learning to perform a certain function or deliver a certain service will not require conscious intervention from the user.

→ A potentially bigger leap in TV intelligence will take place when convergence broadens out to embrace the telephone and other communications devices. The ability to send video through switched networks in the ways described above will require not only TV sets that are transmitters as well as receivers but also high capacity networks.

As we've mentioned before, motion video carries a lot of information: it takes about 1.5 million bits (1.5 megabits) to code the information in a frame of video. The 30 frames making up one second of video thus require some 45 megabits (these estimates are only averages because the amount of information varies widely with the colour range, amount of movement and so on). The lines to carry these vast amounts of information have already been developed. Right here in Canada, IBM and Rogers Communications have installed a one gigabit fibre optic test line. What does that mean? That it can carry information at the rate of one billion bits per second. How fast is that? Well, depending on your page layout, the equivalent of maybe 60,000 pages a second. That's all the print information in 200 medium-sized novels, going by in one second.

Don't look for wires like this in your neighbourhood any time soon. As we'll see in the next chapter, the show business moguls will take a while to figure out what goes into the wires and who gets the money.

Chapter 4

TV & THE MOVIES: HOLLYWOOD HEADS FOR THE LIVING ROOM

"The American movie is now the staple of the earth, the most wanted U.S. export everywhere on this weary old planet."

Jack Valenti to the Royal Television Society, Washington, 1991

We noted early on that our first goal was to describe the new TV technologies, to demystify them and uncover some patterns in how they are being developed and used. Our second goal is to describe the implications of these technologies for Canadians as consumers and citizens, as well as for Canada as a sovereign nation with a fragile culture.

This chapter represents a transition from the first to the second of these concerns. As we provide further descriptive detail on the convergence of TV and the movies, our focus will shift to the dilemmas faced by Canadian policymakers in shoring up our two major cultural industries.

Technology has brought Canada to a crossroads as the box office moves inexorably towards the living room and TV is transformed into a transactional delivery medium. To understand why, we have to look south. This story starts in Hollywood. It's a story that's part pragmatism and part miracle.

A MARRIAGE MADE IN HEAVEN?

Flamboyance and tinsel notwithstanding, Hollywood is essentially very conservative in its approach to business. The Hollywood studios have always been suspicious of change, and nothing has made them more suspicious and downright hostile than the blossoming of network television. This is an attitude that later extended to other new media. Those who know the history of the business will also be aware that the networks have reciprocated in their strangely co-dependent love-hate relationship with the studios.

Stuck in the middle have been the Canadian and American regulators. The CRTC and FCC, normally a study in contrasts, have both played a highly interventionist role in their attempts to keep peace in a disorderly entertainment marketplace. Of course the approaches have differed. With its firm commitment to minimizing regulation, the FCC developed into a kind of referee between the TV colossus on the one hand and the studio colossus on the other. The rules inside the ring were few but have had far-reaching implications for how American entertainment television evolved. Some of these, notably the rules governing primetime access and finance and syndication, were primarily designed to protect the production industry from the once-powerful networks. In most respects, however, the FCC left a wide-open playing field for the exercise of competition and sometimes unusual strategic alliances. With the decline of conventional network broadcasting and the advent of new video delivery technologies, the FCC has shown itself eager to reduce the rules even further and invite in new players, such as the phone companies.

To describe the CRTC's approach as cautious would be an understatement. Let's go back to 1975. That was the year the CRTC held its first hearing on the prospect of pay television (Hardin, p.296). This was long before anyone had started to talk about "narrowcasting" or specialty channels. What the Commission was being asked to consider, in effect, was whether a licensee should be allowed to offer movies or other programming material over a cable channel for a discretionary fee.

By this date, broadcast TV was already no stranger to the movies. Suspicion and hostility had given way, for now, to such a degree that the studios were making movies especially for television, and by 1974 these "MOWs", movies of the week, were making more money for the networks than the theatrical movies

Jack Valenti

they were licensing from Hollywood. NBC had pioneered the concept with the first MOW in 1966. Canadian viewers were beginning to see some of these crop up on their TV sets.

When it came to selling movies to Canadian cable subscribers, however, the CRTC said "no". And it would keep on saying "no" to the idea for another decade, until 1982. The Commission argued persistently that pay-TV would not contribute to the objectives of the *Broadcasting Act* (Hardin, p.296). There was a pretty clear policy rationale for this view. In the U.S., entertainment television was strictly domestic. Thanks to the FCC, prime time belonged to the Hollywood majors and independents. The filmmaking empire had been there for 60 years or more; now TV was making it even bigger, as well as opening it up to smaller producers.

The CRTC's logic in resisting pay-TV was that any such service that was keyed to movies would be overwhelmingly American. The Commission, in short, was protecting Canada's cultural sovereignty.

But that's not all it was protecting. It was also protecting established broadcast licensees by effectively preventing competition. This in itself is not unusual behaviour for a regulatory body. In the more charitable interpretation, the CRTC has always had a responsibility for ensuring an orderly marketplace, one in which existing licensees can enjoy continuity and reasonable profits, the better to make their contribution to the broadcasting system. In the less charitable interpretation, the CRTC, like most such tribunals, becomes the creature of those it is designed to regulate and thus reluctant to allow change of any kind.

The 1975 watershed

By 1975, the handwriting was already on the wall, twice over. In September, the publishing giant Time Inc. had launched the world's first pay-movie channel, Home Box Office, HBO for short. Two months later came the opening salvo in the protracted war to bring paid movie admissions to the living room in another form: Sony introduced its Betamax VCR to the North American market.

From the vantage point of the early 1990s, it is difficult to understand the vehemence with which the Hollywood majors and their allies attacked every new technological development that impinged on their business — first TV, then cable, then pay satellite channels, then VCRs. But according to just about everyone whose opinion has been recorded in print, it was always thus. One producer, interviewed by *The Economist* in 1983, put the following proposition (p.73):

> → When television started in the 1950s, there was a strong view that was the end of Hollywood. When cable came, we thought that would kill our sales to the nets. None of these things happened. Every time the market expands the combination is greater than before. After all it should be immaterial to Hollywood how people see its product so long as they pay.

It is true that cinema admissions had declined precipitously since the introduction of television (which is not to say TV was the sole cause). U.S. movie admissions peaked in 1946 at four billion; by the early 1960s they had already declined by 75%, to one billion.

Even so, by the time HBO and Betamax were arriving on the scene, Hollywood executives should have been too busy counting the TV revenues coming through the door to have taken much notice. It was boom time: earnings from TV rose from $65 million in 1970 to $475 million in 1979 (Balio, p.288). Despite the money, Hollywood lashed out in all directions — perhaps because of the confusion and uncertainty surrounding the new delivery technologies. In 1978, with HBO now in two million cable homes, some of the studios decided to retaliate in the marketplace. That year Warner Bros launched its own Movie Channel.

A year later (1979) Columbia, Paramount, MCA and Twentieth-Century Fox, in response to HBO's ever-growing market power, reached an agreement to form a pay-TV service called Premiere. Premiere was to have exclusive rights to each film licensed to it (including the theatrical output of all four studios) for nine months after release. This provision led to the service's demise after the Justice Department charged Premiere with violation of the Sherman Antitrust Act.

Other studios decided to look after business the all-American way, by-passing the marketplace and heading straight for court. Within a year of the introduction

of the first generation of VCRs, Universal and Disney filed suit against Sony for copyright infringement, since the machines could be used to make copies of their movies. They wanted the court to ban VCRs because of the threat they allegedly represented to their legitimate business interests. The studios weren't fooling around. The suit dragged on for eight years and went all the way to the Supreme Court.

During that period, Jack Valenti, a figure who has since become notorious for his views on the "free" movement of American entertainment products around the world, was busy trying another angle in Washington. As head of the Motion Picture Association of America (MPAA) and Hollywood's chief lobbyist, Valenti tried to persuade Congress to impose royalties on the sale of videotapes and VCRs. That effort ended after a ruling in the "Betamax case" by the U.S. Supreme Court in 1984 found in favour of Sony.

The Betamax decision had its share of ironies. By the year of the Supreme Court decision, the Betamax format had already begun to lose the battle with VHS. And by 1984 as many as 30% of American households had already purchased VCRs of one kind or another. It seemed the VCR was a fait accompli.

Video comes home to roost — and stays

But the biggest irony of all was just around the corner. Home video — a whole new industry — was a bonanza. By 1986, the majors were earning half of all their domestic film revenues from videocassette sales. Meanwhile, HBO had long since become Hollywood's largest single customer. And still stranger bedfellows were climbing under the covers. In 1983, a new studio was formed called TriStar — a partnership between one of the established majors, Columbia Pictures; the most powerful pay-TV service, HBO, still owned by Time; and the "Eye Web", the CBS television network.

Meanwhile, the decline in American cinema attendance still hadn't abated. Whereas in 1946 one third of the American public went to movies once a week, 40 years later only one fifth of the public went once a *month*. Naturally the price of tickets had moved steadily in the opposite direction, so revenues hadn't dropped by nearly the same proportion. Canadian cinema audiences were following suit.

Circumstances have demonstrated that even at their most petulant, the studios are nothing if not adaptable. The degree to which they have become integrated with non-theatrical or home delivery systems — TV, cable, pay-cable, home video — is breathtaking. These links take many different forms. They include joint ventures like TriStar, noted above; exclusive release deals between studios and pay movie networks; and the creation of studio owned and operated services like the Disney Channel (which is available today on about 70% of American cable systems).

Cross-ownership and vertical integration are now the rule, not the exception. The most vivid example is the largest, Time Warner, which not only owns one of the oldest studios (Warner Bros), but HBO, the original pay-movie service (now with over 17 million subscribers). It doesn't stop there. Time Warner controls vast quantities of copyright material through its many publishing interests, ranging from the genteel Little, Brown to the less high-minded *Sports Illustrated.* Warner Home Video is the largest distributor of videocassettes in the world. And the parent company owns cable companies in almost every state in the United States, making it the second largest MSO after Tele-Communications Inc., or TCI. Time Warner has as many basic subscribers in the U.S. as all the cable subscribers in Canada combined.

Why the studios would like you to buy not rent...

In settling the Betamax case for the VCR and against Universal, the high court made another finding whose financial ramifications are still very much with us. The court affirmed the right of video shops to sell or rent the tapes they had purchased from the studios and their distributors. The basis for this decision was the "First Sale Doctrine", which permits the first buyer of a copyrighted work to use that work in any way as long as no violation of copyright occurs (like making unauthorized copies and selling them). That principle means that the copyright holders, majors, independents or otherwise, cannot require payment of any royalty or commission on videocassette rentals. This harsh reality has kept the selling prices to retailers high and the sale of tapes directly to the consumer — known as "sell-through" — very competitive. In 1982 Paramount shook up the business when it released Star Trek II *at $39.95. By 1988, the price pioneer was MCA Home Video, which put* ET *on the market at $24.95.*

Cable Control of Programming...

The major U.S. cable operators own or control most of the basic cable networks and all the major pay channels.

Source: Consumer Reports

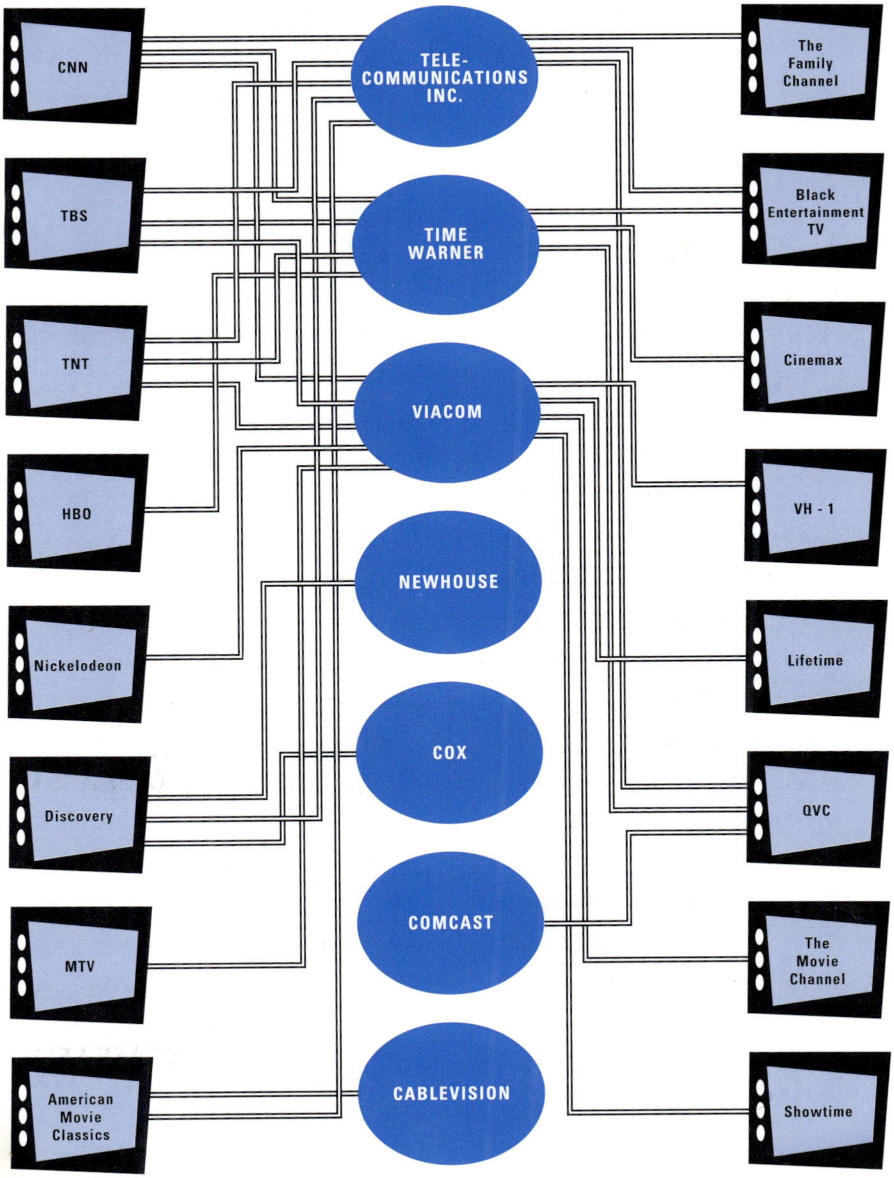

Even in the day-to-day workings of the film business, TV and home video are a constant preoccupation, in two distinct but related ways. First, in the media marketing chain made up of what the trade calls "release windows" or just plain windows (no relation to the computer operating system). Second, in the way movies get financed.

Windows & bucks

In Hollywood's terminology, windows are the delivery or distribution vehicles that bring creative product to the consumer, whether outside or inside the home — though the action is more and more inside, in more and more forms. These "vehicles" are movie theatres, basic and pay cable, home video, conventional television and so on (the new technologies will be adding lots of windows to the "and so on").

Consumers are often baffled at the unpredictable way in which high-profile movies seem to be released. Some disappear from theatres quickly and pop up the next month on videocassette. Others take forever to get to home video, and may or may not be available in the interim on pay-TV. Then there's pay-per-view...

Appearances notwithstanding, there's definitely method to the madness (even if the method doesn't always work out as planned). You don't need to have seen *The Two Jakes* to know that if you want to find out what's really going on, you follow the money — i.e. the highest marginal revenue. Here's how financial analyst Harold Vogel describes the sequencing of release windows (p.73):

→ Sequential distribution patterns are determined by the principle of the second-best alternative. That is, films are normally first distributed to the market that generates the highest marginal revenue over the least amount of time. They then "cascade" in order of marginal revenue contribution down to markets that return the lowest revenues per unit time. This has historically meant theatrical release, followed by licensing to pay-cable program distributors, home video duplicators, television networks, and finally local television syndicators. But the number of households with video recorders has grown so rapidly that release to home video now regularly follows closely after theatrical release and is positioned just ahead of or at the same time as release to cable.

Even though this analysis was published as recently as 1990, it appeared too early to take into account what is likely to be the most important growth area of the decade, namely, pay-per-view. More on that later.

On to the second point, financing. Now that home video and other vehicles have long since overtaken theatres as the major revenue source for movies, those who produce and finance them have to plan carefully for how creative content, marketing, competition and many other factors will affect the "cascade" referred to above.

Films and TV programs get financed in countless ways. A producer might approach potential partners, like home video distributors, who in return for a promised share of the revenues will ante up a certain amount of cash that can then be put towards paying for the production. What our producer is doing in effect is pre-selling the rights to the home video market (or German theatrical market or pay-cable market or whatever). Hence the term "pre-sale". This is not only a favoured way of doing business now; in Canada, where any given window is too marginal to finance productions, co-producing and pre-selling have become necessities.

We should underscore one other aspect of the Hollywood-TV connection. In part thanks to the regulations noted earlier (especially the FCC's "fin-syn" rules), American broadcast TV has been a goldmine for non-movie production by majors and independents in Hollywood alike. They have been the source of practically all of the primetime entertainment series and mini-series — sitcoms, action-adventure, etc — that have appeared on the three commercial networks over the last three decades. A great deal of TV drama went out live from the networks during the 50s (including the CBC). Once Ampex perfected a way to record programming on tape, however, and the FCC decided the networks should go outside for non-news programming, a whole other side of the industry opened up. Although we've concentrated on how movies have infiltrated television, episodic or series programming has accounted for a significant proportion of the TV earnings of the Hollywood production community.

Hollywood commits, Canada committees

The reason we've been concentrating on movies is two-fold. First, the availability of movies through a number of different distribution channels allows us to track the movement of this video form from strictly out-of-home venues to the living rooms of the nation. Second, we have a particular policy concern in this chapter: the need to determine how much public funding and effort should be expended on behalf of Canadian "video" products for theatrical development and distribution, rather than for broadcast and non-broadcast forms of TV.

As American companies were raking in money on the strength of the movie-and-TV marriage, Canadians had to be content with years of committees and public hearings on the subject of pay-TV. It was 1980 and Canadians were, as usual, at a disadvantage. On the production front, precious few Canadian producers were around. Lots of Canadian talent had emigrated to Los Angeles or elsewhere; some had stayed behind and found a home inside the ranks of the CBC. But there was nothing that could be described as an independent program production industry.

On the film distribution and exhibition fronts, things were, if anything, even worse. Canadians may have been spending most of their time watching American material on the small screen; at least the broadcasting system was owned by Canadians. Not so with distributors and movie theatres. Canada's big screens were effectively controlled, programmed and commercially exploited by the distribution arms of the Hollywood majors. Their ability to hang on to this control and to defeat several efforts by Canadian governments to wrest back some control makes a long, sad tale.

By 1980, meanwhile, two major federal committees, outside the CRTC, had pronounced on the subject of pay-TV. Their comments were a familiar mixture of caution, yearning and high-minded ambition. Here is some of what the 1979 Clyne Committee (the Consultative Committee on the Implications of Telecommunications for Canadian Sovereignty) had to say about pay-TV (which was not the focus of its mandate):

> We have heard no evidence that there is at present any substantial demand for

> the introduction of pay-TV. There is thus no need for hasty action, but we believe that the demand will grow and that it would be wise to establish a strategic policy for its eventual introduction.

Having already considered the matter for several years, the CRTC could hardly be accused of "hasty action".

The following year, 1980, the Therrien Committee felt it was perhaps time to make a move:

> Most of the members of the Committee have come to believe, during the course of this inquiry, that pay-TV would offer a new and unique opportunity to foster the beneficial development of the Canadian film and program-production industries while supporting and complementing the Canadian broadcasting system and catering to the needs of Canadian viewers...

But minds were still not made up, for the report went on to say that this majority opinion was "not unanimous".

To make a long story short, it was not until March 1982 that the CRTC finally licensed Canada's first pay-TV services (in CRTC Decision 82-240). Six licences were issued, out of the original 27 applications. In approving the licences, CRTC Chairman John Meisel stated that "Canadian content is the whole purpose of pay-TV". The decision said in part that the Commission viewed "pay television as an integral part of the Canadian broadcasting system which should play an important role in achieving the objectives of the broadcasting policy for Canada set out in section 3 of the *Broadcasting Act*".

Bad news, good news

Many of the ministers, commissioners and committee members who had agonized over the decision to go ahead with pay must have known what lay in store. Their dilemma was real. On one hand, great pressure was being applied by the cable interests and others after all these years of procrastination. On the other hand, the bitter predictions of critics like Herschel Hardin were about to come true — at least in the short term. In 1983, C Channel, the cultural service on which many hopes were pinned, went off the air, less than five months after its launch. Then it was the turn of Star Channel, the Atlantic pay-TV service, which went into receivership almost as quickly.

Other controversies ensued, some of them around the pay movie service First Choice. First Choice was suffering from all the predictable problems: very slow market penetration, a dearth of Canadian-produced material, a cable industry unfamiliar with this new way of selling TV. Then, First Choice struck a deal with the Playboy Channel, which had begun operating in the U.S. in late 1982. The deal was designed to fulfill the network's Canadian content requirement through the co-production of Playboy material in Canada, using Canadian talent. By the nature of the content, the deal was also designed to attract Canadian audiences to program material they had never had a chance to see on television before.

Citytv
News·Movies·Music

The First Choice-Playboy venture attracted more criticism than it did business. Cultural nationalists saw it as a Trojan horse for Americana; prudes saw it as unfit for Canadian consumption. Not unlike the infamous Baby Blue Movies run for a time in the 1970s by Toronto's CITY-TV, the Playboy content was around just long enough to raise conservative ire and then was nudged off the air.

It would be a long time before pay movies made even a dent in Canada's TV marketplace. Even today (and for the last several years), total movie channel penetration has hovered around 10% of Canadian cable households (there are now several such services: First Choice, Superchannel, the Family Channel and their French-language counterparts). In 1986, in the tradition of so many conventional broadcasters, First Choice asked the CRTC to reduce its commitment to Canadian-produced material. The Commission ruled that First Choice/Superchannel would now be required to show 30% Canadian content in prime time and 20% overall, though with a 150% time credit for new Canadian drama. Moreover, the revised conditions of licence reduced the minimum expenditure requirement on Canadian content to 20% of subscriber revenues, down from 45% in the original licence.

By the mid-80s, however, the action in new Canadian TV lay not in the movies but elsewhere: specialty channels. In 1984, the Commission licensed MuchMusic and The Sports Network, which were joined over the next few years by several others. By no coincidence at all, this was the period when the bad news started to trickle into the offices of the conventional broadcasters, especially the networks. Their declining fortunes have been well documented (in particular those of the American networks), and we don't need to retell the whole story here.

In brief, the CTV and CBC networks each lost 25% of their audience in the latter half of the 80s. The lost audience migrated away from general interest television (including American imports) and headed for the specialties (a detailed analysis of these trends will be found in Ellis 1991). They were able to build on a burgeoning cable infrastructure: basic cable penetration in Canada had passed the 50% mark back in 1977. After all the travails of the 70s, pay and specialty television was starting to turn into good news for just about everyone but the conventional broadcasters.

The Canadian film industry: not a pretty picture

In television, the Canadian preoccupation has always been how to get more quality programming on the small screen. On the film side, one refrain has continued to dominate the debate: we can't have a production industry unless and until we have a distribution and exhibition industry.

In 1982, for example, the Federal Cultural Policy Review Committee (known after its chairmen as the Applebaum-Hébert Committee) published a sweeping examination of all facets of the cultural industries and performing arts in Canada. It posed the problem this way:

> As a creative endeavour film is collaborative [...] There must be a working relationship among the three major elements of production, distribution and exhibition. Without such a relationship, a film may be made but not seen. In Canada the tripartite industrial relationship all too often does not work well.

The "made but not seen" syndrome has been echoed in report after report. In 1985, the Raymond-Roth Report found that "no production sector can develop in a healthy and profitable fashion without the financial support of a strong, competitive domestic distribution sector" (p.15).

In the latter part of the decade, however, the conventional wisdom of committee and consulting reports began to shift in emphasis. The new preoccupation of the pundits has been to compare the fate of Canadian film and video production in the theatrical and non-theatrical (TV-related) windows. This is important to us for two reasons. First, this change marks a wider shift in audience behaviour away from theatres towards the home environment. Second, this trend will be accelerated by recent developments in technology, especially those related to PPV delivery.

But how did we get into this mess in the first place?

Integrated we conquer

The answer is vertical integration — the control by one company of several phases of an industrial process, typically including both the creation of some item and its dissemination to consumers. Vertical integration confers market power because it cuts out middle men and extends control of pricing. Until 1949, the Hollywood majors effectively controlled not only the production of movies, but their distribution and exhibition as well. That is, they owned vertically integrated distribution companies and the movie theatres in which the public went to see them. This cozy situation finally attracted the notice of the U.S. Justice Department and, in a consent decree, the studios agreed to divest themselves of their theatre holdings, on the grounds that integration threatened legitimate competition.

Strangely enough, the divestiture coincided with the widespread introduction of television in the United States. As we saw earlier, this gave the studios even more to be unhappy about, as cinema attendance began to slip over the course of the 1950s. But the market power built up by the studios was certainly not about to disappear, either in their domestic market or in the foreign markets they were gradually infiltrating from year to year.

One of the earliest and most important of these was Canada. Here we need to

Highest grossing film in Warner Bros. history

be alert to the distinction between the integration of production with *distribution* and production with *exhibition*. Theatrical distribution is the business of renting prints of a movie to theatres and theatre chains on behalf of the studio that made or financed that movie. Theatrical exhibition is the business of selling tickets to consumers to walk in and watch the movie.

Distributors have high costs, which include marketing, advertising and promotion, making hundreds or even thousands of copies of movies from the negative, as well as the overheads that go with running a big business. But the integrated distribution arms of the Hollywood majors have some major advantages going for them. For one thing, they control access to the movies that everybody wants to see. For another, each of them is now a global business, with representation in scores of countries around the world. This is how the Report of the Federal Cultural Policy Review Committee described the setup (p.257):

> The theatrical market is highly integrated with the United States market; both Canadian and US theatres are supplied chiefly by distribution companies which are integrated with the major Hollywood studios — Columbia Pictures, MGM-United Artists, Paramount Pictures, Twentieth-Century Fox Films, Universal Films, Warner Communications. These studios have the greatest control over what theatres exhibit because they control the "blockbuster" Hollywood releases, which are what the theatres want.

In practical terms, therefore, whether the studios actually own theatres or not has had little effect on their market power in Canada. For many years and until recently, the measure of American domination of Canada's TV screens was that 75% of English-language viewing was devoted to foreign programs (this figure has been dropping slightly since the late 80s). In film, the corresponding measure is the amount of screen time in Canada devoted to "imported" films — 97% — with a paltry 3% left over for Canadian-made films.

As it happens, the Canadian theatrical exhibition market is dominated by two chains, Cineplex Odeon and Famous Players. Cineplex Odeon is a Canadian company that is part-owned by MCA, while Famous Players is owned by Paramount Communications, formerly Gulf + Western. Together they are estimated to control about two-thirds of annual theatrical revenues in Canada (Vogel, p.35).

Even if the two major cinema chains took to the flag-waving indulged in by many broadcasters and cablecasters at public hearings, they wouldn't have much latitude in what they rent for their screens. For not only do the majors have the blockbusters, featuring the bankable stars like Schwarzenegger, they also have package deals. If you want Schwarzenegger, you have to take certain other titles that may not have quite the same drawing power... and some that may have none at all. The cruel law of the marketplace is the theatres have to take the good with the not-so-good. Good or not, the majors are interested in exhibiting *their* films, not what the locals have to offer.

The effects on the Canadian industry have been depressingly predictable. As a 1992 consulting study points out, "in any given year, the volume of foreign films in Canada outnumbered Canadian films by about ten to one" (NGL, p.47). As with television programming, assessments of "popularity" have to take careful account of availability. That means not only how many films get handled and how many screens they get to, but also where those screens are located, how long they play, and — not least of all — how well promoted they are. After you look at all those factors, the proverbial level playing field is tilted sharply in favour of American movies. As the NGL report explains (p. 112):

> Canadian product is being shown, but typically in short play dates in few cities. Canadian films produced in English are technically available in the largest markets, but typically in single-theatre release and for not more than one-week play dates. This pattern means that Canadian films are not very accessible to most Canadians in theatrical release.

Invidious comparisons

We live in a country where we hear routinely about Hollywood movies having opening *weekend* grosses of millions of dollars and record-setting movies are in the

Black Robe

nine-figure stratosphere, i.e. $100 million and more. After one week in release, Columbia's *Honeymoon in Vegas* was reported by *Variety* (September 7, 1992) to have earned over $10 million. (This of course is by no means typical. Most films open to much less business.) These figures do not represent any "foreign" earnings, but only what the studios think of as their "domestic" market. The title given to *Variety*'s regular feature on film earnings is "Weekly Box Office Report (U.S.-Canada)". From Hollywood's perspective, we're all part of one big happy family.

The contrasts between the earnings of Canadian and American films are hard to believe. NGL presents some gross box office revenues earned by Canadian feature films released between 1987 and 1990 in English Canada. The findings include the following (p.114):

- only 3 of the 48 films — 6% — made more than $500,000
- 36 made less than $100,000
- 29 made less than $50,000

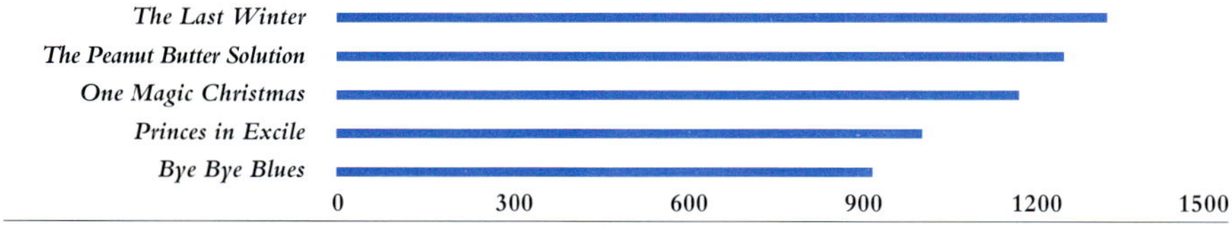

English TV Audiences for Selected Canadian Features
(Thousands of viewers)
Source: Groupe Secor, CBC Research

So far, only two English-language Canadian features have earned more than $1 million at the box office: *Dead Ringers* and *Black Robe*. Then, tucked away in a footnote (footnote 51) on this same page of the report, we read what is perhaps the single most telling comparison of all: "$1 million in box office translates into about 150,000 viewing a film". And that's for the big successes. For the bulk of films released in this period (75% of them), their $100,000 gross thus translates into a total viewing audience of 15,000 people.

Why is this significant? As our theme is the convergence of two media, these figures give us a basis of comparison in audience terms, which for our purposes is more revealing than earnings (which are more difficult to compare in any case). As reported in Ellis 1991, audiences for episodic Canadian drama programs (in the 1990–91 season) were typically over one million viewers per episode. That is an audience over *60 times larger* than the audience for theatrical features making $100,000. The two-hour CBC TV movie *Lost in the Barrens*, for example, captured an audience of over one and a half million in December 1990.

But even these successful Canadian dramas are not the smash-hit TV equivalents of *Black Robe*, which has earned some $2.5 million in Canada. The audience for CBC's English-language mini-series, *Conspiracy of Silence*, was over three million, while the real TV records have been set by the French-language series *Les Filles de Caleb*, some episodes of which have captured a phenomenal four million viewers in Quebec.

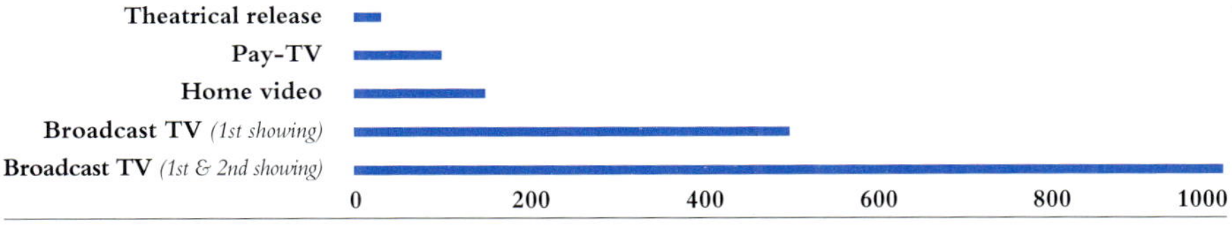

Potential Audiences for Canadian Feature Earning $200,000 at Box Office
(Thousands of viewers)
Source: NGL Consulting

NGL suggests (p.122) that "the premiere showing of Canadian feature films on CBC reaches an average of over 500,000 Canadians and, by the second showing, over 1 million viewers. This reach exceeds the combined viewership of theatrical, home video and pay-TV by roughly four times...". This overall conclusion is corroborated by a 1991 study undertaken by Groupe Secor, which cites (p.67) several Canadian features that captured significant TV audiences in English Canada (see chart).

The NGL report makes passing reference to the crucial baseline comparison of audience levels typically attracted by the four major release windows. It takes the hypothetical example of a film that earns $200,000 as a box office feature. The estimated audiences are indicated in the chart.

If these approximations are valid, the striking contrast lies not in the ability of conventional TV to outperform the other three outlets combined by almost 2-to-1 after only one broadcast, but rather in the *inability* of box office release to come any where close to even pay-TV or home video in audience levels. Pay-TV alone is placed at over three times the theatrical audience, despite the fact that pay-TV is found in only 10% of Canadian cable homes.

These general findings are also corroborated by the financial facts of life. As reported by *Playback* (September 16, 1991, p.9), citing Statistics Canada data:

> While cultural agencies such as Telefilm Canada tend to place a heavy emphasis on the theatrical release of films, distributors recoup most of their investment

Chronology of Intervention into the Canadian Film Industry

1939
Creation of National Film Board.

1967
CFDC (now Telefilm Canada) charged with the responsibility to "foster and promote the development of a feature film industry in Canada".

1968
CFDC budget set at $10 million for equity investment, loans, awards and grants related to Canadian feature film production.

1973
Secretary of State Hugh Falkner negotiates a voluntary quota system with Famous Players and Odeon whereby every major Canadian English language feature is guaranteed at least two weeks of theatre time in Toronto, Montreal and Vancouver.

1974
Federal income tax regulations are amended to grant a 100% Capital Cost Allowance (CCA) for certified Canadian feature films.

1984
CFDC becomes Telefilm Canada.

1986
Federal government announces new $33 million Feature Film Fund administered by Telefilm Canada.

1986
Ontario Film Development Corp (OFDC) begins with operating budget of $20 million.

1987
B.C. Film Development Fund commits $10.5 million over first three years.

through television and home video sales. Only 5% of distributors' revenues on Canadian films are derived from their performance at the box office.

National Film Board of Canada

Office national du film du Canada

What must be appreciated is that the Canadian box office results noted here are recent. They follow many years of intervention on behalf of the theatrical film industry by Canadian governments. This is by no means an industry that has been left to the mercy of the free market. The following cronology indicates just a few of the measures — beginning in 1939 with the creation of the NFB — through which both federal and provincial levels of government have attempted to stimulate production and recapture some of the distribution industry from American domination.

The chronology also shows the frustrations which many of these measures have

1977

Odeon withdraws from voluntary quota system.

1978

CCA changed to allow write-off of entire amount of film investment against taxable income.

1980

CCA tax shelter collapses.

1982

Applebaum-Hébert Report recommends increased funding for Canadian producers and distributors.

1983

100% CCA tax shelter reduced to 50%–50% rule.

1987

National Film and Video Product Bill is introduced to bolster Canadian movie distribution, but is defeated by Hollywood lobby.

1987

CCA is reduced to 30%.

1988

Quebec Cinema Law (Bill 109) is enacted to allow only Quebec firms to distribute films and videotapes within the province, then is watered down.

1988

Creation of Telefilm's Feature Film Distribution Fund.

encountered: the failure of the voluntary quota; the gradual disappearance of federal tax incentives (the CCA); the defeat of a federal film bill after a campaign mounted by Jack Valenti and the MPAA; and the awkward compromises worked out in Quebec to provide some control over the distribution of French-language films.

Bucking trends

It is widely acknowledged that the support provided by Telefilm and other public agencies has played a critical part in both an increase in film production and the creation of opportunities for talent development. And yet the inexorable conclusion is that "regardless of the number and quality of films produced in Canada, they remain obscure and inaccessible to moviegoers and their profitability is severely limited" (Pendakur, p.29).

The reasons for this are not far to seek. In addition to American control of distribution, questionable policy measures, and the perennial issues of budgets and production values, the simple fact is that Canadians are staying home more and going out to the cinema less. This is not a new trend, according to Statistics Canada ("Focus on Culture", p.8):

> Going to the movies is declining, and the lost ground taken over by television and video. Motion picture theatre attendance figures, continuing their downward movement, fell to 79 million in 1988–89. The 7% decline from 1987–88 figures continues the downward trend which followed the high observed in 1980-81, when admissions totalled 101 million. Motion picture theatres have generally been able to offset the drop in attendance by raising ticket prices.

These figures indicate that over the course of the 1980s, as more and more public money was being pumped into the support of theatrical production and distribution, *Canadian theatrical attendance was dropping by a cumulative 22%.* The same Statistics Canada catalog reports that as far back as 1986 Canadians were already spending more money watching videos at home than on movie tickets. In fact, "average family spending on motion pictures plunged to $41, while spending on videocassettes averaged $58."

Fully two years after this turnabout in the leisure pursuits of Canadians, the Canadian government was committing itself to a new instrument, the Feature Film Distribution Fund. The Fund was established by the minister of communications in 1988 to

> enable Canadian theatrical distributors to become better capitalized in order to provide sufficient financing to Canadian productions and to more successfully compete for the Canadian rights to film products intended for distribution in Canada, thereby ensuring the ongoing stability, professional and economic development of both the distribution and production sectors.[21]

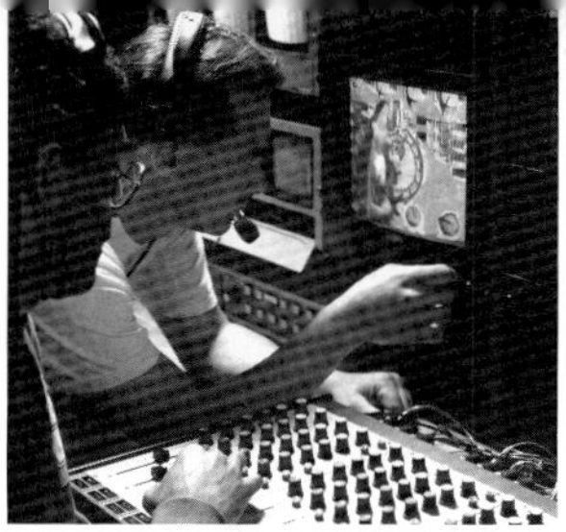

The general notion of a boost to distribution, placing less emphasis on the supply side, was based on the received logic that support to production alone would never get Canadian films past the mesmerizing threshold of 3% of screen time. The idea had the blessing of the 1985 Film Industry Task Force, which decried American domination and its ill effects.

The architects of the new measure may have been right on logical grounds. What they didn't seem to do was question whether the *goal* was right: to concentrate effort and public money on theatrical distribution. While some accommodation has been made of late to the blossoming of home video and pay-TV, the basic rationale of the Fund lies decidedly outside the home.[22]

Meanwhile, Telefilm Canada was certainly not inactive on the television front. In 1983, as part of the federal government's new policy on broadcasting, Telefilm Canada was given responsibility for yet another fund, the Canadian Broadcast Program Development Fund. As the name suggests, it was designed to stimulate production for the small screen.

What is most interesting from our perspective is this. The CFDC (later Telefilm) was never mandated by Parliament to intervene in the broadcasting industry; its bailiwick was film. And for the first 15 years of its existence, CFDC/Telefilm had no direct role to play in television. The Fund was in some ways a rescue attempt made on behalf of the independent production community in the wake of the collapse of the film industry after 1980. Whatever its real genesis, the Fund was a kind of afterthought, which even today is administered under a Memorandum of Understanding (MOU) between Telefilm and the minister of communications.

Yet this "afterthought" has for several years now consumed a far higher proportion of Telefilm's budget than the Feature Film Fund. The Broadcast Fund placed almost four times as much money in TV production (about $78 million) than the Feature Film Fund placed in theatrical production (about $21 million). Moreover, the Broadcast Fund is credited with having stimulated the creation of a production infrastructure that was virtually non-existent in 1980 — even if other public measures, like CRTC content quotas, must be given some credit as well.

Telefilm, it seems, has succeeded far better in television than it has in the theatrical market, even though, ironically, that is its real beat. In an interview with *Playback* (Anson-Cartwright, p.28), filmmaker and columnist Peter Pearson, who was executive director of Telefilm from July 1985 to November 1987, was asked the following question: "Although on paper Telefilm says it is supporting more commercial [film] projects, in English Canada it hasn't been able to make a dent at the box office. What do you attribute this to?" Here is his response:

> From the very beginning of the CFDC at its very initial impulse, it was supposed to have been not only a production organization but one involved in distribution. Michael Spencer, for the first ten years [of the CFDC] constantly fought against the frustration of not being able to get the films to the theatres and that problem has never been resolved.
>
> In my time, there was the Raymond Roth task force and again it was recommended that all distribution in all forms be through Canadian distribution companies in Canada. That's never been solved. So the kind of clout the Broadcast Fund had — knowing that the productions were to go to air because of Canadian content regulations — has never existed in the theatres.
>
> And so it's Telefilm's and the CFDC's huge failure that for all of the [film] productions that have been made, very few of them have been seen by Canadian audiences [...]. [That's] in contrast to the Broadcast Fund productions where they are all exposed to the public and a lot of big popular support. In Quebec, for example, the whole of the Quebec television culture is now centred around stuff that's come out of the Broadcast Fund essentially.

The rise of the living room

What we've been looking at so far is a tug-of-war between in-home and out-of-home entertainment media. We've noted structural reasons for the seemingly hopeless battle to get Canadian movies into Canadian cinemas where Canadians can watch them. And we've questioned whether it is prudent to subsidize theatrical distribution in an era when demographics, leisure patterns and other factors seem to be keeping people home more to consume video products.

What we haven't done yet is look at how emerging technologies may affect the balance of power between cinema and living room. We'll therefore take a quick tour of three different technologies: home theatres, pay-per-view and IMAX.

The home theatre

Until fairly recently, movie buffs could be forgiven for not wanting to watch either classics or new releases on a regular TV set, whether by broadcast or VCR. A 21-inch, low-resolution TV with monophonic sound coming through a tiny speaker was typical equipment in the living rooms of the 1970s and early 1980s. A set with these limitations couldn't possibly do justice to the production values of even a "B" Hollywood movie, compared to the big-screen, big-sound experience of a cinema hall.

This is not to suggest that movie-goers are motivated merely by technical and aesthetic considerations. People go to the movies for many other reasons than the size of the screen and the Dolby sound system, like dating rituals and escape from loneliness. However, even though technology cannot easily replace the laughter and applause of a large crowd in a dark hall, it has moved ahead in leaps and bounds in its ability to overcome the limitations of the NTSC standard, conventional TV sound and the natural constraints of an average home environment, such as room size.

Austin, in "Home Video: Second Run Theatre of the 1990s" suggests (p.340) that

> with home video so prevalent, theatres that specialized in showing revival pictures are being forced to quit the business or to change their format. One distributor estimated that there were 200 movie houses in the United States in 1980 that showed revival films, 75 of them exclusively. By mid-1987, the latter figure had dropped to a mere 15 sites. As would be expected, videocassette entertainment has begun to usurp the place formerly held by 16mm film on college campuses. With lower priced VCRs and inexpensive rentals, students are opting

> to view films in the comfort of dorm rooms rather than travelling across campus to see the same picture in an auditorium.

However, it is not suggested that the VCR will ever completely replace the movie theatre. The importance of this venue is well articulated by the former film critic of the *New York Times*, Bosley Crowther (in Austin, p.343):

> The total effect of a motion picture is conditioned to a greater or lesser extent by the environment in which it is shown... The fun of movie-going, pleasure that is derived from the experience of spending a few hours in the movie theatre, includes a lot more than the experience of observing the film. It is the amalgamation of a series of pleasurable stimuli — the initial anticipation, the warmth of companionship, the congeniality of the surroundings, the freedom to use and partake of all the facilities, the feeling of elegance. The final satisfaction is in the total experience.

In the turf war between the living room and the cinema, each has been poaching a little from the other. Many cinemas have been trying to become cozier, friendlier places, with cafés featuring espresso and pastries to complement the popcorn and soda. But the real changes have been taking place in home entertainment systems and the attempt to bring some of the theatrical viewing experience into the home. This has spawned a whole new branch of consumer electronics which goes by the name "home theatre".

This is not one technology as such, but an audio and video component setup for the home that can provide greatly increased quality and fidelity, as well as user convenience. Perhaps the most fascinating aspect of the home theatre concept is the wide range of options available on the market — truly a system to suit every budget.

For example, the *Consumer Reports 1992 Buying Guide Issue* opens with a 50-page section on home entertainment, one part of which is devoted to "Setting up a home theater". It begins modestly (p.8):

If there's a stereo system near the TV set and VCR, all you might need to set up a home theater is a $5 cable. Another simple solution: hook up the stereo TV set to a pair of self-amplified loudspeakers, which cost about $150.

The *Buying Guide* describes not only how to spend more money on more elaborate equipment, but, as befits its mission, how to avoid poorly designed remote controls, how to calculate the power requirements of the sound system using their power multiplier formula and why it makes sense not to treat the TV set as the central component of the home theatre. This kind of advice tells us that home theatre is becoming institutionalized.

Across the whole spectrum, the emphasis has been less on picture improvements than sound improvements. It seems to have taken consumers a few years to realize that while the theatrical experience could be better approximated with a larger TV or projection screen, the sense of being swept away by the action depended every bit as much on the depth and dynamic range of sound reproduction. Even theatre-goers get reminded that "The Audience is Listening", the promotional slogan that accompanies the THX movie sound system developed by George Lucas of *Star Wars* fame. Lucas also markets a home version of the THX system that costs $8,000 or more.

If you think that's expensive, try Frox. In the fall of 1991, a startup high-tech firm in Sunnyvale, California introduced the most advanced system in the world for home entertainment — the Frox Interactive Home Theater, which can cost anywhere from $10,000 to $50,000, depending on the configuration. It can operate a dozen or more peripherals with the one-button remote control FroxWand simply by clicking on icons that appear on the monitor screen. The system uses a SPARC II computer chip borrowed from high-end engineering workstations, up to four 100-disc CD changers and image processing circuitry that can perform over 20 million pixel manipulations a second, to achieve resolution matching 1050-line HDTV technology. Its digital capabilities include the capture, storage and display of library and viewing information transmitted over the air on the vertical blanking interval ("Frox Introduces Interactive Home Theater").

The Frox isn't for everybody. Even *cheap* home theatre isn't for everybody. As we suggested above, technology can't replace social intercourse — though Virtual Reality may soon do a good job of simulating it.

Nevertheless, it's our contention that cinema attendance in Canada will keep dropping through the 90s, except for attendance at large-format venues like the IMAX installations described below. One of the most fascinating areas of speculation concerns the possibility that new home entertainment technologies may increase the per capita hours Canadians spend with their TV sets. For the last two decades, per capita weekly TV viewing has barely changed from roughly 23 hours. The question, therefore, is whether time spent with the home theatre or entertainment centre will gradually expand the viewing hours historically spent with broadcast television, or simply further fragment existing audience shares.

There are numerous indications that Canadians will continue to spend more of their entertainment hours in the home than outside the home. In a 1992 Decima sport and entertainment survey, 55% of respondents in Ontario reported that they were more likely to pursue enterainment activities in the home than outside the home, compared to two or three years ago. Only 8% reported that they were less likely to do so.

Technology & the in-home "cascade"

It would be risky to predict that more and more leisure time will be spent in front of smart-TVs, home theatres and their equivalents strictly on the basis of superior technical quality and versatility. To paraphrase Syd Silverman, nobody's going to buy into home theatre to watch it eliminate digital artifacts. As usual, they're going to want programs to watch.

The home theatre concept is focused for the time being on quality of reproduction and ease-of-use. What we have to keep in mind is that with the advent of smart technologies, the TV set will become receptive to more and more sources of programming. This is partly a function of expanding channel capacity. It's also a function of decoders, and storage and manipulation devices like interactive receiver-transmitters. To receive pay-per-view programming in quantity, for example, you need both lots of channels and an addressable descrambler.

Television is in turmoil these days because we have at least four different models of TV delivery all in transition, all at once:

- over-the-air, general interest broadcasting
- specialty and pay services
- pay-per-view (PPV)
- non-broadcast technologies based on tape and discs

Market share and money are cascading down from conventional broadcasting, which has lost its primacy in the broadcasting systems of both the U.S. and Canada over the last decade. The cascade has paused at the second "tier", pay cable, which has shown strong growth in the last several years. The latter two, PPV and non-broadcast, have not yet come into their own.

The more these latter technologies become available in the marketplace, the more of a threat they pose to established broadcasting interests. In Canada, this threat is captured in the vocabulary broadcasters use to characterize what is going on — like "Deathstars" and "audience fragmentation". These are not viewer concepts. They are not even producer concepts. These are concepts belonging to broadcasting's old guard, which is now under siege from three different directions:

- New competitors, both domestic and foreign, have many avenues opening up to the living rooms of the nation.
- The end of free television and the rise of transactional television mean decision-making power is shifting away from broadcasters to the viewer.
- The ability of the regulator to regulate — and protect the established interests — is being steadily undermined.

Let's recall three other facts of life. First, when it comes to drama and entertainment television, broadcasters don't produce, producers do (the CBC being a notable exception). Second, the "cascade" approach to release windows isn't suddenly going to go away; as technology alters and multiplies the in-home release windows, those who produce the programs and hold the copyrights will keep fine-tuning their marketing strategies. Third, Hollywood's influence over the entertainment business is going to have a profound effect not only on what we see on TV but how it gets there.

Yet the technological cascade has even Hollywood feeling threatened — again. Why?

Many unconventional entrants are developing their own entertainment and related products, especially for new delivery systems. As we would expect, some of these entrants have old-boy connections. Warner New Media, for example, is owned by Time Warner and located in Burbank, a stone's throw from the Warner Bros. studio. Its mission is to put games, reference and educational materials, and ultimately movies onto non-broadcast media, mostly optical discs of various types. A 1991 release was a CD-ROM package called *Desert Storm: The War in the Persian Gulf*. The breakthrough everyone's waiting for is being able to put full-length movies on 5-inch discs whose quality on the screen is at least as good as VHS tape. Regardless of how and when the breakthrough comes, Hollywood will not be alone in going after the consumer's business.

Five Years of Video

Rental Market

	Units (billions)	*Average Unit Price ($)*	*Total Market ($ billions)*
1987	3.3	$2.25	7.42
1988	3.74	$2.30	8.60
1989	4.06	$2.40	9.74
1990	4.13	$2.70	11.15
1991	4.09	$2.50	10.23

Sell-through Market

	Units (millions)	*Average Unit Price ($)*	*Total Market ($ billions)*
1987	115.6	$21.32	2.47
1988	147.7	$19.53	2.89
1989	195.5	$17.83	3.49
1990	231.0	$16.14	3.73
1991	290.7	$15.93	4.63

source: Alexander & Assoc.

Pay-per-view: the next bonanza?

In a survey conducted in December 1991 among 1,000 American adults, the Electronic Industries Association (EIA) found that 67% of those polled would

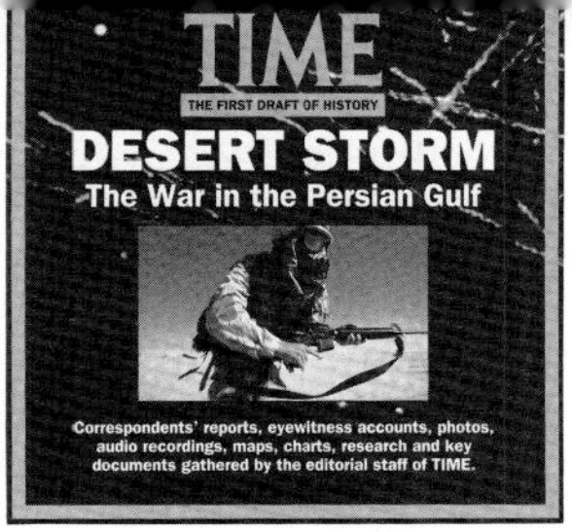

prefer to stay home to watch a movie, compared to just 22% who said they would prefer to go out.

This is the kind of survey finding that deserves cautious treatment, especially since details about the questions asked, sampling methodology and so on were not available. The EIA, moreover, is an industry group whose members make and sell consumer electronics products like VCRs. They have a vested interest in results that show consumers would rather stay home and use their products than go out to see a movie. One important ambiguity in this summary response is a breakout of how those who would prefer to stay home would rather procure their movie for viewing — pay-cable, pay-per-view, cassette rental?

But even allowing for these pitfalls, the tendency revealed in this response is certainly corroborated by other evidence. We've noted the steady drop in cinema attendance throughout North America. Meanwhile, home video continues to expand — though, as we'll see, with a significant shift taking place as between the rental and sell-through markets. The data in the accompanying chart are for American rentals and sales; these are more recent and comprehensive than the data available for Canada. It is safe to assume that the five-year trends indicated for the U.S. are generally applicable to Canada.

If we add together the annual totals for rental and sell-through, we find that the total home video market rose 50% in dollar terms from 1987 to 1991 (from $9.89 billion in 1987 to $14.86 billion in 1991). This aggregate figure conceals some interesting price and unit volume differences. Over the same period, the average *rental* price rose slightly — 11% — whereas the average *sell-through* price actually dropped 25%. This pricing differential would help explain in part why the rental market rose in unit volume by 24% over the five years (dropping off slightly in 1991), whereas the sell-through market rose a staggering 150%.

Vogel offers (p.84) the following assessment of these recent trends in home video:

> In all likelihood, PPV will noticeably dampen the growth of home video demand and alter the sequential release patterns for certain types of films. Already, there is evidence that the frequency of home video rental — which has averaged almost one

> tape a week for the typical VCR-owning household of the late 1980s — is declining despite the low cost of overnight rental (an average of around $2.50 in 1989).

Vogel seems to have missed the significant shift from rentals to sell-through. It may well be that sell-through will also be negatively affected by new intrusive technologies like PPV, but for the moment that does not seem to be the case. As prices drop, consumers are treating movies more and more like books and recordings, as durable products to own rather than ephemeral products to rent or view on broadcast television. This suggests that a strong market will exist later in the decade for disc-based products, especially movies and other heavily promoted material.

It should be noted that the combined consumer spending on buying and renting videocassettes provided above by the Video Software Dealers Association (VSDA) and Alexander and Associates is considerably higher than the figures provided by Paul Kagan Associates. Kagan's figure for total consumer spending on home video in 1991, for example, is $11.2 billion, as opposed to the $14.86 billion total noted above. This discrepancy may be explained by the inclusion of late charges and other such factors.

The big question on the minds of the home video folks is about the new kid on the block — pay-per-view (PPV) — and just how it will affect the positioning and revenues of the home video window. Let's begin our analysis of the situation by looking at the current market base.

Market base & economics

The PPV market is highly dependent on distribution technology, and a highly intrusive technology at that, based on the addressable descrambler. In the United States, roughly 20 million cable households are now served through these boxes ("Cable bill looks less relevant than ever as veto backers hit stride", p.13). That represents 36% of basic cable households (totaling 55 million), or about 22% of the 92 million television households.

By contrast, VCR penetration stood at 77% of American TV households as of January 1992, three and a half times higher than the figure for addressable boxes

Event pay-per-view: World Wrestling Federation

(source: VSDA and Electronic Industries Association, EIA). VCR penetration is somewhat lower in Canada, at around 70%. In both countries, however, home video is a mature industry, while PPV is still marginal in terms of audiences and revenues.

Once the PPV market starts to expand, it will cut into the revenues of home video retailers, with the smaller operators likely to suffer the most (see Prince 1992). But producers and distributors who hold the rights to popular movies — Hollywood again — stand to gain handsomely from such a shift in the market. Why? It's back to Vogel's cascade, based on highest marginal revenue. As reported in *Variety* (March 23, 1992, p.128), "pay-per-view funnels between $0.45 and $0.50 of every subscriber dollar into the pockets of the studios, compared with only $0.20 of every videocassette dollar and $0.15 of every paycable dollar, according to a March 2 Goldman Sachs report". The Hollywood majors have a powerful vested interest in seeing pay-per-view succeed.

In 1992, however, this is far from a head-to-head fight over how movies get into the living room, since movies are not yet the biggest draw on PPV. Indeed, the FCC reported in a 1991 study that the overwhelming majority of revenues realized by American cable operators from PPV derived from sports and two sports in particular — boxing and wrestling. And outside of movies, wrestling still clearly dominates the medium. In the words of Stephen Tapp, general manager of Viewer's Choice Canada, "Hulk Hogan drives event pay-per-view".[23]

Furthermore, the expansion of PPV as a home viewing medium is constrained by not one but two factors: the set-top box and channel capacity.

→ The *set-top box* represents a direct, out-of-pocket cost to subscribers. Naturally there's a close relationship between the number of such boxes in use, and marginal revenue potential. To take a hypothetical example, let's say a particular movie gets a healthy 10% of the potential U.S. market of 20 million addressable homes. At a charge of $4.00, that represents gross proceeds of $8 million, about half of which — $4 million — would go back to the studio that released it. Above that $4.00 price point, consumer resistance starts to set in — at least for a movie that is already in circulation.

But the real number-crunching starts in two other arenas: events which go out live, like a prize fight, and special movie events, in particular the potential launch of a high-profile movie on PPV as the first window, prior to both theatrical and home video release. At the moment, PPV is well down the hierarchy of release windows. To take a movie right to PPV, even before theatrical release, would mean a dramatic hike in the viewing charge.

According to Greg De Prez, vice-president for PPV at the largest cable operator in the United States, TCI, "a one-time debut or PPV exclusive film would have to charge $20 or more to return significant revenue". Using the same example as above, a takeup of 2 million "admissions" would mean gross revenues of $40 million at a $20 fee. If we project a future installed base of twice as many boxes, 40 million, a 10% takeup would mean a gross of $80 million *in one night.*

According to *Variety* (May 18, 1992, p.21) the cascade is already beginning to modulate in tune with changing times:

> In a move that could rearrange the aftermarket food chain, two pay-per-view networks are negotiating to get the rights to unreleased theatrical movies before they hit the video stores. Although no titles have surfaced, Action Pay-per-view and Cable Video Store both say they'll have some world-premiere movie experiments on their schedules before the year is out. But the homevideo industry is not welcoming this experiment with open arms. Homevid currently aces out PPV by anywhere from 30 to 100 days for just about all theatrical movies that roll off Hollywood's assembly lines.

→ The second constraint on PPV growth is *channel capacity.* Despite all the talk about the multichannel universe, many cable systems are running out of capacity. Compression is here to help, but it costs money and takes time to implement. As of October 1991, for example, less than 10% of American cable systems had 54 or more channels — although these serve almost 29% of all basic subscribers (source: National Cable Television Association, NCTA). Indeed, *Variety* reports that new cable networks, like the Turner Cartoon Network, TCN, are bribing cable operators in desirable markets by making cash offers to find channel space for them (Dempsey, p.1).

We alluded earlier in this study to the connection between channel capacity and the slow trend to near video on demand (NVOD). Multiple channels are needed not merely to offer a wide choice of film titles, but also a wide choice of start times. The staggered starts spread over many channels — as implemented on Time Warner's Quantum service in New York — are the PPV equivalent of the VCR timeshifting phenomenon. We now read predictions that "by as early as 1995, hundreds of cable systems throughout the [United States] will be feeding 30 to 100 new PPV movie channels to their subscribers. That could catapult PPV into the most lucrative aftermarket for theatrical movies." (*Variety*, March 23, 1992, p.128).

Viewer's Choice Canada (VCC)

Stephen Tapp of VCC has referred to PPV as a "true retail, transactional business" (1992 Festival of Festivals Symposium). VCC, like its American counterparts, gets direct and almost immediate price signals that tell them not only how they're doing as a service, but also how subscribers are reacting to their individual movies and events. As Tapp says, "we can find out the next morning how our programs have done".

This kind of consumer feedback should not be confused with the "overnights", the program ratings that the broadcast networks buy from A.C. Nielsen and other ratings services. These are based on very limited samples of the viewing audience and may have large margins of error. There is, moreover, a big difference between knowing how many viewers "watched" a free program and knowing how many paid $3.95 to see their program...

VCC is a year old as of this writing and still a small player on the small screen. It is licensed to serve Eastern Canada and currently has access to about half a million cable homes equipped with addressable descramblers. This represents less than 13% of their potential market — four million cable homes. While this may appear to be a modest beginning, what it means to Tapp and his colleagues is huge growth potential.

It is difficult to assess how quickly that growth will come. General manager Tapp will only say that his buy rates are "running ahead of the U.S. average". Whatever their short-term financial picture, VCC is operating from strength: it is co-owned by Astral, Rogers Communications Inc. and TSN Enterprises.

All of this confronts us with two questions. Are Canadian viewers going to keep staying home more and going out less? And if so, are they going to find their movie watching shifting more and more to PPV?

We've already seen the evidence of devastation in the theatrical market for Canadian movies. As far as the living room is concerned, it's only a matter of time before the constraints on PPV find their engineering solutions. Take channel capacity. Thanks to compression, Tapp stated in an interview that he envisages being able to program as many as 50 Viewer's Choice pay-per-view channels by 1994. The penetration of addressable descramblers can only increase in the meantime.

What about the built-in advantages of home video? A rented tape can be stopped, restarted, rewound and so on. A purchased tape becomes part of a permanent library. In a few years, however, digital technology will have levelled this playing field as well. Microchips will be available that will allow the capture and manipulation of PPV signals coming into the home. And smart-TVs will eventually allow viewers to choose either a one-time viewing session at one set price, or the opportunity to make a copy on a rewritable compact disc for another, higher price.

VCC is a distribution outlet for movies that is entirely controlled by Canadians. Does that mean VCC will finally get Canadian-made movies together with Canadian audiences? In other words, will they succeed where our movie theatres, and movie policies, have failed and keep on failing?

The best reason for believing PPV is on the verge of a boom is Hollywood's bottom line — and the cascade theory. If that's where the bucks are going to be, Hollywood's deal-makers will be giving technology a big push — our favourite example of technological determinism working backwards. But of course having Hollywood as part of a PPV solution is a golden opportunity for Hollywood to become part of another problem. That other problem could be DTH/DBS.

PPV has developed until now as a cable-delivered service. Despite competitive advantages over other delivery technologies, such as cable's billing and marketing infrastructure, there's nothing inherently natural or permanent about PPV's cable connection compared to satellite delivery to the home. Cable has a long headstart and three-quarters of the market. In one respect, however, cable's well established roots and its distribution plant may turn out to be a disadvantage.

One thing DTH/DBS has to offer is much faster deployment at much less cost — the only imponderable being how many consumers will actually sign up for PrimeStar, Hubbard, SkyPix and the other planned services when the time comes. Small dishes, competitive prices and even novel program offerings will not necessarily be enough to dislodge the cable monolith. If DTH/DBS does manage to get a foothold, however, it will be well placed to aggregate small but highly motivated audiences across North America.

Since we have been talking so much about movies, it is worth a reminder that PPV has fingers in other programming pies. Not just wrestling and rock concerts, but, according to VCC's Stephen Tapp, perhaps team sports and even Broadway plays. In that respect, the "Hollywood" monolith will be developing a few new tentacles...

It's the year 2000. VCC and several competing services are in millions of Canadian homes. Virtually everyone is equipped to decode their signals by means of their smart-TVs. VCC alone programs 400 channels. Among these are a whole tier devoted to Canadian movies, plays, rock concerts and other cultural events — not to mention the three Virtual Reality channels, a real Canadian niche. They programmed Canadian material originally because the regulator obliged them to. When content was deregulated, VCC kept on its Canadian movies and events because it keeps finding viewers who want to pay for them. Of course, the big moneymaker is still wrestling...

Curtains for theatres?

We close this chapter with a few comments about how new technologies will affect the use of leisure time. Our particular concern is the degree to which home entertainment will not only diversify, but actually take time away from other activities. The most obvious candidate is going to the movies.

We know two things. First, cinema attendance is declining and has been for many years. Second, cinemas are only one among many out-of-home entertainment venues, all of which serve an important social function. The escape from home, whatever the motive, can take the individual to video arcades, malls, museums, bars, skating rinks, amusement parks. One thing that many of these venues have in common is that they too have been touched by new video technology — whether it's the sports bar with the satellite dish or the museum with the interactive, touchscreen laserdisc displays.

So where does that leave movie theatres? They're certainly not going to disappear. But theatres will soon have to start offering something that positions them as a real alternative to everything that's cooking in the living room. Dolby and THX sound systems are one recent example. As we noted earlier, however, even complex technologies like THX are becoming available for the home — albeit at quite a price.

Let's recall also that cinema attendance was declining long before technology offered the faintest hope of giving people that theatre-in-the-home feeling. The many widescreen cinema formats have been around since the early 1950s; advanced home entertainment systems have only been around since the mid-1980s. What is true is that starting in the 1970s TV offered a lot more choice, whether real or perceived, thanks to the advent of cable and the VCR. When combined with a steady climb in the cost of going out to the movies, we would expect the movies to lose out.

What does not seem to have happened, however, is a jump in average weekly hours spent with TV by Canadians and Americans. In the last decade or so, per capita viewing has held steady around 23 or 24 hours a week — though big viewing differences have always existed between demographic groups, like older women versus teenage males.

So no simple transfer of time and loyalty seems to have taken place from cinema to TV. Yet while overall viewing remains stable, audiences are being exposed to more and more movies at home, from more and more sources — and the conditions for viewing them (and listening to them) are improving by leaps and

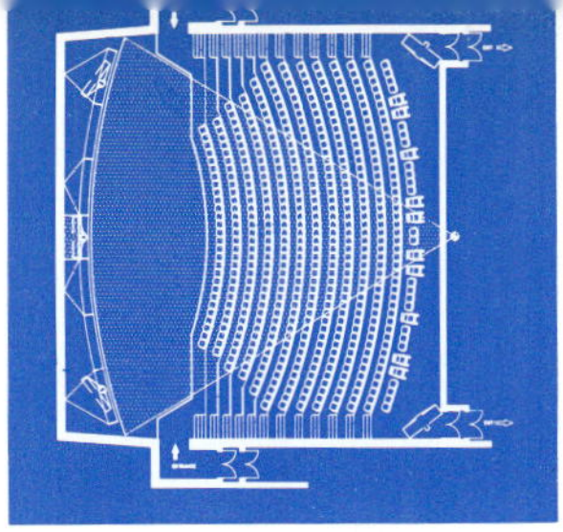

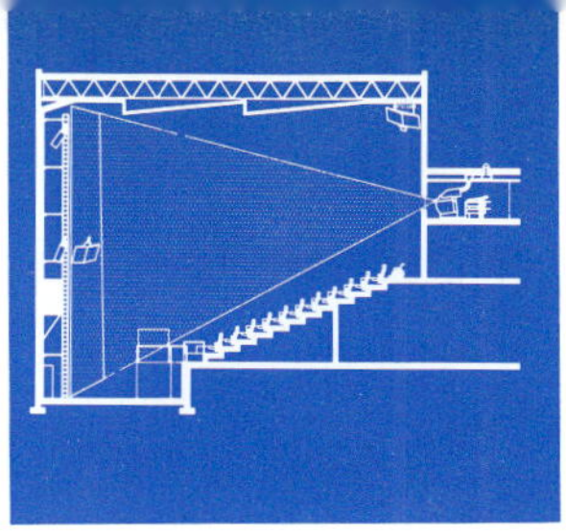

bounds. It is inconceivable given these developments that Canadians will be lured out to see domestically produced films in greater numbers, no matter how much more sophisticated Canadians get at marketing theatrical features.

That raises the tough policy question: why are Canadian taxpayers subsidizing not just the development and production of theatrical feature films, but also their distribution and marketing, even as the financial and audience results at theatres continue to disappoint their most ardent champions? And not just as federal taxpayers through Telefilm Canada but also as provincial taxpayers in Ontario and Quebec and British Columbia.

Every effort should be made to stimulate the *creation* of films with theatrical production and artistic values. Traditionally, of course, television has been very much regarded as a second-rate medium for films, compared to theatres — not just for technical reasons but for all the concerns associated with advertiser sovereignty, the ratings game and so on. Given the growth of home entertainment and transactional TV, however, there is less reason than ever before to continue putting resources into the theatrical *distribution* of Canadian material.

Compare the current funding initiatives with two other reference points: the CBC and IMAX.

→ The CBC captures French and English audiences 50 to 100 times larger for Canadian-made movies and mini-series than can be drawn to theatres for any feature short of a *Black Robe* or *Naked Lunch*. Yet the CBC's budget — 80% of which comes from government-approved tax dollars — has declined in real terms every year from 1984 to 1991. Is the federal government in its zeal to create a Hollywood North throwing good money after bad?

→ Imax Systems Corporation is a different kind of Canadian success story. Through its proprietary camera and film systems, this Ontario-based company is responsible for creating some of the most spectacular cinematography ever seen in theatres. Though IMAX is rarely part of discussions on the future of the Canadian entertainment industry, attendees at the 1992 International Festival of Festivals Symposium were given the opportunity to hear about some of the technical and artistic achievements on the IMAX project slate. Gordon Harris, manager of research and development for IMAX, discussed breakthroughs in 180° 3D installations that rival the most advanced special effects installations in the world (see accompanying box).

In addition to designing and building both permanent and temporary installations in countries all over the world from Spain to Japan, IMAX has been involved in numerous film production projects. Harris himself designed many of the optical, lighting and power systems which went two and a half miles down into the Atlantic Ocean for the filming of *Titanica*. IMAX is undoubtedly the only company in Ontario, perhaps in Canada, which has managed to get to the leading edge of entertainment technology.

IMAX systems are not about to rejuvenate cinemas across the continent. For one thing, they're very costly; for another, existing films can't be simply transferred into the IMAX format — they have to be shot that way. But what is eminently clear is that as conventional cinemas, like conventional broadcasters, languish in the wake of new technologies, the future of out-of-home entertainment belongs to the big theatrical experience. Some, like the Rolling Stones concert film *At the Max*, can be enjoyed in Canadian venues like Toronto's Cinesphere. Others, like Universal Studios Florida, may require not only a few hours on the plane, but a serious commitment of time and energy. One of the most popular rides at USF is *Back to the Future*, a simulation which allows customers to ride in DeLorean cars moving in synch with the movie, projected in an IMAX-designed theatre.

IMAX & the BIG theatrical experience

According to Gord Harris of Imax Systems, the electronic media have not quite cornered the market in storage capacity, special effects and the ability to wow an audience. In a September 1992 address, he described some of the remarkable features of film in general and IMAX film in particular…

An IMAX 70mm film frame has about 10 times the area of a 35mm frame. One IMAX print can resolve over 17 million pixels — the equivalent of more than 80 megabytes of digital information, the entire contents of a standard desktop computer hard disk.

Moreover, film continues to be a much cheaper storage medium than the magnetic media used by computers. Harris notes that while computer memory will still cost as much as one dollar U.S. per megabyte by the year 2001, a Kodak 70mm print costs about one-third of a cent *per megabyte today!*

IMAX frame

70mm frame

35mm frame

Whatever critics may think of *Terminator 2* and its inevitable sequels, the drawing power of special effects on a grand scale has not been lost on Hollywood — or IMAX. The day may well come when some of the most costly and spectacular Virtual Reality installations, now the domain of cinespheres and theme parks, will find their way into our living rooms. Yet parents will still want to take their kids to Wonderland, Disneyland and all their clones and surrogates.

By moving into our living rooms, Hollywood may have found a more comfortable place to settle down. Meanwhile, new technologies will also be pulling consumers out the door. As they do, we're witnessing yet another kind of convergence, as cinemas become more like theme parks and theme parks go a lot more high tech. We know this must be a trend: not content with a piece of every other conceivable form of entertainment, Time Warner now has interests in theme parks as far away as Australia.

Chapter 5

Road to Avonlea

CANADIAN PRODUCERS, CANADIAN CONTENT

"All that channel capacity has a voracious appetite for product. There will be a shift in emphasis, and in fortunes, from program deliverers to program producers."

Andrew Roman, Miller Thomson, 1992

As we noted in the preceding chapter, two axioms have always ruled the financial life of Canadian broadcasters. One, American entertainment programs are cheap to buy and yet make a high return in advertising dollars. Two, Canadian entertainment programs are expensive to buy — so expensive in relation to their potential return that they are almost invariably a losing proposition in purely business terms.

Stiff competition among our broadcasters for American entertainment programming has pushed up the prices of American programs to a considerable degree in the last few years. But this has done little to correct for the discrepancies that have made the domestic fate of Canadian programs so precarious. It is these discrepancies that originally prompted the regulator to create Canadian content quotas, which require our private TV broadcasters to air no less than 60% Canadian programming throughout the broadcast day and 50% in prime time (the figures are more demanding of CBC).

Let's look at the problem from the perspective of the independent producer. Broadcasters pay independent producers a "licence fee" for the right to air their programs, usually expressed as a percentage of the original production budget or "negative cost" (i.e. the cost of getting everything completed to the point of a finished film negative, from which copies are made). In the United States these days, despite tougher economic times, successful American producers often receive TV licence fees covering up to 80% of their production budgets. In Canada, on the other hand, where broadcasters have traditionally covered only 20% of a program's budget in the form of a licence fee, the situation has deteriorated even further, according to public statements made by leading producers like Robert Lantos, Chairman and CEO of Alliance Communications. At the 1992 Festival of Festivals symposium, Lantos described Canadian broadcast licence fees as being in a "free fall".

Even a cornucopia of federal and provincial subsidies and rebates has not been able to bring relief: the amount of money available in this country, whether public or private in origin, is limited by the size of our domestic market. Inevitably, therefore, Canadians began looking beyond our borders for international partners and investors. What is fascinating about this trend is that it crosses the line between purely commercial initiatives and those led by government. As we'll see in a moment, the federal government has encouraged the international option by negotiating bilateral co-production treaties with nearly two dozen other countries.

The growing globalization of home entertainment and its financing has not been solely prompted by developments in technology. It is certain, however, that the expansion of distribution channels, the looming increase in channel capacity and the shift to transactional viewing will all have a long-term impact on how TV producers conduct their business. Will these technological developments be good for Canadian producers?

On the basis of interviews and other research, it would seem that more prospects are being opened up than foreclosed. Even the decline of conventional television in the U.S. and fierce competition from the cable networks have worked to the benefit of Canada's larger producers, who are now doing a landslide business with both camps. And yet, while the prospect of any new release window created by technology is another potential source of production financing, highly publicized developments such as the launch of "Deathstar" direct-to-home satellite

Conspiracy of Silence

services (discussed in the next chapter) seem to have little to offer except as financial "backenders". As usual, the news from the technology front isn't all good or all bad.

The independents we are alluding to are part of a small group of Canadians who are — outside the CBC — largely responsible for making the kinds of TV which embody Canadian cultural values, i.e. drama and entertainment programs. We've noted that these producers are doing more and more of their business abroad and finding unprecedented acceptance among the American networks. One of our purposes in this chapter is thus to ascertain whether the way these producers define commercial success in Canada, the United States and elsewhere will continue to enhance our national cultural goals — as well as the supply of "quality Canadian programming".

The growth of independent production

Independent production of Canadian programming is a relatively recent phenomenon in the history of television. In 1983 the industry got a shot in the arm with the creation of the Canadian Broadcast Program Development Fund (the "Broadcast Fund", or just the "Fund"). The Fund was set up to promote the production of high quality, culturally relevant Canadian programming and is administered by Telefilm Canada, the public funding agency for our film and television industry. At about the same time, the CRTC began imposing stiffer Canadian content requirements on broadcasters as part of their conditions of licence. These have come to include commitments from broadcasters as to how much money they spend on Canadian programs, how they schedule these programs, how they contribute to talent development and so on.

Together with provincial initiatives, these measures created a boom in Canadian program production and made far more domestic entertainment programming available to Canadian viewers than ever before. The greater volume of work and better viewing shares that came about did not, however, solve the underlying structural problems. High quality Canadian programs are still prohibitively expensive to produce relative to the size of the market and have no

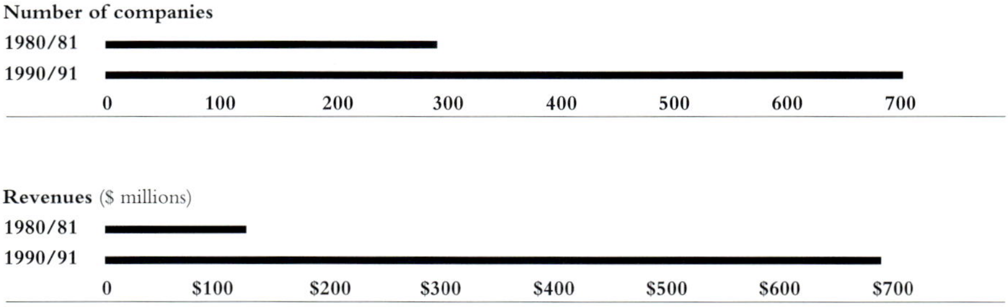

Growth of Canadian Film & Video Companies
Source: Statistics Canada

hope of recouping more than a fraction of their budgeted costs from Canadian TV sales. The business dilemma is that the CRTC's regulations and conditions of licence still require that TV broadcasters invest in independently produced Canadian material.

The broadcaster's temptation is to pay as little as possible to independent Canadian producers for their series and TV movies. While this has always been an issue in the TV business — as we said, even American producers don't finance 100% of their costs from licence fees — the situation has become critical in Canada. While the costs of production have been rising ahead of inflation, broadcaster licence fees, traditionally around 20% of budgets in Canada, have not kept pace. Conventional broadcasters in particular have suffered a major downturn in advertising revenues since the late 1980s and many have been forced to slash costs. Meanwhile, their high-end program suppliers need more money, not less, to get their programs made as scripts and production values become more competitive.

International co-production

Like their counterparts all over the world, even the Americans, Canadian producers have taken to seeking out international partnerships, pre-sales and joint ventures in order to make a living. In fact, the particularly small size of the

Canadian market has obliged our producers to develop considerable skills in finding, building and maintaining these international relationships.

The push to internationalize has come not just from the producers themselves, but has also been encouraged by the federal government. This encouragement has taken the shape of bilateral co-production treaties, which the Canadian government has negotiated with some two dozen other countries in recognition of the importance of international co-production (see accompanying box).

Generally speaking, Canada has participated in three kinds of international co-productions:

→ Canadian-originated projects with indigenous content, such as *Bordertown*, a Canada-France co-production

→ international co-productions where the Canadian production partner is creatively involved but the subject is not Canadian, such as *Sword of Gideon*

→ international co-productions where Canada plays a financial role, such as the mini-series *The French Revolution*, which Canada co-produced with partners in France, the U.K., Italy and Germany

Recent Canadian television co-productions include the mini-series *First Circle* (with France), *Young Catherine* (with the U.K.), *Golden Fiddles* (with Australia) and *The Sound and the Silence* (with New Zealand and Ireland); the series *Sweating Bullets* (with Mexico) and *Tarzan* (with Mexico and France); and the animated series *Rupert* (with France).

Whereas Canada and its co-production partners generally regard the treaties as both useful and successful, they are an irritant to the United States. That's because they are seen as conferring an unfair advantage and being at odds with the most favoured nation principle of the General Agreement on Tariffs and Trade, or GATT. Canadians, on the other hand, see them as an advantage in their efforts to finance programs without American money and enter foreign markets dominated by American product.

Some Americans, particularly at the Hollywood majors, complain about the treaties. Others, however, see them as an indirect advantage, through co-ventures with Canadian production companies. Ironically this is for the same reason that the treaties are seen as helpful by Canadian producers — they act as an opening into foreign markets. Take, for instance, Astral Inc., a Canadian packager and financier of many international television projects, which also operates First Choice, the Canadian pay-movie service. Astral recently signed a co-venture deal with Warner Bros. International Television. Under the deal, shows produced by the co-venture — called Warner-Astral Europe — will meet both Canadian and European broadcasting quotas. Warner International Television President Michael J. Solomon has stated that the deal is beneficial to Warner precisely because "Canada has [co-production] treaties with over 22 countries and the U.S. doesn't" (*Variety*, July 13, 1992, p.40).

Like all co-production arrangements that cross national boundaries, projects enabled under a bilateral treaty create their own difficulties. These difficulties stem from the division of responsibility and control, both financial and creative, typical of such partnerships. Since the co-producers in question come from different cultures, and usually have different broadcasting and legal systems, each partner has particular creative demands of a project, a potential source of conflict. Some of the most successful projects are those in which one country takes the lead creatively, while the other partners have approval.

How Co-Production Treaties Work

Canada's co-production treaties are negotiated by the Department of Communications and administered by Telefilm Canada. These treaties aim to facilitate foreign participation in the financing of indigenous film and television projects. Under the terms of such treaties, co-productions qualify as domestic content in each of the participating countries which are signatory to them. Thus, even though a production may not conform with the letter of the rules governing domestic content, it will still qualify as such.

Canada has official co-production treaties with 23 countries around the world. A film or television production produced under the terms of a treaty qualifies as domestic content in each of the co-producing countries, i.e. a Canada-France co-production such as The Adventures of the Black Stallion *is considered a Canadian content program in Canada and a French content program in France.*

There are also difficulties surrounding the desire of English-speaking producers to shoot co-productions in English, whereas France, Canada's strongest co-production partner, is naturally partial to French-language productions. Canada has yet to co-produce a continuing series with English-language partners in either the U.K. or Australia, possibly because of cross-cultural and business barriers.

This is true even if the lion's share of the production budget for that series is raised and spent in Canada. In fact, as little as 20% of the production budget can be spent in any one partnering country. Over the course of several years, however, there must be an overall balance to the amount of financing contributed in total by Canada and each of its co-production partners to their co-production projects.

Since official co-productions are considered domestic programming, they are eligible for public funding in each partnering country, if it is available. An official Canada-France co-production can apply for funding from Telefilm Canada, for example. Broadcasters in Canada, and in other countries with domestic program content regulations, will also pay higher licence fees for programs considered to be indigenous.

Canada does not have such a treaty with the U.S. and would not benefit from the existence of one because the U.S. does not have any broadcast content regulations. Formal co-production deals between Canadian and American partners — i.e. deals that involve some prior financial commitment, rather than just a sale after completion of production — are often referred to as "co-ventures".

Treaties are not the only way international productions get made these days — nor the only way Canadian producers secure relationships with foreign partners. Indeed, the various options have now become remarkably complex. The prime-time action-adventure series *Counterstrike*, for example, is a co-venture between Alliance Communications in Canada, a production company in France and broadcasters in Canada (CTV), France (TF1) and the U.S. (the USA Network). Without all these partners it would have been virtually impossible to raise the production budget of approximately $1 million per one-hour episode. Yet despite perennial difficulties in selling a story to a foreign audience, this kind of action-adventure series is arguably the least difficult genre to co-produce internationally.

In the past, Canadians have usually been able to finance projects as either Canadian-European co-productions or as Canadian-American co-ventures, which would subsequently be sold in Europe. As the *Counterstrike* example shows, however, the heavy costs and high risks associated with producing fiction television have accelerated the trend towards trilateral projects, where three territories are major participants. Adding a third set of partners from another culture and another television jurisdiction makes the creative juggling act even more demanding. Yet so strong is the appeal of American-style programming that even the prospect of a tug-of-war over money and "final cut" does not seem to have deterred many European producers and broadcasters.

European financing is now vital to many projects that have both Canadian and American money. A case in point is *Forever Knight*, a late-night drama series about a vampire cop. Produced by Toronto's Paragon Entertainment, this series has been licensed to the CBS network in the U.S. and Glen-Warren Entertainment (a division of Baton Broadcasting) in Canada, with TriStar Television as the U.S. distributor. Financing was not complete until European distribution rights were picked up by German broadcaster Tele-München. According to Paragon president Richard Borchiver, the German financier was as important in the deal as the American distributor TriStar.

Paragon is not alone in this strategy. Even Atlantis Films, which has made a practice of developing series like *Neon Rider* and *Mom P.I.* with Canadian broadcasters, now has a drama series in development with German broadcaster ARD. Established producers like W. Paterson Ferns, president of Primedia Entertainment, are employing the co-production treaties more often in order to take advantage of benefits such as tax-shelters and bring in as much financing as possible.

Content rules & the "Top Cops" syndrome

We've just seen that the road to success for many Canadian producers now leads to the four corners of the globe and complex financing deals. The further internationalization of production, with the participation of more foreign partners, will enable our producers to tackle bigger projects, in the style of TV epics like *The French Revolution*, which Canada's Alliance Communications helped to finance. But that kind of success raises questions about just how far benefits can be expected to extend to Canadians. Michael MacMillan, president of Atlantis Films, suggested in

Nelvana's

Babar

a 1992 interview that internationalization may put both professional opportunities and creative content at risk:

> [Program] content and engagement of people tend to follow where the money comes from. [...] The less Canadian money in the project, in general, the less it will provide jobs here and the less it will reflect this country. That's a general truism.

Not all of MacMillan's colleagues see this as a truism. At the 1992 Festival of Festivals Symposium, Michael Hirsh, president of Nelvana, now one of the world's leading animation houses, gave examples of just the opposite. He alluded to co-productions with France — where Nelvana has established a major studio — that have created significant volumes of work for Canadian animation artists back in Toronto.

It's only natural that different producers should have different perspectives on these issues. Yet there's one issue that just won't go away: when is a Canadian TV program not Canadian any more?

Canadian content is defined for regulatory and funding purposes according to the so-called "point system". This codified federal system assigns points — up to a maximum of 10 — to TV programs according to the nationality of the creative personnel responsible for its creation. The most important collaborators, the writer and director, get two points each, while others, like the editor and composer of the score, get one point each. Along with factors like how much of a production budget is spent in Canada, the point total qualifies individual programs and series for certain privileges — like Telefilm funding, tax rebates and broadcast quotas. A program that achieves the requisite number of points is "certified" as a 6-pointer, 8-pointer or 10-pointer.

Whereas the system is applied for a cultural purpose, it uses what is essentially an *industrial* definition of "Canadian", based on place of residence, not on anything intrinsic to the theme or values of the program itself. A problem arises as soon as a Canadian producer begins to share creative and financial responsibilities with one or more foreign co-producers. That's because there is a strong business incentive to lure financing — especially American financing — by yielding control to larger, wealthier foreign partners, while at the same time trying to maintain the Canadian status of a production.

The first and most famous example of a Canadian-American co-production that epitomized this dilemma was the series *Night Heat*. The series, which aired on CBS from 1985 to 1991, signalled a new and enduring era in Canadian television production. Originally commissioned by CTV, it was the first late-night dramatic series produced with Canadian participation for a U.S. network. The show's creators, Grosso-Jacobson Productions of New York and Los Angeles, were approached by CTV and decided to shoot the series in a co-venture with Alliance Entertainment (now Alliance Communications).

Because it was more cost-effective to do so, the series was shot in Canada. *Night Heat* was popular and showed American network executives and producers that an American-style series could be produced just as well in Canada as in the U.S. As critics have been fond of pointing out, however, the producers went to great pains to ensure that viewers would have no clue that the program had any connection whatsoever with Canada. By altering or disguising street signs, currency, licence plates and other cultural symbols, the producers managed to create a disembodied setting for the show that could have owed its origins to almost any medium-sized North American city. In other words, the show was Canadian in name but not in spirit.

The hybrid genre created by *Night Heat* has encouraged other American producers and broadcasters to shoot in Canada. Grosso-Jacobson has itself continued to shoot in Canada with Canadian partners. In fact, the Canadian content certification of *Top Cops*, another series created by Grosso-Jacobson and produced by CBS Broadcast International in Canada, sparked concern in the Canadian independent production community about the effectiveness of Cancon rules.

Like its predecessor, *Top Cops* is produced, directed, written and acted by Canadians. *Night Heat* and *Top Cops* (now in its third season) have something else in common: the average television viewer tuning into the program, whether on Global Television or CBS, is unlikely to distinguish it as a Canadian production. It is derivative of the American "reality show" format, which is cheap to produce and short on artistic insights. Even though the stories may emanate from Canada, reality programming has a way of blurring the lines of program nationality.

Despite it all, *Top Cops* exemplifies a growing production trend. Far from seeing Canada as a television backwater, many American producers now actively seek out Canadian colleagues to "line-produce" (perform the hands-on producing chores) or to enter into a co-venture arrangement in order to produce programs that qualify for Canadian content status and its attendant financial benefits. These benefits include a higher licence fee from the Canadian broadcaster and the opportunity for tax-shelter financing.

The content certification rules were intended to prevent unscrupulous Canadians from having their cake and eating it too — handing over control of a production to an American partner, while still enjoying the advantages of certification. Among other things, the rules are designed to discourage Canadian producers from relinquishing claims to future revenue on programs by giving away distribution rights to their foreign partners. In the real world, however, entertainment lawyers are in business precisely to square this kind of circle. The certification of *Top Cops* as Canadian did not come about as a result of, say, peer adjudication at a festival, but as a result of skilful legal work.

The Cancon rules do not pose an impediment to most American producers who shoot in Canada with Canadian producers, and meet the minimum six out of 10 content points and various expenditure requirements. As a result, increasingly large numbers of productions with significant U.S. presales (and the influence that comes with such financing) have applied for or been granted Canadian content status. Some of Hollywood's most powerful producers are getting in on the act. Spelling Television, producer of the hugely successful *Charlie's Angels* and *Beverly Hills 90210*, plans to develop Canadian content programs from its office in Vancouver. Cannell Films, which has had a production base in that city for several years, shooting series such as *Street Justice* and *The Commish*, also seems poised to produce Canadian certifiable programs with the help of Canadian producers.

The involvement of American partners does not necessarily signify that the originality or nationality of a program is being compromised. Yet how ironic that the Canadian content rules, originally intended to protect domestic programming from the American onslaught, are now being used by shrewd American producers to finance "Canadian" content for foreign markets, all with the help of tax expenditures from Canadian coffers. Even those who have been the beneficiaries in the past are lodging complaints. Consider the position of Steven DeNure, senior vice-president of creative affairs for Alliance Communications, who is quoted as saying that the "glut" of Cancon projects now on the market is driving licence fees down. This glut, he said, is a result of projects that are developed in the U.S. but produced in Canada as Canadian content, thereby making it more difficult for Canadian producers to develop, finance, produce and sell their own programs to Canadian broadcasters (*Playback*, October 12, 1992, p.7).

The situation poses several dilemmas for industry.

First, when broadcasters buy an American-style Cancon program, they may be meeting their Cancon regulations technically without doing so in spirit. This may be of little concern to broadcasters, who pay a fraction of the price for a Cancon program like *Top Cops*, which is already financed by a U.S. sale, compared to a wholly Canadian program such as *E.N.G.*

Second, Canadian producers who work as line producers with Americans on Cancon programs stand to lose over the long term. Without foreign distribution rights, they miss out on benefitting from what can be the most lucrative part of the business. The short-term industrial perspective is that such productions create jobs. But what really builds up this industry, in terms of both revenue and market clout, is a library of programming for which a production house shares in distribution rights, just as a book publisher capitalizes on the strength of its backlist.

Third, under the current system, it's the broadcasters who are calling the shots and even Telefilm must dance to their tune. Broadcasters choose which programs they want and a production cannot apply to Telefilm's Broadcast Fund without a broadcaster's commitment letter. The Cancon regulations allow broadcasters to pay more attention to the deal that can be constructed than to the artistic merits of the program in question.

Road to Avonlea

Market fragmentation & niche audiences

We turn now from an examination of the content dilemma created by the internationalization of production, to an analysis of how the Canadian production community is likely to be affected by the vast increase in channel capacity afforded by compression and other technological developments.

Over the past several years, as we observed, the creation of American cable networks, combined with the erosion of the broadcast networks, paved the way for new partnerships and financing opportunities for Canadian producers. The new cable networks needed partners to produce less expensive series than TV was used to. Meanwhile, the broadcast networks passed on the effects of audience fragmentation by lowering their licence fee payments to American producers, who now found themselves in need of deficit financing. (Deficit financing refers to monies which must be found to cover the difference between a program's total production budget or negative cost and the licence fee paid by the commissioning or first-run broadcaster.) In both instances, Canadian producers were able to step in, providing more affordable programming for cable and deficit financing for the production of other material.

American cable networks have become the most important source of financing for many Canadian drama series, after public sources such as Telefilm Canada and the CBC. The Disney Channel, the USA Network and the Family Channel, among other U.S. cable networks, are currently contributing between 20% and 60% of the budget of some programs, and in most cases, between 30% and 40%. This country's busiest program suppliers, such as Alliance Communications, Atlantis Films and Paragon Entertainment, all sell heavily to American cable and pay-cable clients. In the case of certain programs, a Canadian broadcaster may pay as little as 10% of the budget, while as much as 50% might come from an American deal.

Examples of Canadian series airing on U.S. cable networks include *Road to Avonlea* (The Disney Channel); *Counterstrike* and *Beyond Reality* (USA Network); and *Maniac Mansion* and *The Adventures of the Black Stallion* (The Family Channel).

The introduction of pay and specialty services in Canada like YTV and First Choice has affected Canadian production in three ways: it has offered producers new outlets and sources of financing for their programming; it has caused conventional broadcasters to reassess their attitudes to programming and audiences, particularly as they pertain to advertising; and it has contributed to the decrease in licence fees paid by broadcasters to producers for their programs.

Specialty services have encroached on the advertising turf of the conventional broadcasters because, as narrowcasters, they offer advertisers targeted marketing opportunities with their niche programming approach. They have succeeded in attracting both advertisers and audiences. Canadian specialty and pay services accounted for almost 13% of television viewing during the 1990–91 season, up from less than 2% in 1984–85. YTV, the youth and family service, and Family Channel/Le Canal Famille, which all began broadcasting in 1988, have played an important role in expanding financing and production opportunities for Canadian producers. Although many specialty services do not represent a market for performance programming (drama, entertainment, variety), YTV counts Canadian series such as *Maniac Mansion* and *The Adventures of the Black Stallion* among its roster of programs.

Many industry observers expect this trend to niche programming to continue. In many ways, however, niche programming is only an optimistic response to the well-established problem of audience fragmentation in television. Whatever else may happen to the industry, it's a safe bet that the future holds a lot more channels and thus a lot more fragmentation.

Will further fragmentation be beneficial to Canadian producers?

Yes and no. Yes, because new opportunities will be created by the expansion of domestic distribution channels. And as we've already noted, these channels will in all likelihood offer both more economical and more direct ways of reaching consumers. No, in the sense that a more fragmented broadcasting marketplace will mean lower licence fees from any one source. That in turn will mean that producers will have to show all the more skill in putting together the disparate pieces of complex deals and aggregating the resources to get their projects realized.

Canadian producers interviewed on this subject were not of one mind. Pat Ferns of Primedia was cautious about the new technological prospects:

> I think the technology that allows the consumer, the viewer, to have more is forcing a different set of marriages among the people who cause programs to get made. We have to be more imaginative about the ways we find the financing because it's getting trickier and trickier.

Michael MacMillan of Atlantis was more optimistic:

> The splintering phenomenon will actually work in our favour on a global basis because it will force other large markets to be co-operative. And who are they going to co-operate with? Well, probably an English-speaking country that is near to America, that has a lot of [international co-production] treaties and an excellent production infrastructure.

However optimistic the view, the consensus is that Canadian producers, already juggling a host of American and European partners, will have to find even more partners on the deals of the future. The challenge to Canadians will be to ensure that they can exploit rights to the various markets involved in a program's financing.

At present, several American cable services, like USA Network, are serving well as sources of financing for Canadian producers. Because these services are not available in Canada, no potential conflict exists over Canadian rights. A Canadian producer can thus presell to a Canadian broadcaster on the one hand and to a U.S. cable network on the other. But in the case of an Arts and Entertainment or PBS, which are available in both the U.S. and Canada, a sale to one of these services in New York or Los Angeles will automatically pre-empt a sale in Canada.

In the future, technology will only make the rights problem more complicated. This will be particularly true of satellite services, whose signals, though intended primarily for the American market, will spill over into the most populous areas of Canada. One possibility is that satellite operators will delete the signals of programs for which they hold only U.S. rights. Another possibility is that they may view transmission of such programs as a problem for the Canadian rights-holder or broadcaster to deal with. The challenge for the producer, who wants to maximize sources of financing, will be to sell to an American network, as well as to a Canadian broadcaster, then have both parties agree on the scheduling of the program.

New services: good news for producers?

The satellite services to which we've just alluded are known as direct broadcast or direct-to-home (DTH). In Canada, they've also come to be known as "Deathstars", because of the alleged threat they pose to the broadcasting system. While we will be reviewing some of the issues related to Deathstars in the next chapter, our primary concern in this context is to ask whether these new services represent an opportunity to Canadian producers.

These American DTH services will have an enormous appetite for programming, because they will take advantage of compression technology to provide 60, 80 or even 100 channels to those equipped to receive them. It is unlikely, however, that their appetite will be of any help in financing new Canadian production.

For the most part, DTH services will be seeking the rights to programming that is already produced — movies, in particular. Instead of acting as sources of risk or equity financing, they will obtain pay-per-view rights from program producers or rights-holders, then pay them based on the audience their program draws. For Canadian distributors of movies and those with substantial catalogs, DTH services are likely to be nothing more than potential new markets for old programming, a chance to bring in a little extra revenue. The cost of providing the huge amount of programming these services propose to offer will inhibit them from investing in original program production.

One of the most significant effects of the mere *prospect* of American DTH services in Canada is the reactions of broadcasters and cablecasters. As we'll see in more detail in the next chapter, neither segment of the distribution infrastructure welcomes the perceived threat of more American competition on such a massive scale. Views differ on solutions, however.

Private broadcasters favour, or once favoured, a moratorium on new specialty or narrowcast services, on the grounds they would result in further fragmentation of the broadcasting system. A formal request to the minister of communications, which sought a three-year moratorium on Canadian licensing of new services, was eventually turned down. Meanwhile, Canada's cable industry has been moving in exactly the opposite direction, looking for the CRTC to allow the licensing of *more* specialty services — though not necessarily Canadian ones. What Canadian cable operators have in mind is the need to compete with DTH by offering more services to their subscribers. Ideally, they would like many of these to be the very services that American DTH operators will be offering in a couple of years.

A third option has emerged, one shared by industry leaders as different as Kevin Shea, the head of YTV, and Jay Switzer, vice-president of programming at Toronto's CITY-TV. Both Shea and Switzer have expressed their desire to see a number of new Canadian specialty services licensed as quickly as possible. At a conference on broadcasting policy held by the Law Society of Upper Canada in the spring of 1992, Switzer argued that getting Canadian services up quickly was the only way to ensure they would gain a competitive foothold before the arrival en masse of new American services, whether by DTH satellite or other distribution vehicle.

This is a concept generally endorsed by Pat Ferns, who, in addition to his role as an independent producer, has also been chair of the production committee of Advanced Broadcasting Systems of Canada (ABSOC). Ferns takes the idea one step further, suggesting in an interview that Canadian-originated specialty services should consider launching themselves internationally and take advantage of the same technology that is propelling DTH/DBS into Canada:

> Where the technology is going to help is when, with digital compression and so forth, you are able to deliver signals more cheaply than is the case when the only way you broadcast is with transmitters all across Canada. If you can bump it up on a satellite over the whole of the U.S., and you can find half a million people who are interested in that kind of service, you can sell a certain kind of advertising and charge a certain fee, and that may make sense.

For the moment, however, the whole debate has been forestalled by the timetable imposed by the CRTC's structural hearing, slated for March 1993. The Commission has announced that it will not hear applications for new Canadian services until a thorough review of the ground rules takes place under the auspices of this hearing. As it indicated in Notice of Public Hearing 1992-13 (September 3, 1992):

> The Commission is [...] aware of the need perceived by certain parties that it license new Canadian services [...] particularly as a response to emerging foreign-based multichannel distribution systems. Consequently, the Commission considers that it is also appropriate, in the context of this review, to explore the criteria that should govern the licensing and authorization of potential new broadcasting undertakings [...].

The supply-side view of Canadian content

The "supply-side view" of Canadian content recognizes that Canadian broadcasting does not operate as a free marketplace where supply and demand can be counted on to ensure the production of distinctive Canadian programming — especially drama and entertainment programming. This view goes on to suggest that distinctive Canadian programming should not be produced according to either the economics of private broadcasting or even the perceived demand of the Canadian viewing audience.

Instead, public policy should ensure that such programming is produced in significant volume and then given a reasonable chance to find its audience. You do not conduct market research to determine whether viewers would like the opportunity to see a program with the working title *Street Legal*. A producer and creative team follow their artistic instincts and start producing the show, which then may need to be nurtured through two or three or more seasons by a patient broadcaster, so that the new show and its untried audience can find each other. (Ted Turner is alleged to have said in connection with his bold way of starting up broadcasting businesses, that if you had asked people in a survey 100 years ago

Street Legal

whether they'd be interested in the concept of paying to sit on a hunk of vibrating metal and be flown around 20,000 feet above ground, then airplanes might never have been invented.)

Some would argue that this supply-side strategy is already in effect in the Canadian TV marketplace. Even if we grant that it is, however, there is considerable evidence that both the distinctive programming and the strategy itself are coming under seige.

First of all, we've just seen the extent to which the content regulations are being more honoured in the breach than the observance. The result is a new breed of "Cancon" programming encouraged by ambitious American producers with the connivance of regulation-weary broadcasters. The precipitous drop in licence fees offered by private broadcasters has also obliged some production companies to consider financing their Canadian projects without support from Telefilm's Broadcast Fund. Without Telefilm support, however, it is likely that such programs will be financed through complex international deals and that their Canadian content will be diluted as a result.

The second problem is that as new multichannel distribution technologies bring more foreign programming into Canada, we will need to re-evaluate the regulator's ability to protect the

Are we different?

As Canadians know only too well, the promotion of a distinctive national culture, especially in a small jurisdiction, depends on much more than responses to market demand. The development of Canadian services, whether new or established, must have some opportunity for the exercise of creative vision. And some opportunity for a "supply-side" strategy, whereby distinctive Canadian programs can be produced and then given a reasonable chance to find their audience. Distinctive Canadian programs can be expected to enshrine values that are different from American values.

There is some evidence, for example, that Canadian TV dramas have managed to avoid sex-role stereotyping much more than their U.S. counterparts. This difference undoubtedly has a lot to do with deregulation and the fact that the U.S. networks are not required to adhere to any sex-role guidelines at all. Other examples of distinctive values might include a non-commercial approach to entertaining children and a preference for resolving dramatic conflict in non-violent ways.

broadcasting marketplace. In other words, the whole support system comprising the content regulations, conditions of licence, the Broadcast Fund, and other federal and provincial initiatives, may be put at risk by new technology. Even if we were to refrain from finding fault with the way the goal of the content regulations is being subverted, we will argue in the next chapter that a plausible argument can be made that technology will force the federal authorities to reconsider the role of regulation in the broadcasting system of the 1990s.

Three observations might be made here by way of concluding remarks to this chapter.

→ First, some see the new and more fragmented marketplace as offering the opportunity to segment Canadian programming efforts into two major categories, one for mainly domestic consumption, the other for mainly foreign consumption. One such observer is Primedia's Pat Ferns. He predicts that the indigenous production industry could be pulled in two different directions. One of these would be towards less expensive ways of producing domestic programming, driven less by high production values and more by characters and stories. The other would be towards more costly, high production value international programming that requires more partners and, possibly, more diffuse storylines to interest those partners. Local programming would then become cheaper, while international programming would become bigger and more "event-oriented". This segmentation of production values and budgets could help Canadian producers reduce their risks in the development of new projects.

→ Second, while its future role seems perpetually clouded in uncertainty, thanks largely to the vagaries of public funding, a strong case can be made that the CBC is the only Canadian broadcaster that can ultimately be depended on to produce distinctive Canadian programs. In the past, the CBC has been the primary source of much of this programming, partly because it has access to two streams of public funding (its own and Telefilm's), and partly because it is, despite commercial sales, not in the business of maximizing profits. A recently announced CBC initiative — the export of Canadian-made programs through its new Northstar satellite service — suggests that the Corporation sees an aggressive export offence as the best defence against the incursions of foreign-based multichannel distributors, like American Deathstars.

→ Third, and as a logical extension of the previous point, we cannot discount the possibility that the CRTC might elect some day to relieve private broadcasters of their performance program content obligations, in return for some other consideration, such as a tax on revenues or operating profits. One prominent Canadian producer we interviewed, who declined to be identified, suggested that CTV and Global be relieved of any obligation to produce 10-out-of-10 point, wholly Canadian programming. His argument is that if we want Canadians to find their cultural reflection somewhere in the 100-channel universe, then the only viable solution is to concentrate our efforts on the public broadcaster. The continuing effort to police a system that goes against the grain of every business principle is, he suggests, a drain on resources that Canadians can no longer afford.

Split Screen

Chapter 6

TECHNOLOGY: THE ULTIMATE DEREGULATOR?

"So the whole dreary game with which we have become all too familiar over the years, in which various broadcast executives troop through CRTC hearings making solemn commitments on content in return for fat profits, only to come back for more hearings on why they should be relieved of those commitments when profits turn out to be a little less obese than expected, is over, even if neither the regulators nor the industry are quite willing to admit it yet."

Editorial, The Globe and Mail, *September 5, 1992*

In the previous chapter, we suggested that some cracks had appeared in the regulatory apparatus put in place many years ago to promote the production of Canadian programs. We looked at how certain Canadian producers are now inclined to define their success in the international marketplace, rather than in strictly domestic terms. We also looked at how other producers and broadcasters are skirting the spirit of the regulations to create a half-breed genre known as Cancon programming.

Meanwhile, consumers are facing a range of entertainment choices they have never had available before. Even as the amount and variety of products multiply, the ways of delivering them to the consumer will become more numerous and complicated.

We described earlier how these developments are hastening the decline of conventional over-the-air TV broadcasting. Yet the whole regulatory apparatus for administering and controlling television is based on a decades-old relationship between viewers, broadcasters, advertisers and regulators. Given these changes to traditional television, we have to question whether regulations created for an industry dominated by a handful of conventional networks are appropriate in an era of narrowcasting, digital compression, pay-per-view and direct broadcast satellites.

Our task in this chapter therefore is to examine how new technologies have undermined or altered the traditional rationales for the regulation of broadcasting. Whatever our opinion of the rationales themselves, new technologies will have another effect: they will make it increasingly difficult for regulators to put their principles into practice and to enforce the rules.

The leading example of this problem, which we discuss in some detail, is that of the American-based, direct-to-home satellites known as "Deathstars". Rather than dwell on conventional concerns about the damage Deathstars will allegedly do to the broadcasting system or Canadian culture, we stress that those who have spread most alarm about them are those who have most to lose — Canada's broadcasters and cablecasters. To demonstrate the importance of this point, we examine some of the ways in which the current regulatory framework has helped to entrench the market power of the conventional distribution firms — often at the expense of consumers and video providers. We therefore come to question whether this regulatory framework continues to operate in the public interest as defined in section 3 of the *Broadcasting Act*.

To begin with, however, let's see what justifications can be found for the regulation of broadcasting in the first place.

Rationales for the established regulatory framework

In creating a regulatory framework for broadcasting, neither the Canadian nor the American government has explicitly codified the various reasons that would justify such regulation. Section 3 of the *Broadcasting Act*, for example, provides a much clearer sense of the goals of regulation than it does of the reasons or what we will term "rationales" for the regulation of broadcasting. Nevertheless, we can infer a series of rationales from years of policy pronouncements, jurisprudence and regulatory decisions. In this chapter we propose to discuss five of these: *spectrum scarcity, intrusiveness (including potential for harm), intangible cultural benefits, advertiser sovereignty and merit goods.*

This enumeration does not purport to be exhaustive. Yet we believe it accounts for the most important concepts underpinning the actions of the CRTC in the realm of broadcasting. We also believe that these rationales have now been largely overtaken by developments in technology and by changes in the structure of the industries concerned. We begin with a brief description of each rationale.

Spectrum scarcity

According to the spectrum scarcity rationale, television broadcasters make use of a scarce public resource — the electromagnetic spectrum. Television signals were originally carried in only one small part of the electromagnetic spectrum, i.e. the Very High Frequency (VHF) band. Because the part of the spectrum devoted to broadcasting is limited and uncontrolled use of over-the-air spectrum would result in chaos, it was seen as the duty of government to regulate the allocation of channels so as to maximize the public benefit.

Prime Minister R. B. Bennett invoked the spectrum rationale when he introduced Canada's first broadcasting legislation in 1932:

> The use of the air [...] that lies over the soil or land of Canada is a natural resource over which we have complete jurisdiction [...] and I cannot think that any government would be warranted in leaving the air to private exploitation and not reserving it for development for the use of the people.[24]

The public nature of the spectrum is reflected in section 3(b) of the 1991 *Broadcasting Act*, which provides that "the Canadian broadcasting system [...] makes use of radio frequencies that are public property". Spectrum scarcity has been judicially recognized in Canada as justifying government intervention into the broadcasting industry, even though such intervention may, for example, infringe freedom of expression. This is in sharp contrast to the print media, which are virtually unregulated.

The scarcity rationale was introduced into American jurisprudence in 1943 by Justice Frankfurter, who used it to find against the NBC network, which had objected to being regulated on grounds of freedom of expression:

> Freedom of utterance is abridged to many who wish to use the limited facilities of radio. Unlike other modes of expression, radio inherently is not available to all. That is its unique characteristic, and that is why, unlike other modes of expression, it is subject to governmental regulation.[25]

Spectrum scarcity has probably been the rationale most often invoked in support of the regulation of broadcasting. Ironically, it is the one rationale most directly affected by new developments in technology, as we'll see below.

Intrusiveness & potential for harm

The distribution technologies used in broadcasting are known to lawyers and other specialists as "intrusive". The long-standing distinction between intrusive and non-intrusive technologies is based on the idea that the former are "scarce" and public, like signals carried on the electromagnetic spectrum, while the latter are unlimited and private, like books, records, CDs, videocassettes and so on — the "take-home" technologies.

Intrusiveness combines the closed, finite distribution system with the principle that broadcast signals intrude into the home in ways that are only partly under the control of the end-user. Ever since broadcasting began, this distinction has helped bolster the legal wall that separates cultural activities subject to regulation, like TV broadcasting, from those, like print publishing, that are entirely unregulated (apart from matters such as obscenity, tax liability and other general provisions of business and criminal law).

The idea of intrusiveness or pervasiveness is closely associated with that of potential for harm. Over the years, Canadian and American regulators have kept a watchful eye on licensees, to guard against activities that could, for example, be construed as obscene or slanderous. In a notorious 1978 decision, involving the use of "offensive" language by comedian George Carlin on a radio show, the U.S. Supreme Court argued that broadcasting was subject to a greater degree of government intervention than other forms of communication, such as the print media:

> First, the broadcast media have established a uniquely pervasive presence in the lives of Americans. Patently offensive, indecent materials presented over the airwaves confront the citizen, not only in public, but also in the privacy of the home, where the individual's right to be let alone plainly outweighs the First Amendment right of an intruder.
>
> Second, broadcasting is uniquely accessible to children, even those too young to read [...]. The ease with which children may obtain access to broadcast material, coupled with the concerns recognized in Ginsberg, amply justify the special treatment of indecent broadcasting.[26]

While the distinction between intrusive and non-intrusive technologies is fast eroding, we'll note later on that the advent of new distribution technologies is now raising related issues, particularly around the question of privacy.

Intangible cultural benefits

This rationale posits that Canadian content in television programming strengthens national culture and identity. But Canadian programming, particularly drama, is prohibitively expensive to produce, given its limited return on investment and the availability of cheap, popular American programming. All this acts as a powerful disincentive to the production of Canadian programs. This disincentive is compounded by the fact that the market does not take into account the positive, though intangible cultural benefits to the Canadian nation when the true costs and benefits of Canadian programming are being weighed. Economists often refer to such intangible benefits as *externalities.*

In purely economic terms, it is assumed that the TV market is "inefficient" because it produces too few Canadian programs with positive cultural benefits. These benefits or "positive externalities" arise when a certain good is purchased and used by a consumer, and this purchase and use benefit another individual not involved in the transaction. The purchase and use are "worth" more to "society" than what the actual purchaser paid for it or was willing to pay for it.

In the case of TV content, an external benefit arises from the positive cultural spillovers generated by Canadian programming. Not only will a typical viewer derive a certain entertainment or educational benefit from viewing Canadian content, but the nation as a whole will benefit because viewing Canadian shows will enhance national and cultural identity. Thus, according to this rationale, intervention by the CRTC into Canadian television broadcasting through content quotas is justified because it corrects for the discrepancy between strictly economic value and cultural worth.

Television as a "Public Good"

There are important economic differences between advertiser-supported, over-the-air television and the user-pays television we have described as part of a "transactional" model of the new technologies. Economists describe the first kind of television as a "public good". Public goods are defined as being both "non-excludable" and "non-rival" in the way they are consumed. Once a public good is disseminated to a certain number of consumers, the additional cost of another person consuming that good is zero. Moreover, it is expensive and often impossible to prevent anyone from consuming the good even if they are not willing to pay for it. Thus, public goods are normally supplied to consumers for free.

Advertiser sovereignty

The fourth rationale recognizes that, in advertiser-supported broadcasting, broadcasters do not "sell" their programs to audiences; what they do instead is sell audiences to advertisers. This means programs are a cost of doing business, not an end in themselves, and programming decisions are made to maximize viewing levels without any direct evaluation of individual viewer preferences. The influence exerted by advertising over programming decisions discourages the creation of programs that appeal to minority or specialized tastes, and may therefore work against the public interest.

Over-the-air broadcasting was and is financed directly by advertisers, not viewers. Although programs financed by advertising revenues will allow viewers access to television programs for free, *the programs aired will reflect the number of people who view those programs, and not the value people place on them.* Conventional broadcasters therefore have no efficient means for discerning which particular programs will enhance viewer satisfaction. Instead, they are compelled to provide programming that will draw the largest audiences and thereby the largest advertising revenues.

Programs with high audiences, however, would not necessarily generate the most revenue if financed directly by viewers. Consider an episode of a typical sitcom and a special presentation of an opera.

A television program distributed free over the airwaves can be characterized as a public good. This has consequences for the efficiency of both program production and distribution. Once a program has been produced and broadcast, the price of over-the-air television viewing is essentially zero. If John is already watching Street Legal, *it costs nothing more to allow Susan to watch it as well. A television program is thus non-rival in consumption — unlike the last piece of pie, which John and Susan also have their eye on.*

Before the advent of scrambled or encrypted signals, it was impossible to prevent anyone with the proper equipment from receiving a television signal, just as it is impossible to prevent a ship from using a lighthouse for guidance. In order for the TV market to be "efficient" in economic terms, therefore, the price of television viewing had to be set at zero.

While the sitcom may draw ten times the audience of the opera, the sitcom viewers may value their program far less than the opera viewers, typically because people watch sitcoms for distraction, while viewers of the opera are more deeply engaged. Consequently, the viewers of the opera might be willing to pay $10 or more for the privilege of viewing the opera, while the viewers of the sitcom might not be willing to pay anything at all. Thus, if we multiply the number of viewers by the level of preference (based on what viewers would be willing to pay for either program) the opera might well "outperform" the sitcom.

In conventional broadcasting, the opera may well be considered more valuable to its viewers, but it's the sitcom that gets aired because it generates the highest audience levels. Because of the power of advertising to affect program exhibition in this way, regulators have felt obliged to mitigate the influences of advertising.

Merit goods

The final rationale for the regulation of conventional broadcasting is that certain kinds of television programming, in the manner of art galleries, should be available to Canadians whether a measurable market demand exists for them or not. Such commodities are termed *merit goods.*

The premise is that such programs have some inherent artistic or cultural merit and are therefore deemed worthy of special protection. The financing of opera and ballet companies is often justified on this basis.

Merit goods and their support are difficult to justify on objective grounds. In the case of Canadian television programming, Hoskins and McFadyen have argued (p.17) that "the taste for cultural products is a cultivated taste and government support for cultural activity, like government support for education, is justified largely by the objective of moulding the public's wants".

Many economists see government support of so-called merit goods, like cultural programming, as paternalistic. Their reasoning provides an interesting contrast to the previous rationale concerning advertiser sovereignty. In that case, the problem is seen to be that viewers have pent-up demand for certain kinds of programs, which the conventional system is not equipped to provide.

In the case of merit goods, the argument is made that there may well be no significant demand for the products or services in question. Nevertheless, regulators like the CRTC have encouraged or required the production and dissemination of programs that would have little chance of seeing the light of day under free market arrangements.

New technologies, new rules

Despite uncertainties about a sound basis for regulating broadcasting, we will suggest later that government must continue to regulate — but in new ways. One of the goals will be to ensure that the providers of information services — like broadcasters, cable operators and telephone companies — do not abuse their increasingly powerful market positions.

We turn first to an evaluation of how the traditional rationales for regulation have been undermined by new technologies.

Technology has largely wiped out the problem of **spectrum scarcity** and therefore eliminated it as a rationale for the regulation of broadcasting. We say "largely" because the demand for channel space on many cable systems in North America has outpaced the ability of operators to expand and upgrade their existing plant. However, that is, or will soon become, an issue not of scarcity but rather of fair and equitable access to broadband networks for competing information providers — a rationale for a very different kind of regulatory framework.

Four different but related factors have been at work here:

Multiple delivery media. Over-the-air broadcasting was originally limited in both its geographical range and the number of frequencies available to it in the VHF band. During the last two or three decades, broadcasting has not only expanded into the UHF band, but has been able to take advantage of several other delivery media, including coaxial cable, fibre optic cable, satellites and wireless transmission.

Compression. Within each of the new media just alluded to, digital video compression has made it possible to increase channel capacity (i.e. available spectrum) by factors of 4-to-1 or more. These ratios will increase steadily from year to year as engineers write more efficient compression algorithms and overcome problems associated with bringing broadband networks into the home. At the time of writing, Cable Television Laboratories (CableLabs), a research consortium funded by the American cable industry, is developing a cable network technology that would increase bandwidth to 1 GHz or more, enough to carry 150 analog TV channels.

Transactional delivery. Under the old arrangements, a handful of broadcasters in each market sent out their signal for free reception by the general public — everybody with a TV set. (This is a form of "point-to-multipoint" delivery.) Because reception could not be controlled *technically*, other factors were and are still controlled instead, like content, hours of transmission, program types and so on. Today, however, cable transmission, addressable converters and other technologies make it possible, indeed necessary, for viewers to enter into transactions with distributors for delivery of particular channels or programs (a form of "point-to-point" delivery). Control of what is made available, how much, when, etc. has shifted towards viewers to such an extent that anyone offended by, say, the material offered on the Playboy Channel can choose not to have it delivered to their home.

Convergence. The distinction between intrusive and non-intrusive technologies has collapsed with the advent of digitization and convergence. Intrusive technologies like TV are now far more under the control of the viewer, far more plentiful and far more part of a private rather than public "transaction". In the years to come, ordering a digitized movie by phone from a pay-per-view service and recording it on a disc will be difficult to distinguish from ordering a digitized movie on a disc from a video store.

Some commentators have taken the position that these technological arguments are simply irrelevant because the scarcity rationale was never an issue in the first place. Interestingly enough, two camps have arrived at this position regarding scarcity for diametrically opposed reasons. The leading exponent of one view, Ithiel de Sola Pool, wrote in 1983 that "scarcity" was a made-up problem (p.151):

> The time has come to bury the old cliche that spectrum is a scarce resource. It is an abundant but squandered one. Like any resource as paper, trees, printing presses, wires, or television sets, it is plentiful [...] there is much of it to be had. It is renewable: when a user has used it for an hour or a nanosecond, it is there again for the next person to use.

Others, particularly economists, have argued that the spectrum should not be singled out as a scarce good or resource in a manner that suggests this is somehow unusual. In economic theory, all goods and resources, with few exceptions, are scarce relative to the level of demand for them. At the very best, therefore, scarcity of spectrum is not materially different from the scarcity of other resources, but only different in degree. This economic concept has also found its way into American jurisprudence. In a 1986 case involving the FCC, Justice Bork argued as follows:

> Employing the scarcity concept as an analytical tool, particularly with respect to new and unforseen technologies, inevitably leads to strained and artificial results [...]. It is certainly true that broadcast frequencies are scarce but it is unclear why that fact justifies content regulation of broadcasting in a way that would be intolerable if applied to the editorial process of the print media. *All economic goods are scarce,* not the least newsprint, ink, delivery trucks, computers, and other resources that go into the production and dissemination of print journalism. Not everyone who wishes to publish a newspaper or even a pamphlet may do so.[27]

Other legal arguments have been advanced against **intrusiveness and potential for harm**. For example, Mark Fowler and David Brennan have contended (pp.228–229) that "the assertion of the pervasive influence of individual licensees is a gross exaggeration of the licensee's real impact". The reason for this is that

> the viewer always retains ultimate control over what enters his home; he may choose to turn the channel [...]. Other media are also "pervasive". One can

hardly argue that a one-newspaper town is not "pervaded" uniquely by the orientation of its newspaper.

When viewers pay for the programs they watch, they are able to express their preferences for those programs directly. Under this transactional model, the incentives for program production are improved; minority tastes are more likely to be satisfied; and **advertiser sovereignty** recedes as an issue (and as a rationale for regulation). This description oversimplifies the current structure of television in one important respect, which is that many widely viewed specialty services in both Canada and the United States are financed from a dual revenue stream — subscriber fees and advertising sales.[28]

While new technologies correct for some of the inefficiencies associated with advertiser support by requiring direct viewer payment, the very fact that viewers have to pay creates a new inequity and a new regulatory issue: those who are poor have to pay the same as those who are rich.

The treatment of **intangible cultural benefits** associated with Canadian-made drama and entertainment presents a problem. That's because it's not clear whether new technologies will help correct for the discrepancy between the perceived

Transactional TV Arrives

In case you had any doubts about the trend away from ad-supported to transactional television, consider this. In 1991, American consumers spent more in direct payments for their TV viewing than business spent on all TV advertising. The numbers are impressive: whereas total ad expenditures for that year came to $28 billion for both conventional and cable TV, consumers spent $32 billion — $20 billion in cable fees and over $12 billion in videocassette sales and rentals (data from FCC). Note that this consumer spending does not *include any hardware or equipment purchases.*

We've noted frequently that one way to gauge the spread of transactional TV is to look at the proportion of viewers who pay cable companies to get their "free" TV. In Canada that proportion is now 75%; in the U.S. it's over 60%. As long as cable TV has operated in North America, it has never had to pay a dime for the use of local, over-the-air signals. Cable subscribers have always paid for this "free" TV, but not the cable benefits of such programming and the actual demand for it in the marketplace. The analysis depends to a large degree on how much influence is ascribed to the various technologies. One possibility is that compression and satellite spill-over will swamp Canadians with so many American signals that viewers will be even less inclined to insist on Canadian choices.

operators. Subscribers were traditionally willing to pay something for convenience, expanded choice, clearer signals and so on, even though many of the "products" in question, the local TV signals, were actually public goods and free for the taking. Station operators were in many cases willing to have this use made of their signals because they enjoyed the indirect recompense of larger audiences and a correspondingly larger advertising base. Enter retransmission consent.

Retransmission consent requires that cable operators seek the permission of local broadcasters before distributing their signals to subscribers — and with that consent goes payment of a fee. Despite vociferous opposition from Jack Valenti and the MPAA, this provision has survived in the final version of the U.S. Cable Television Consumer Protection Act *of 1992, or bill S.12. It means that for the first time in 40 years, "free" TV will become transactional TV not only for cable subscribers but for operators as well.*

To the extent that new technologies do *not* enhance cultural benefits, the so-called "externality" rationale for regulation would still carry weight. The expansion of transactional video services may have the effect of increasing the supply of Canadian programs and thereby help create new viewer demand. There are two reasons for this. First, a multiplicity of channels offering inexpensive distribution will give specialized and minority-oriented services a better chance of competing for viewers than in the far more restricted and costly world of network broadcasting. Second, Canadian viewers who place a high value on Canadian programs and their intangible benefits will be able to express their preferences through a direct financial transaction. This is not possible in a television system based on advertiser support, which has always favoured the more highly rated American entertainment programs.

Technological developments are not likely to affect consideration of Canadian programming as **merit goods**.

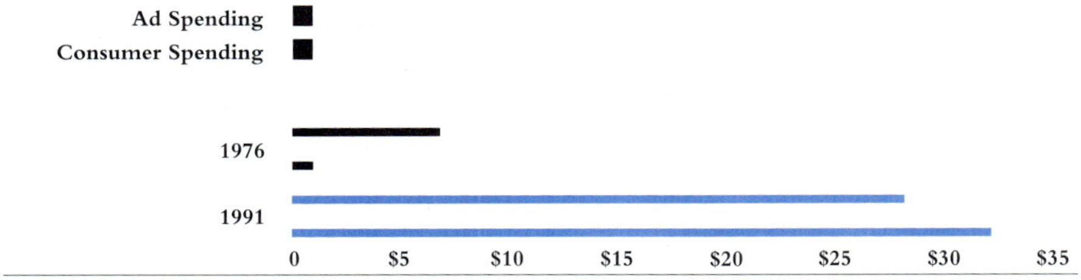

Ad Spending on TV vs Direct Consumer Spending for Home Video and Cable
(U.S. Data: $ billions)
Source: FCC

WHO'S AFRAID OF DEATHSTARS?

The evidence suggests that the rationales for our traditional regulatory framework are being undermined by new technology. As we said at the beginning of this chapter, however, the technological challenge involves more than principles. It also means that the regulations in place will be increasingly difficult to enforce, justifiable or not. Arriving in tandem with both recession and national discord, these challenges sweeping through the electronic media have raised industry anxiety to new heights.

The lightning rod for all this anxiety has been something called "Deathstars", American direct-to-home satellite services, which sometime in 1990 or 1991 acquired their notorious nickname — a play on "DTH" (for direct-to-home) and perhaps "Darth Vader". This is the kind of satellite that sends signals intended for direct reception by viewers, by means of a dish antenna, rather than by cable operators or other intermediaries. To judge by the press reports, it would seem as though the enemy had already landed on our shores. As it turns out, however, Deathstars still haven't made it off the launchpad.

Why Deathstars? What technological developments have propelled these satellites to centre stage in the current debate? Although communications satellites have been around for years, a couple of new developments have created an infant industry and a lot of controversy.

Deployment of communications satellite

Power. The first of these involves the power with which satellites retransmit their signals back to earth. (Like light bulbs, their power is rated in watts.) There's a direct relationship between transmission power and the size of the backyard dish antennas used by individuals to receive satellite-delivered television signals: the higher the power, the smaller the dish. Up until now, "backyard" dishes, as the term suggests, have been large (as much as 10 or 12 feet in diameter) and no fun to install (unless you enjoy pouring concrete). Nevertheless, according to estimates provided by Market Facts, 3% of Canadian households owned an installed satellite dish in 1991 (the same proportion as in the United States). That translates into just under 300,000 dishes across the country. Other estimates place the number closer to 400,000.

A new generation of mid- to high-powered satellites is now off the drawing board and up in the heavens. The most obvious and marketable difference these make down here on earth is that they require a dish antenna that's more the size of, well, a dish — a small serving plate. Not only that, they are designed to sit on a window sill and even be moved around.

By the way, the size of dish you need does depend on one other important factor and that's where you live in relation to the equator: the farther north, the more attenuated the signal and the bigger the dish required. According to data published in the newsletter *CVRO Viewer's Connection* (Fall 1991), adequate reception of a Ku-band signal from the SBS-6 satellite (from which the SkyPix service is to be delivered) would require a four-foot dish in Toronto or Halifax, but an eight-foot dish in Winnipeg or Victoria and a ten-foot dish in Regina. As so often in Canadian history, geography has managed to make a privileged class of those Canadians who live closer to the American border.

Compression. The second new development, which is even more important, is our old friend digital video compression. Compression, you'll recall, can be applied to any medium used for transmitting video signals. And because compression squeezes more signals into less space, it saves money. Nowhere is this more cost-effective than in satellite transmission. Compression allows more than one channel to be transmitted on each satellite transponder or relay transmitter, the leasing costs of which are expensive.

This is the technology which has enabled the Canadian pay movie service First Choice to embark on its "Multiplex Theatre" experiment. In a promotional letter to subscribers published in the October 1992 edition of *Feature* (the pay-TV magazine), First Choice announced it was about to begin using compression to deliver its main service plus three new extra channels. These channels are designed to offer First Choice subscribers the chance to pick from several movie titles — four altogether — at any given time of the evening. As the letter notes: "It's the convenience factor we at First Choice want to emphasize: the opportunity to select from up to twelve movies every night during prime-time viewing hours".

Although First Choice has now started Canada down the road to near video on demand, this four-in-one multiplex service is still small potatoes compared to what the Deathstars allegedly have in store for us: one or more satellite-delivered services, each comprising anywhere from 60 to 100 channels of movies, sports and other entertainment programming, and available to individual subscribers in much the same way as cable is now. These DTH services would feature many channels devoted to pay-per-view options, in the spirit of the Viewer's Choice and Time Warner Quantum services we described earlier.

What's wrong with this picture?

The big problem for Canadians is that all of the services of this kind being developed are American and their programming is, in the tradition of broadcast television, unlikely to have any significant amount of non-American content. As we noted in the last chapter, American DTH or DBS providers will be at best "back-enders" for Canadian producers looking for budget money. This problem would be nothing more than history repeating itself, except for two things: the huge quantity of programming involved and the size of satellite footprints. Because satellites don't respect international boundaries, the footprint or coverage area of these services will spill over the 49th parallel far enough to be available to the vast majority of Canadian households. Moreover, the signals from DTH satellites can't be stopped or controlled by the regulator like signals in a wire. A November, 1991 *Globe and Mail* article suggested that the launch of Deathstars in December 1993 means that

> the Canadian television industry as we have come to know it, the whole symbiotic ecosystem of politicians, regulators, broadcasters, specialty services, cable carriers, producers and various other hangers-on has two years to live.

The most widely discussed services — and none is operating as we go to press — are SkyPix and the Hughes and Hubbard initiatives. (Several other projects, in various stages of development, are being backed by some of America's largest communications companies, including TCI, Scientific Atlanta and AT&T.)

SkyPix was supposed to be up and running with its 80 channels (70 of them PPV) in early 1991, then late 1991, then early 1992... It has been plagued by resignations, financial setbacks and rumor-mongering about its failure to secure movie deals with the Hollywood studios. Through it all, it has still managed to maintain a

Canadian operation, known as Aladdin, which has been marketing the as-yet non-existent service. This presence in Canada, combined with the long-awaited and much-postponed launch, have made SkyPix the focus of anxiety among Canadian broadcasters — and candidate for the position of Deathstar One. Ironically, it seems far more likely that the service being organized and financed by U.S. Satellite Broadcasting, and led by Stanley Hubbard of the Minneapolis broadcasting family, will actually go into service first and stick around long enough to make money.

No matter who gets up there and lives long enough to tell about it, Canadians now have two issues on their minds:

- First, there's the regulatory question: what, if anything, do we do about the Deathstars?
- Then there's the marketing question: will Canadians actually fork out money for the receiving equipment, as well as for subscriber and other fees? Remember, satellite spillover doesn't mean you can just turn on your TV and start watching hundreds of movies. This is transactional TV (though some services may be "free" — i.e. ad-supported).

Legal battle lines drawn

The Canadian legal community is divided over what can and should be done about the Deathstars. The reason there's a debate in the first place stems from the decades-old concern about the threat posed to Canadian cultural sovereignty by the massive presence of American programs on the television screens of the nation. What's at stake is the desire expressed by some parties to have American DTH services either kept out of our system or, failing that, to have them licensed and obliged to adhere to Canadian regulations and conditions of licence. Thanks to the power of technology, the regulatory debate has some new twists, as reflected in the following questions:

- Can these satellite services be legally regulated in Canada? In other words, do they fall under the jurisdiction of the CRTC?
- Even if they do, is it possible in any practical sense for the CRTC to enforce the rules of the *Broadcasting Act* against them?

→ And even supposing the answer to these questions is "yes", is it appropriate to try to regulate them?

Canadian communications lawyers such as Peter Grant, of McCarthy Tétrault, and Christopher Johnston, of Johnston, Buchan & Dalfen, have made a strong case that American-based satellite services do fall within the provisions of the *Broadcasting Act* and therefore within the jurisdiction of the CRTC.

Grant prepared a widely circulated opinion for Telesat Canada that addressed the particular circumstances of the SkyPix service and its Canadian agent, Aladdin. He suggests first of all that once an American service begins transmitting and is receivable in Canada, it would be "carrying on a broadcasting undertaking in part within Canada" (p.5). If it did so and did not have a licence, such a service would be operating contrary to section 32(1) of the *Broadcasting Act.*

As Grant recognized, it's one thing to argue successfully for jurisdiction. It's quite another to be in a position to enforce the rules against a delinquent broadcaster — especially one that doesn't have any assets in Canada. Grant goes on to argue, however, that the CRTC would have two ways of enforcing its authority over Skypix, thanks to the presence of its affiliate in Canada, Aladdin. The first approach is "to prosecute Aladdin and its agents and individual affiliates as parties to an offence under section 32(1) of the Act, based on Skypix's activities in Canada and the assistance rendered by the defendants to the Skypix operation".

The second, and in Grant's opinion, more favourable approach, is to

> hold an inquiry under section 12(1) of the Broadcasting Act, followed by the issuance of a mandatory order under section 12(2) forbidding Skypix, Aladdin and their officers and employees, and Aladdin Associates and any other person who may have knowledge of the order from directly breaching section 32 of the Act or aiding and abetting Skypix to breach section 32 of the Act, which would also constitute an offence by virtue of s.21 of the *Criminal Code.*

On the other side of the issue, regulatory lawyer Andrew Roman, of Miller Thomson, argues that preventing American DBS services from gaining access to

Canada is like erecting a "CRTC-constructed Berlin wall around Canada" (p.2). He rejects the Grant opinion that the CRTC has jurisdiction over American DBS services. Arguing that U.S. satellite services fall within the *Broadcasting Act* because their signals spill over into Canada, Roman says, would be akin to arguing that U.S. border broadcasters can be regulated in Canada because *they* spill over the border.

As Roman goes on to say (p.6),

> a national broadcasting regulator cannot regulate signals coming in internationally. Unless we are prepared to turn the country into a police state, there is no practical way the CRTC could regulate the proliferation of new, international satellite services from Europe and the U.S., which are currently being planned. National governments cannot control information and entertainment transmitted internationally via satellite, directly to the home.

Numerous other legal technicalities are involved here, and the lawyers will continue to argue over them. While it's not our job to comment in detail on the merits of these arguments, let's just say that serious doubts have been raised over both jurisdiction and enforcement — i.e. over the CRTC's *right* to regulate American DTH services, as well as over its *ability* to do so.

That leaves one other big question that is more political than legal in nature. Putting aside the precedents and fine print, is it a good idea to attempt to regulate foreign DBS? The answer requires that we be more specific: good idea for whom?

Among the options open to the regulator as to how American DTH services should be handled, two of particular interest to us are outright ban and unrestricted access. Let's examine each of these briefly.

→ **Outright ban.** Nobody can say for sure what the public reaction would be to such a ban (setting aside the question of practicality). There are some indicators to give us a clue:

→ Canadian cable subscribers have shown in the past that they do not take well to CRTC-imposed restrictions on access to American broadcast services. Indeed, rebellions have occurred in response to mere changes in the channel

Satellite tracking station

lineup of the big three networks. One mitigating factor is that not many ordinary viewers will be cognizant of all these developments. Even the 300,000 or more Canadians who own satellite dishes will be operating at a disadvantage because the receiver-decoders that are in wide use in this country will have to be changed for a new technology to accommodate the transmission parameters of DTH.

→ Meanwhile, a new interest group is working away in the background to organize the fight against a variety of restrictions on viewers. Though it is called the Canadian Viewers Rights Organization, its published statements indicate that its real constituency is viewers who happen to be satellite dish owners. (The abbreviation CVRO plays on "TVRO", for television receive-only earth station.)

→ Public reaction may be conditioned by the ethos that has developed around the phenomenon of cross-border shopping. As Free Trade becomes more entrenched and the economy threatens to sag for several more years, we have no reason to believe that in the world of transactional TV, Canadians will see shopping for TV services as any different from shopping across the border for gas for the car or clothes for the kids. In broadcasting, patriotism has been a popular refuge for scoundrels. When it comes to the pocketbook, patriotism is a luxury many Canadians may not be able to afford. And that goes directly to the issue of if and when the regulatory apparatus will make room for competition in the provision of video services, or continue to rely on the cable operators as the monopoly gatekeepers.

→ Canadian editorial writers will undoubtedly exercise some influence over public opinion. The lead editorial published in the *Globe and Mail* on September 5, 1992 (and quoted at the head of this chapter) is entitled "The withering away of the CRTC, at last". While it does not pronounce on this particular issue in detail, the paper is clearly hostile to the whole notion of the continued regulation of content in any form. Elsewhere in the newspaper, senior writers like Stephen Godfrey have not exactly been wishing for the CRTC's demise, but have been warning that the CRTC's future role "will clearly be weaker" — thanks in large measure to new technologies like DTH services (see Spectator column, September 19, 1992).

→ **Unrestricted access.** Whether Deathstars kill off anything or anybody depends a great deal on whether ordinary viewers buy foreign DTH services in large numbers — and what they're prepared to forsake if they do. So far, since there aren't any Deathstars, there isn't any hard evidence about what kind of effect they'll have on the Canadian broadcasting system. Given the notoriety of the subject, however, there has been plenty of speculation — and one detailed study, carried out for the Canadian Association of Broadcasters (CAB) by NGL Consulting and released in June of 1992 (*Potential Market for U.S. DBS in Canada*).

The NGL study asks in effect whether and to what degree American DTH or DBS services will damage the broadcasting system. Its purpose is to predict "damage" by using consumer uptake as a proxy for such damage. And, moving right to the bottom line, we find the following forecast (p.7):

> If launched and established in the North American market, high power U.S. DBS could cause about 4.6% of Canadian basic cable subscribers to disconnect by the year 2000; however, the cable industry should continue to experience basic cable growth despite the forecasted incursion of U.S. DBS.

The study draws this conclusion on the implicit grounds that the interests of Canadian viewer-consumers match those of Canadian broadcasters and cablecasters. The logic of the analysis is complex, but the ultimate conclusion is simple enough: American DBS services do not pose a threat to Canada because the forecast shows that only 4.6% of cable subscribers are likely to forsake cable in favour of DBS.

In a covering memorandum dated July 7, 1992, the study client, CAB president Michael McCabe, notes that "earlier fears that U.S. DBS would result in massive cable subscriber disconnects should give way to a more reasoned assessment". McCabe goes on to say that "market entry by U.S. DBS *will not result in the serious damage to the Canadian broadcasting system or its Canadian distribution infrastructure*" (emphasis added).

Consider for a moment the moral tone implicit in this position: that Canadian cable subscribers who, next year or in the year 2000, disconnect from cable in favour of a foreign satellite service, should be characterized as having done "serious damage" to a national institution. So, it's good for Canada if few cable subscribers defect and bad if many do. What's going on here is that Canadians who might opt out of the "system" are being stigmatized and made into video pariahs. Is this what the lofty goals of the *Broadcasting Act* have come to?

The issue at hand is not how many Canadian cable subscribers will actually defect or what "damage" Deathstars may bring about in our culture — if any. The issue is how vested interests are using this and other new technologies as weapons in their defence of the market power that has gone hand in hand with protectionism, quotas, subsidies and monopolistic control of distribution. Let's stop demonizing foreign market power long enough to take stock of what's happening to market power in our own back yard.

By way of example, cable industry representatives have been lobbying hard to get their hands on the new U.S. services, promising a better deal for Canada than if new services are allowed to run amok in a free TV marketplace. Wouldn't you know: we heard it all two decades ago when the country was agonizing over what to do about pay-TV. The pay-TV lobby painted a stark dilemma: either get completely swamped by American pay, with no countervailing benefits; or else give us what we want and the quid pro quo will be work for the Canadian production community. That goal, promised the lobby in 1975, would be achieved by offering 15% of gross revenues to Canadian production. The technique was dubbed "Canadianization through Americanization" (Hardin, pp.293, 296). Industry leader Ted Rogers had already described the choice facing policymakers in terms reminiscent of the current Deathstar debate. As Hardin summed it up (p.300):

> Despite the Therrien Committee's pay-TV go-ahead, the cable industry, led by Ted Rogers, kept up the pressure, becoming more truculent. It argued that the cable industry would lose apartments to satellite dishes (and American pay-TV) in a big way unless it had pay-TV of its own quickly.

As we saw in the last chapter, having our own pay and specialty services has been of *some* benefit to the Canadian production community — as well as to Canadian viewers. The fact that the benefits, in percentages of revenue, never materialized as originally promised was only part of the problem.

Moreover, the benefits to Canadian producers were not given gratis, but in return for an important quid pro quo granted to the cable industry — the right to continue controlling access to TV for the majority of Canadian viewers.

Viewed in this light, the whole Deathstar controversy fits a long tradition of flag-waving scare tactics used by the cable industry to maintain its grip on television distribution in Canada. As we'll see shortly, these recent tactics come at a time when the CRTC is giving a freer hand to the cable industry in the ways that it requires payment from subscribers.

Regulation & the quid pro quo

The regulation of television broadcasting in Canada is something of a sacred cow. Its two most important components are: the control of content through the imposition of general TV quotas and conditions of licence; and the control of distribution through the conditions imposed on cable operators, who act as gatekeepers to the system on behalf of the regulator. These are controversial measures, but only up to a point. Until recently, it was virtually impossible to raise the prospect of a deregulated or even less regulated broadcasting system. Apart from the tangible benefits already noted, the Bush and Reagan administrations have given deregulation a bad name.

Now the prospect of Deathstars and other threats to the status quo have Canadians wondering what's next. As we've tried to suggest, public discussion of these matters has taken an alarmist turn — technological change is equated with loss of control and de facto deregulation, which in turn are equated with damage to national sovereignty. Some disruptions may lie ahead in our technological future. But that should not stop us from asking whether we're still getting our money's worth from the regulatory apparatus.

First of all, let's be clear what we mean by "regulate". The regulation of broadcasting in Canada does not signify a set of prohibitions and responsibilities with no corresponding privileges and powers. What regulation tends to do, in fact, is confer and entrench market power, not for those who make programs or for those who watch them, but for those who deliver them — broadcasters and cablecasters.

The irony is that the public interest provisions of the Broadcasting Policy for Canada, enshrined in the *Broadcasting Act*, suggest exactly the opposite. In return for the privilege of using part of the broadcast spectrum, broadcasters are faced with onerous-sounding responsibilities. Creators and audiences are supposed to be the beneficiaries, at least by some interpretation of the provisions. But the reality is otherwise, as we'll now illustrate by looking at how first broadcasters and then cablecasters are faring under the "yoke" of regulation.

Broadcasters & Cancon

A television licence confers remarkable privileges, especially in larger markets. At the same time, Canadian content regulations have been flouted for years by exactly those broadcasters most able to carry them out in good faith. The hard times that hit conventional television in the late 1980s can be traced to technological and economic forces largely beyond the control of either licensees or regulators. Most TV licensees stand to lose, not gain, from any radical form of deregulation or re-regulation precipitated by technology. Consider the following...

Broadcasting undertakings are quasi-monopolies. Canadian broadcasters do not enjoy strictly monopoly privileges, but they come close. No TV broadcaster in Canada has ever lost a licence for violation of regulations or conditions of licence, nor seen their licence awarded to another bidder after a competitive bidding process. Broadcasting licences may no longer be licences to print money, as a famous Canadian said, but they certainly entrench market power. The wealthiest market area of Canada, the province of Ontario (representing 50% of English-speaking Canada) is a virtual duopoly, at least as far as domestic licensees are concerned. Domestic conventional broadcasters offer little competition in this market, which is shared between the CanWest-Global operation headed by Izzy Asper and ONT (Ontario Network Television), part of Baton Broadcasting (whose stations include about half the affiliates of the CTV network).

Among the interested parties who see some injustice in this situation are Canada's major independent producers. The producers have no hope of securing a TV broadcasting licence, at least not an over-the-air licence. Broadcasters, on the other hand, have few restrictions on entry into the production industry, apart from conditions of licence requiring them to buy a certain volume of programs from outside production houses. At the 1992 Festival of Festivals Symposium, Paragon Entertainment CEO Jon Slan reported that Canadian broadcasters are becoming more aggressive in taking creative control of "independent" projects, as well as credit for their original development.

Private broadcasters are publicly subsidized. Most Canadian broadcasters enjoy substantial public subsidies for airing Canadian drama and entertainment programs. In *Networking*, we demonstrated that for all English programs assisted by Telefilm in fiscal 1989–90, having total program budgets of about $157 million, broadcasters paid an aggregate total of 21% for the licence and investment costs of the material they aired. Canadian taxpayers paid an aggregate total of 33% of these budgets through the Broadcast Program Fund — *half as much again as the broadcasters*. Other investors paid the balance.

Broadcasters are protected from competition — not only by enjoying de facto ownership of their licences, but through several policy measures. These are: the unavailability of many American services in Canada; the use of simultaneous substitution, whereby Canadian signals must be substituted for identical American signals on most cable systems; and a tax measure known as Bill C-58, which disallows the deduction of costs for advertising placed on U.S. border stations by Canadian firms. The combined annual financial benefit of these last two measures to Canadian broadcasters is well over $100 million.

Broadcasters enjoy priority carriage on cable. In Canadian policy, cable systems are treated as gatekeepers who control what is available to most Canadians on their TV screens. That's because three-quarters of Canadians subscribe to cable; cable operates as a monopoly; and the CRTC's Cable TV Regulations specify the priorities for the services cable operators may carry. Local, over-the-air broadcasters are considered "foundation" services and get priority treatment in the regulated channel line-up.

The goal of this elaborate superstructure is the "maintenance and enhancement of national identity and cultural sovereignty", as provided by section 3(1)(b) of the *Broadcasting Act*. How are we making out?

One of the leaders of the production community, Robert Lantos of Alliance, has had some harsh things to say about both the achievements and the motives of Canadian broadcasters. In the fall of 1991, when private broadcasting was still reeling from the worst financial results in history, Lantos summed up his views in a keynote address on the new realities of independent production:

Canadian broadcasters had it made. Historically, they were a privileged class,

> protected by legislation from direct American competition and from foreign ownership. They enjoyed government issued licences to print money and when it came to the issue of drama, the very heart of the television schedule, they did not need to be broadcasters at all. They were, and largely continue to be, *rebroadcasters*. There isn't another sizeable country in the western world which showcases as little indigenous drama on its privately-owned airwaves as Canada [...] With very few notable exceptions (and those in the past few years), they have contributed outrageously little to the skills, infrastructure and creative genius required to produce drama. Their philosophy was, "Reap maximum profits now without worrying about planting seeds for future harvests". Their long-term strategy had about the same amount of foresight as the clear-cutting of forests.[29]

The crux of the question lies in the CRTC's Canadian content regulations and the conditions of licence that help to implement them. Like discussions of technology, discussions of content quotas tend to get polarized. One camp sees them as a permanent fixture and the price that must be paid for the preservation of a national culture. The other camp (or at least *an* other camp) sees content quotas as a travesty, an infringement of free expression.

The truth seems to lie somewhere in between.

→ First, quotas have certainly benefited the independent production community, in conjunction with other policy measures, as we've noted elsewhere. Canada would not have an industry able to compete in the international market without the massive government interventions represented by quotas, the Broadcast Fund and so on.

→ Second, Canadian programs represent a serious opportunity cost, as CTV and other broadcasters have long complained (see, for example, the CTV calculations reported in *Networking*, pp. 140-41). Canadian entertainment programs are costly to make and not very popular with many advertisers, whereas much American programming is cheap to buy and returns far higher revenues.

This much is pretty well known. So why do private broadcasters put up with it? Well, they do and they don't. They mostly put up with it because the CRTC has handed them a very attractive quid pro quo — fill your quota and be subsidized, protected and entrenched. Sometimes broadcasters don't put up with these obligations. In 1982, the CTV network went to the Supreme Court to fight CRTC conditions of licence that for the first time spelled out what kind of dramatic programming they would have to do, how much and so on.

We do not suggest that CTV was necessarily wrong to do so. One respected commentator, for example, law professor Hudson Janisch, has questioned whether the Supreme Court was justified in the way the CTV challenge was "impatiently dismissed out of hand", in view of the "unquestioned" promise of the *Broadcasting Act* of "the right to freedom of expression and the right of persons to receive programs...".[30]

Ten years later, broadcasters are staying out of court, but compliance is still about as grudging as it ever was. Let's look at what is, in financial terms, the most successful broadcasting operation in English Canada, Canwest-Global. If anybody is in a position to put costly Canadian programming on the small screen, it's Global Television and its affiliated stations in Western Canada.

According to publicly available data compiled by Burns Fry Ltd, CanWest-Global outperformed the Toronto Stock Exchange TSE 300 from the fall of 1991 until the spring of 1992. That means CanWest did better as a public company than the composite index of 300 of Canada's leading business firms. For the 1986–91 period, it also outperformed by wide margins the other three most powerful TV owners in the country, the WIC, CHUM and Baton broadcasting groups. CanWest did so on not one but several standard financial measures, including revenue growth; earnings before interest, depreciation and taxes; and earnings per share.

Many of these resources apparently did not find their way into the production studio, according to the CRTC's 1992 decision renewing the Global Communications television licence (Decision 92-220). In it the Commission had some harsh things to say about Global's programming performance and renewed its licence for only four years, instead of the anticipated seven. It said, among other things, that Global "may not have contributed to the Canadian broadcasting system as fully as it should have, given the resources available to it". The decision pointed out that in its previous licence term, Global had met its Canadian content requirements by scheduling a disproportionately high number of cartoon re-runs and failed to schedule a suitable proportion of its Canadian programs at peak viewing times, when most Canadian viewers are available. And despite Global's apparent financial prowess, the Commission also charged it with questionable accounting practices:

> Global's practice of not netting Canadian programming syndication revenues against Canadian programming expenses is not an industry-wide practice. Moreover, the Commission does not consider this method to be an acceptable accounting practice for regulatory purposes.

Some of these findings were documented in *Networking* (pp.187–88), where we compared

> the amount of money put into Telefilm-assisted program production by the networks and the number of hours of first-run [Canadian] programming that resulted from these financing activities. The data [...] showed that, dollar-for-dollar, Global managed to sponsor a *proportionally* much higher number of first-run hours than CTV (or for that matter CBC) — i.e. as a ratio of investment dollars to program hours. Whereas CTV contributed 42% of the total financing from the three networks, it aired just 37% of the network hours (74 hours). Global, on the other hand, contributed 3% of the funds, yet banked 14% of the hours (29 hours).

In other words, Global has made a practice of putting as little of its own money as possible into Canadian productions, while leveraging its investments into a lot of time credits for purposes of its Canadian content obligations. Content quotas have given us sham Canadian series like *Top Cops*, the American-style reality series which has been airing on Global in the 1992–93 season. That may explain why in a comparison of program availability and viewing data, *Networking* showed (p.63) that Global's Canadian drama programming had the lowest ratio of viewing to availability of any of the three English networks in the 1988–89 season. It had the least audience appeal or "quality", we would surmise, because it had the least investment in artistic integrity and production values.

This is how the TV business operates in Canada and it's all perfectly square and above board. But let's not kid ourselves. If this is the best cultural contribution the most financially *successful* private broadcaster can make, perhaps it's time to acknowledge that the Canadian content regulations as they now exist have outlived their usefulness. Perhaps it's also time to start looking for the silver lining in the technological cloud hanging over our collective consciousness.

Consumer protection & cable rates

Earlier in this chapter, we showed how both cable companies and broadcasters are using the advent of multichannel distribution vehicles like Deathstars as part of a scare campaign. Canada, they say, is in for a massive invasion of new American video services. They can't be stopped or regulated and the broadcasting system — read cable and broadcast financial interests — will suffer serious damage as a result. As far as the cable industry is concerned, it must be allowed to head off the Americans by Americanizing cable and retaining Canadian subscribers. This means cable must have "flexibility" in its service packaging and pricing.

As we'll now demonstrate, however, cable operators are neither the patriotic Canadians nor the consumer advocates they would have us believe they are.

The financial success of CanWest-Global has made it something of an exception in the television industry. By contrast, the cable industry as a whole in Canada has performed well in all but one or two years of the last decade. Cable companies continue to be among the most financially successful communications companies in Canada. From 1982 to 1989, according to data from Burns Fry, the Canadian cable industry experienced a three-fold jump in its return on equity (ROE), while the ROE for television fell in every year but one. While television revenues merely doubled in the 1980s, cable revenues more than tripled, from about $400 million in 1981 to over $1.3 billion by 1989.

We've mentioned elsewhere the growing phenomenon of "tiering up" in the

Canadian and American cable industries. This refers to the practice of moving more and more services away from regulated, omnibus tiers onto unregulated, discretionary tiers. The practice has two general purposes. One is to promote so-called targeted marketing, which allows cable operators to isolate service transactions by channel and by program or event — also known as "unbundling". This trend can be seen in the growth of pay channels and particularly pay-per-view offerings. The cable industry says consumers prefer to have such personalized choices. The industry has also made it apparent that future growth opportunities do not lie in bundled basic cable tiers, but in new, discretionary areas like video on demand and personal communications services (see, for example, *A Clear Vision*, p.22).

What is not made so clear is the other purpose of tiering up — the evasion of rate regulation. Cable operators in both the U.S. and Canada must observe certain rules about the services they carry on their "basic" tier and how much they're allowed to charge for that tier. But cablecos are squeezed two ways on the bottom tier: this tier must include services like the community channel and second-language channels, which have little subscriber appeal, while the amount operators can charge for this tier is kept relatively low and subject to regulatory scrutiny.

Cable industry comes to defence of Canadian consumer...

The Canadian Cable Television Association (CCTA) intervened against the CBC's 1992 Newsworld licence renewal application, filing a detailed written brief, then giving a one-hour oral presentation of its position on March 13, 1992. CCTA head Kenneth Stein came to the hearing armed with ammunition to mount a vehement attack on the Newsworld application. The Association was not content to do a mere internal staff review of the application's merits. Instead, they hired both the Angus Reid Group and Peat Marwick to discredit both the survey research and the business plan presented by CBC in evidence.

That was only a step along the way to more important pronouncements by Stein, the chief among these being that the 84% fee increase requested by CBC for anglophone markets was not only unreasonable but not "supported by cable subscribers" (brief, p.3). The CCTA therefore called for a fee increase over seven years of zero.

Stein referred in the hearing to his association as the representative of Canada's six million cable subscribers. A surprised Keith Spicer had to ask Stein three times to acknowledge that the CCTA was there in fact to represent not cable subscribers *but cable* companies.

The myth of the basic tier

If most subscribers had been content to stay on basic — that kind of basic — it would have been bad news for cable operators. So a solution had to be found: create a kind of basic basic, a minimum tier that meets regulatory requirements and then create enticements to move subscribers up to a higher tier — known as "extended" or "full" basic — where the services are more attractive and the rates are, in the industry's favourite euphemism, "flexible". The ruse has worked beautifully. In its Notice of Public Hearing 1992-13 (dated 3 September 1992), the CRTC noted that "as of May 1992, approximately 4.1 million of the 4.5 million cable households having access to such packages have, in fact, chosen to subscribe to them, representing a penetration rate of 91%". Industry predictions are that the uptake will keep getting higher as more systems offer extended basic packages. And all it takes is a couple of dollars a month more. Or instead, you can *save* a couple of dollars a month by staying on basic (basic basic, that is).

The policy rationale for allowing the basic basic and extended basic formula is that Canadians would continue to get access to Canadian program services at affordable rates. Yet the CRTC's own regulations on extended basic discriminate

Adding further to the confusion, the CCTA, far from decrying the service provided by Newsworld, described it as "valuable" and "vital". Despite the chair's characterization of the CCTA's professed concern for the consumer as so many "crocodile tears", the Association stuck by its position that it was defending the consumer from untimely and exploitative price increases. In its brief, the CCTA asked (p.7):

> Has the CBC changed its objective from providing a service at an affordable cost as originally proposed or are they seeking to change the service, at whatever the cost, at the expense of the consumer?

Then, in a final flourish (p.16), the brief paid homage to the "stated commitment of the cable industry to a distinctive Canadian broadcasting system".

The CCTA also referred to "the challenges of a competitive future" (p.15), as well as to the need for what it called "flexibility". How did the CCTA operationalize the notion of flexibility? By asking for an amendment to the Cable Television Regulations that would allow its members to keep the valuable and vital Newsworld service off basic cable... and allow them instead the option of selling Ted Turner's CNN news service on the tier of their choice.

against Canadian services in both a quantitative sense and a qualitative sense. First, the regulations covering what's called "linkage" — how foreign services can be packaged with Canadian ones — allow two authorized U.S. satellite signals on an extended basic tier for every Canadian specialty service. Second, the regulations make no attempt to specify what *kind* of Canadian signals must be made available on extended basic. So cable operators are left free to put up the cheapest Canadian fare they can find, with no regard for its value to producers or audiences, then mark them up by as much as they can get away with.

In a promotional letter sent out by Rogers Cablesystems in March 1992, we read that this new service, called Full Cable Service, would feature — in addition to several American specialty services — one new Canadian service, namely TV5, a French-only service produced by several Canadian and European broadcasters. The reader will not be surprised to learn that TV5 is of extremely limited appeal in English Canada and also carries a very affordable wholesale rate to cable operators: 5 cents per subscriber per month, compared to the 59 cents requested by CBC Newsworld — and denounced by the CCTA in its intervention before the CRTC (see accompanying box).

This letter and a colourful brochure emphasized that this offer was being made "with no increase to your current cable rate". In the fine print, we read that "annual rate adjustments will take place in January". Then, in early October 1992, another brochure was mailed out by Rogers with a cover announcing the bad news: "Your cable rates are changing. Here's why". Inside we discover that Full Cable Service is going up after exactly nine months at the "no increase" rate, from $17.18 a month to $19.04 a month, a jump of $1.86 or 11%, well over twice the rate of inflation.

The really fine print reveals that the increase is actually made up of several little increases: one for Canadian specialty service pass-through costs; another for capital expenditure recovery related to system upgrading; and a third for "a special circumstances increase of $1.23 per month to offset capital and operating expenditures to improve the quality and dependability of the cable service". A full 23 cents of the total rate increase represents the cost that Rogers is allowed to pass through to offset the 55-cent rate increase won by CBC Newsworld, which the CCTA had fought so hard to protect the consumer from.

Meanwhile, the CCTA was calculating that to compete in the environment of the 1990s, it would have to spend collectively, as an industry, somewhere between six and 12 *billion* dollars on upgrading and new technologies. As it wrote in *A Clear Vision* (p.27):

> Upgrading existing networks to "digital-ready" capability as well as extending service will require an investment of approximately $6 billion over the next 10 years. Achieving universal addressability and/or information and two-way services would add several billion dollars more to this investment requirement. Further, depending on how aggressive the industry becomes in developing new services and addressability with DVC [digital video compression], the estimated $6 billion investment could easily double.

When we return to the numbers provided in the Rogers mailout, we discover that of the $1.86 rise in Full Basic Service, only 26 cents is allocated to Canadian specialty channels — i.e. gets passed on to program-providers. The entire remaining amount — $1.60 or 86% of the increase — is to be retained by Rogers to help the company improve its own fixed assets through the introduction of "innovative fibre optic and digital transmission systems". No explanation is provided by Rogers as to the differences between "upgrading" their system and "improving" it, nor why these factors should occasion two separate and incremental rate hikes of such magnitude.[31]

If the Canadian cable industry spends billions of dollars in an undisciplined way on new technology, then the whole nation will pay the price in both consumer dollars and missed opportunities. In theory, only two options are available for ensuring that these massive infrastructure investments are carried out in a way that meets the public interest: one is the discipline of public policy, i.e. regulation; the other is the discipline of the marketplace, i.e. competition.

Neither the behaviour of cable companies nor the regulations in place bode well for the Canadian consumer. More and more cable transactions are being allowed to become discretionary and unregulated. This freedom of action would be unobjectionable if cable companies were subject to effective competition. But there are few signs that the regulator will allow competition any time soon or that it will tamper with the monopoly status of cable. As Deathstars and other technological innovations threaten to topple the regulatory superstructure, Canadians could be placed in the unenviable position of being captive to a monopoly supplier, while being prevented from seeking competitive options from other sources.

Not everyone agrees with this view of the situation. Michael MacMillan of Atlantis Films, for example, believes that whatever happens to strengthen cable as the preferred delivery system is to be encouraged. As he pointed out in a recent interview:

> We'd much rather cable be the way that consumers consume programming as opposed to DBS because DBS is not regulatable, or it's a lot less regulatable than cable. It's through Canadian content regulations that a healthy and predictable market for Canadian programming is maintained. My attitude is to keep cable as a more attractive option for consumers.

MacMillan is a producer who has built a successful business on recognizably Canadian programming. His goal is an orderly marketplace in which domestic broadcasters create reliable demand for domestic programming. It would suit everyone if the goal could be achieved. That, after all, is the intent of the content regulations, the use of conditions of licence to stimulate demand, the resort to cable as the gatekeeper.

But changes in the marketplace and technology have made the goal more remote than ever. All the evidence suggests that further entrenching cable's market power will work *against* the goal of Canadianizing the broadcasting system rather than for it. So too with the regulation of content: the cure has become worse than the disease.

S.12: REGULATING CABLE AMERICAN STYLE

It should be obvious by now that this chapter is not an argument for simple deregulation, if deregulation means taking the cap off cable rates but not allowing effective competition. The re-regulation of cable has been one of the most hotly contested political battles in Washington all through 1992. Indeed, as we go to press, Congress has managed to override George Bush's veto of S.12, the 1992 *Cable Television Consumer Protection Act* — the very first time in his tenure at the White House that any Bush veto has been overridden by Congress.

Why be concerned with what the Americans are up to? For two reasons — despite evident differences between our two systems, not the least of which is that American cable operators are licensed and partially regulated by municipalities. First, the American government has already experimented with cable deregulation, the net effect of legislation passed in 1984. One of the principal reasons for drafting S.12 in the first place was the feeling in many political quarters that ever since the deregulation of rates in 1984, consumers had been victimized by the cable industry.

Second, and in a wider perspective, the Americans have been struggling recently with whether to discipline the cable market through some form of regulation or enhanced competition. While forces in Congress marshalled on the side of re-regulation (not all of them for the same reasons by any means), the Bush White House and the FCC have been promoting the idea of competition as the only workable solution. The administration's philosophy has been evident in the White House moratorium on regulation, the views of Chairman Sikes and many commissioners and staff, as well as formal policy initiatives such as the announcement of support for video dial tone. Their strategy is to check market power and promote consumer interests by encouraging new entrants into the delivery of video services — cable overbuilders, MMDS and wireless technologies like 28 GHz, DTH satellite services and, as announced in July of 1992, the telephone companies through the use of video dial tone technology. In testimony to the U.S Senate in 1989, FCC Chairman Alfred Sikes staked out his position:

> Any [cable TV] price regulation, of course, should be applied only to the extent that competitive marketplace forces are demonstrably inadequate to safeguard customers' interest. If price regulation is to be reimposed, as a number of interest groups have urged, it is important at the same time to take steps aimed at engendering the kind of pro-entry, pro-competitive policies which, over time, will facilitate phasing out any such regulation.[32]

The competition model also found support in both FCC and independent economic studies showing that competition in cable franchise areas lowers rates to subscribers, typically by 20%. Nevertheless, while S.12 represents a defeat for the stance on competition, virtually everyone in Washington agreed that something had to be done to restore order to the cable marketplace.

Cable operators have naturally seen the events of the 1980s in a somewhat different light. (Various other interested parties, including the NAB and the MPAA, fought a bitter fight over certain provisions of S.12.) In April of 1992, participants at the Financial Post Conference on broadcasting in Toronto had a chance to hear the industry perspective from Ron Osborne, the president and CEO of Maclean Hunter Ltd. Its extensive holdings in the print and electronic media include dozens of cable systems in Canada, the United States and the United Kingdom, making it the second largest cable MSO in this country after Rogers Cablesystems. Here is what Mr Osborne said in his address on the subject of cable rates and rate deregulation:

> Let me dispense with the myth that somehow cable operators in the U.S. have been gouging cable subscribers ever since deregulation in 1984. In 1984 the average basic rate per subscriber, for just the basic service, was $9.20. In 1990, some 6 or 7 years later (I'm never sure if that's inclusive or not), the average was $17.58. Well, when you consider that cable had gone through 3 or 4 years of constraints, absolutely no increases prior to 1984, an increase from $9.20 to $17.58, at a time when the number of services delivered as part of the basic service expanded expedientially [sic], that is one bargain. I doubt

whether many of you are selling products that haven't had per unit price increases that match and exceed that.[33]

The basic rate figures quoted by Mr Osborne represent a cumulative increase of 91% or about 15% a year on an annualized basis. According to data supplied by the National Cable Television Association (NCTA), moreover, the *total*, not average, number of national cable video networks available in the United States rose from 49 in 1984 to 73 in 1990. That's an increase over the whole period of roughly 49%, not exactly exponential ("expediential"). In other words, rates grew in this period about twice as fast as the number of cable services. Whether or not a rate of increase three times that of inflation still represents a "bargain" is a moot point.

NCTA data also tell us that Mr Osborne's claim that there were "absolutely no increases prior to 1984" is misleading. Citing Paul Kagan Associates, the NCTA reports that from 1980 to 1984, average monthly basic cable rates rose from $7.85 to $9.20. That's an increase over the period in question of roughly 17%, or about 4% a year for each of the four years. Thus, there may have been little or no increase relative to inflation. Despite what is conveyed by the "absolutely", rates did in fact increase even prior to deregulation. *After* deregulation, in any event, the rate of average annual increase itself increased by a factor of almost four times (15% vs 4%).

These rate hikes were the principal, though not the sole reason, that Congress was moved to action in 1991. Here is some of what was read into the record on the floor of the U.S. Senate when an amended version of S.12 was introduced on January 31, 1992 (*Congressional Record* — Senate, S 760):

Since rate deregulation, monthly rates for the lowest priced basic cable service have increased by 40 percent or more for 28 percent of cable television subscribers. Although the average number of basic channels has increased from about 24 to 30, average monthly rates have increased by 29 percent during the same period. The average monthly cable rate has increased almost three times as much as the Consumer Price Index since rate deregulation.

> [...] Most cable television subscribers have no opportunity to select between competing cable systems. Without a sufficient number of local television broadcast signals and without the presence of another multichannel video programming distributor, a cable system faces no local competition. The result is undue market power for the cable operator as compared to that of consumers and video programmers.

The issues touched on here are too vast for us to cover in anything like a comprehensive manner. So let's stick with the simple example we introduced above — the issue of "tiering up" from basic to create unregulated or semi-regulated service packages, such as the Full Basic Service offered by Rogers. Consumer acceptance of extended basic in its various forms across the country means that 10% or less of the subscriber base will continue to subscribe to "basic basic" — the alleged basic tier. This formula makes good business sense, because it is profit-maximizing. But it makes a mockery of rate regulation and flies in the face of the CRTC's own professed goals in using cable as its cultural gatekeeper.

An elegant solution to the consumer protection dilemma was provided in an early version of S.12. It proposed an amendment to the rate regulation provisions of the *Communications Act of 1934*, which read in part as follows (*Congressional Record* — Senate, January 31, 1992, S 762):

> If the [Federal Communications] Commission finds that a cable system is not subject to effective competition, the Commission shall ensure that the rates for the provision of basic cable service [...] are reasonable; except that if fewer than 30 percent of all customers to that cable system subscribe only to basic cable service, the Commission also shall ensure that rates are reasonable for the lowest-priced tier of service subscribed to by at least 30 percent of the cable system's customers.

Understandable differences of opinion might arise over the notion of a "reasonable" rate, as well as over the choice of 30% as a cutoff point. But it's the principle that counts: you don't decide to guard the henhouse, then let the fox decide exactly what constitutes a henhouse.

Regulation vs competition

Canadians face some tough choices down the road. Unlike our free-marketeering neighbours to the south, we have clung to government intervention and protectionist measures to build our television industry — and we've been largely vindicated over the years for having done so.

Now we're caught in a pincer movement. On one side a mature industry has caught up with and overtaken the regulatory apparatus, which seems to be more in touch with the business community than with the public interest. On the other side the inexorable march of technology has thoroughly undermined the traditional basis for the regulation of broadcasting. Few Canadians, however, are well disposed to the idea of giving up the structure that seemed to form the very foundation of our national culture.

The current obsession with Deathstars and damage projections misses a fundamental point. We are not going to be unravelled by one technology beaming down from unfriendly foreign skies. The changes we've been describing are neither confined to a single technology, nor are they part of some external conspiracy being foisted on us against our will.

Given current trends, it seems inevitable that we will one day have competition in the supply of video services to Canadian homes — whether we plan on it or not. But planning on it doesn't mean we throw out the baby with the bathwater. Current trends point just as compellingly to a mixed model that combines regulation with competition. We don't need to stop regulating; we need to start regulating differently. In the next chapter, we will describe the two major forces impinging on how we use and regulate television in the 1990s: convergence and globalization.

Chapter 7

CAUTION — MERGING TRAFFIC

"The leading media companies see the world dominated by a few giant concerns by the end of the century, each company controlling a vast empire of media and entertainment properties that amounts to a global distribution system for advertising and promotion dollars."

The Wall Street Journal, *March 7, 1989*

In our three preceding chapters, we looked at several developments that are changing the way broadcast television is consumed, financed and regulated in Canada. We saw evidence for the following conclusions:

Transactional television is the norm. Consumers are spending more and more entertainment dollars in the home, in many cases because of a lack of disposable time and money to go out. Rights holders and distributors of movies, sports events and other program material are using new video technologies to move the box office into the living room — accelerating the changeover from free TV to pay-TV.

The regulatory framework is outmoded. Technology has undermined the existing rationales for regulating broadcasting and will make such regulation more difficult to apply in the future. At the same time, the rules in force covering program content, affordable rates, etc, are working much more to the advantage of broadcasters and cablecasters than video suppliers and consumers. Technology will help initiate a re-evaluation of the ground rules for TV at a time when these ground rules have become inadequate or outmoded for other reasons anyway.

It's a producer's world. The domestic market in Canada has always been too small to provide adequate economic support to any of the cultural industries, including film and television. A few years ago, it was largely up to our TV broadcasters to aggregate sufficient financial resources within Canada to get indigenous drama and entertainment programs produced. Today, that task has fallen to the production community. The constraints of our domestic market have also obliged Canadian producers to rely on the international marketplace for financing partners — with the sanction and encouragement of the federal government.

The purpose of this final chapter is to expand on these conclusions in relation to a development we've met before in several guises — convergence. We'll pursue this part of our discussion from two perspectives:

→ First, we'll look at how broadcasting services in Canada and elsewhere are slowly converging with telecommunications services — less in terms of regulation or infrastructure than in terms of functionality, as part of a larger "information industry". This raises two points. Not only will this kind of convergence force a re-evaluation of the current regulatory framework for broadcasting, but it will also raise a whole new set of consumer protection issues for "broadcasting", issues more associated with telephony and other telecommunications services. These include rate discipline, whether achieved through regulation or competition; access to distribution networks for both service providers and end-users; service diversity and innovation; and a number of emerging issues, the most notable of which is privacy. These issues need to be examined in the light of our earlier comments on the viewer benefits of choice, control, quality and interactivity.

→ Second, we'll return briefly to the international stage to look at how convergence is affecting the way the world's media multinationals conduct their business these days. A pattern of globalization is emerging typified by both vertical

integration and horizontal consolidation. By way of a case study, we'll describe the most spectacular example of this strategy in action, namely Time Warner, the world's largest entertainment company.

Broadcasting vs Telecommunications

Most of us have grown up seeing TV technology and telephone technology as two completely separate and unrelated animals. And for good reason. While they shared a few technical elements in common — analog processing, communicating over distance and so on — the differences were always more important than the similarities. These differences were of three kinds:

Technical. TV is a broadband technology using point-to-multipoint public communication. Telephones utilize a narrowband technology and operate through switchable networks to enable point-to-point private communication.

Functional. TV is a video medium that developed historically as a passive, in-home entertainment device. Telephony developed historically to carry interactive voice, then data traffic and has always been as important for business applications as for residential applications.

Economic. Conventional television is a free "public good", supported by advertising and distributed over the air to members of the general public without discrimination. Telephony was always considered a "natural" monopoly and telephone services are financed by subscriber fees and toll charges.

From the perspective of 1992, this sketch of the differences seems somewhat simplistic and artificial — even though we still tend to consider TV to be for leisure and the telephone to be a vital link with the outside world. Indeed, a number of regulatory principles are reflected in the traditional differences between a TV show and a phone call, between a free TV service and a paid subscription to the phone network, between a cultural policy and a consumer protection policy. And these principles have been institutionalized in the way the CRTC administers broadcasting on the one hand and telecommunications on the other.

When we say that broadcasting and telecommunications are converging, we need to be more explicit about how we are using convergence in this context.

Technically, TV has moved closer to telephony with the spread of cable delivery and the introduction of addressable descramblers. Important differences remain in terms of bandwidth and interactivity: the transmission of high bandwidth video or TV signals by cable does not lend itself easily to the two-way, switched interactivity of a telephone network. But the largest and most influential communications companies — like TCI, Apple, IBM and Time Warner — appear to have set the eradication of these differences as a long-term business goal, on the way to providing services like video on demand. The combination is often referred to as "switched broadband".

Functionally, and despite lingering technical constraints, the convergence of video and telecommunications has been realized in a number of services and products. Two obvious examples are videoconferencing and videotex. Videotex is a two-way interactive service that allows a user to call up information from a remote databank and conduct transactions like home banking. The home terminal can be a standalone device, a computer terminal or a regular television set with a special attachment. The user can gain access to particular pages of information by pressing a button on a remote control or keypad. Is this broadcasting or telecommunications?[34]

Economically, we have noted at many points that TV is no longer free for the majority of Canadians and most new TV services will be marketed at some discretionary cost to the viewer, whether from cable companies or other video suppliers. More and more TV services are taking the form of private, two-way transactions, like pay-per-view, while the traditional model of telephony as a natural monopoly has now faded away, even in Canada.

Let's be clear what we do *not* mean here by the convergence of television and telecommunications. "Convergence" sometimes refers to what was formerly called "plant integration" — the idea that the physical plant owned by the telephone companies should be integrated with the network plant owned by cable companies serving the same areas. The rationale was that it would be more efficient and economical to supply subscribers with their communications services by sending them through one drop line into subscriber homes, rather than through two — the cable company's coaxial cable and the telephone company's twisted copper pair.

This was, however, an idea whose time never seemed to come. Two obstacles stood in the way. First, CRTC regulations require that cable companies own their own physical plant. The concern is that if they leased network facilities from a third party, such as a telecommunications carrier, then it would be more difficult to hold cable companies accountable for the broadcasting services they provide. Other statutory restrictions prevent common carriers from entering the cable business.

Second, the idea of combining cable's high bandwidth network with the "switchability" of the telephone network *in one line into the consumer's home* has been fiercely resisted by both cable and telephone interests. To no one's surprise, neither sector has been willing to forego the opportunities associated with the ever-expanding palette of new services made possible by technologies like digitization. The industry experts interviewed in the course of this study were unanimous in the view that plant convergence, especially at the local network level, is now exceedingly unlikely. And if anything, the passage of time will make this eventuality even more remote, as fibre optic and wireless transmission technologies become less expensive and more flexible.[35]

What we are seeing in Canada, therefore, and to an even greater extent in the United States, is not so much a convergence of cable and telephone as a crossing of traditional boundaries. This is partly a matter of the two industries going after each other's existing turf. Cable companies, a few of which are already providing high-speed private digital networks to large businesses, have shown some inclination to compete head-on with the telcos for voice communication services, using wireless technologies. The American phone companies have been given a green light of sorts by the FCC to undertake development of video dial tone technology to allow them to compete with other video suppliers to the home.

While it is unlikely that the telcos will be able to mount effective competition against cable in their mainstream services, more crossing of lines can be expected in what the CCTA refers to in *A Clear Vision* (p.17) as the "unclaimed territory" which the telephone, cable and DBS industries all have their eye on:

> Between the telephone industry (voice communications and enhanced services) and the cable industry (broadcast, pay and specialty television), there exists a broad array of new services ('the unclaimed territory') that can be distributed to in-home and business users. These include telemetry, information services and enhanced entertainment services. As both the cable and telephone industries adapt newer technologies and add new services, the gap between them will shrink.

The CCTA document predicts that the unclaimed territory will be "occupied" by the year 2001.

The regulator's dilemma

The CRTC, which regulates both broadcasting and telecommunications, handles its two sets of duties under entirely different statutes, with two rather different interpretations of the public interest. In Canada, cable has always been treated as an integral part of the broadcasting system and is therefore assessed in terms of the benefits it brings to Canadian culture. On the other hand, telephone companies are treated as utilities and regulated with a view to providing universal service at the lowest possible cost.

While the CRTC began life in 1968 as the broadcasting regulator, it later inherited the job of looking after the telephone companies. Not unlike its sister agency, the Department of Communications, which one day found itself looking after both culture and technology, the CRTC operates under two distinctive mandates and administrative traditions. Whereas the CRTC administers broadcasting under the 1991 *Broadcasting Act*, the telephone companies or "common carriers" have been regulated under the *Railway Act*, the *National Telecommunications Powers and Procedures Act* and the *Telegraphs Act*.

This regulatory lawyer's dream has been cut down to more streamlined proportions by Bill C-62. What Bill C-62 does not do is reduce the sharp contrast between the treatment of telecommunications carriers on the one hand and broadcast and cable licensees on the other. Telecommunications hearings are much more punctilious than broadcast hearings, and include judicial procedures

like rights of reply and cross-examination. Telecommunications carriers are, moreover, subject not only to specified rates of return on their investment, but also to rigorous cost separation and accounting safeguards.

What is perhaps most significant from the perspective of the public interest is that although the 1991 *Broadcasting Act* stipulates in section 3(1)(t)(ii) that distribution undertakings should "provide efficient delivery of programming at affordable rates", no rigorous provisions are in place — like those for the phone companies — to ensure whether cable companies are allocating their costs and revenues for regulated and unregulated services in due and proper fashion.

We said at the beginning of this chapter that the de facto convergence of what were once distinctive broadcasting and telecommunications services would have two effects: one, render the separate regulatory treatment of broadcasting and telecommunications more difficult; and two, introduce a whole new set of consumer protection issues for broadcasting. Let us look at a brief illustration of this first point, before going on to give a treatment of several new issues.

The separation of content & carriage. We've seen that broadcasting and telecommunications have been subject to different regulatory treatment and that convergence is rendering this situation more and more untenable. One of the long-standing traditional obstacles to convergence is the principle of the separation of content and carriage required of common carriers.

Under its enabling legislation, the *Bell Canada Act*, Bell is explicitly forbidden not only from holding a broadcasting licence but also from in any way controlling the contents or influencing the "meaning or purpose of messages transmitted" through its facilities. In other words, it has to stick to its knitting as a telecommunications common carrier. Although only Bell Canada is subject to this legislative provision, the entire telecommunications industry is generally regulated on the basis of a separation between content and carriage. The main rationale behind this restriction is — or was — to prevent common carriers from using monopoly control over communications infrastructures to restrict freedom of expression. Given Bell Canada's long history of predatory pricing and other anti-competitive practices, there was good reason to write these safeguards into the legislation.[36]

Looking again at cable, we find that the *Broadcasting Act* takes a completely different view of content and carriage. Section 3(1)(t)(iv) provides in fact that distribution undertakings (cable operators)

> may, where the Commission considers it appropriate, originate programming, including local programming, on such terms as are conducive to the achievement of the objectives set out in this subsection [...].

Not only are cable operators in Canada allowed to originate programming — in fact they're *required* to originate community programming — they are also allowed to own or control services distributed on their networks. Rogers Communications, for example, Canada's largest cable MSO, owns a controlling interest in YTV (jointly with CUC Broadcasting), as well as Canada's Home

Shopping Channel. Under the regulations for broadcasting, therefore, undertakings that distribute content or program "messages" to their subscribers are not obliged to observe the content-carriage distinction, on the proviso that the regulator is satisfied they are continuing to promote our national cultural goals, such as giving priority to the carriage of Canadian services.

Enter technology — and a dilemma for the regulator. The rationales for regulating the two communications sectors are based on traditional differences that are fast disappearing. Consider the following:

- The content-carriage distinction developed in an era when transmission technology was based on "dumb" networks that acted as pure conduits for private messages. Today, however, networks incorporate fibre optics along with digital signal processing, packet switching and compression techniques. These features are the basis for "intelligent", broadband networks which can be used to enhance and manipulate messages in ways that will make it increasingly difficult to distinguish content and carriage — if only because many end-users now *want* carriers to provide custom ways of handling their data. What is more, such networks are being designed and implemented by both cable and telephone companies.
- The content-carriage distinction was originally designed to protect the public from the monopolistic market power of the telephone companies. Broadcasting services, by contrast, were originally distributed in a regulated but competitive marketplace without direct charge. In Canada, the situation has been turned upside-down. Since the CRTC's order to allow Unitel to compete with Stentor, the established monopoly telephone consortium, long-distance telephony is competitive (pending a court appeal). Cable companies, however, still enjoy monopoly licensing and, as discussed in the last chapter, are steadily consolidating their market power as they liberate services from rate regulation.
- The content-carriage distinction could be applied differentially to telephone and broadcasting undertakings because they provided separate and distinct services. Now both sides have plans to go poaching on each other's existing

turf, in addition to preparing for battle over the "unclaimed territory" noted above. In a few years, the two sides will — conditions permitting — be offering many of the same digital electronic services on a fee basis.

Notice that our concern here is not whether the telcos are being treated unfairly because they are being kept out of TV — or whether they are likely to enter the business of supplying entertainment services to the home by such-and-such a year. Once again, what is at stake is the larger principle of how the CRTC will continue to justify its differential treatment of services and service providers that technology is making less and less distinguishable — a dilemma we can call "regulatory lag".

The idea of curing regulatory lag through some type of reform or re-regulation does not necessarily imply that particular benefits will flow from cable-telco competition. We can put the idea in relief by recalling how and why our neighbours to the south have responded to this particular convergence issue. American regulators are letting the telcos — and other new entrants — compete in the provision of new services to the home for three main reasons: to check the market power of cable TV; to reduce the regulatory load on government; and to provide market incentives to have broadband networks serving American homes as soon as possible. In 1988 senior FCC policymaker Robert Pepper wrote the following positioning statement:

> If it is true that fibre optic integrated broadband networks promise to become the electronic infrastructure of an information-dependent economy and society in the next century, it is important that such networks be permitted to evolve free of unnecessary government constraints. Today, however, significant regulatory barriers exist to integrated broadband deployment. In addition, other regulatory and policy questions create additional uncertainty that may slow broadband deployment. Policymakers should remove regulatory barriers and uncertainties and replace them with a framework that will permit technological and service deployment while ensuring a competitive environment.

Ted Rogers

Four years later, in July 1992, the FCC followed up on this position by adopting a video dial tone (VDT) scheme and called for development of VDT proposals from American telephone companies. In the same spirit it approved a 5% equity stake by telcos in cable program companies. Some industry pundits have waxed enthusiastic, as in a 1992 *Variety* article (Whorton, p.24):

> VDT — two years away from experimentation — carries vast implications for Hollywood studios, broadcasters and the home video market as film studios, broadcasters and independent program packagers presumably could bypass local cable systems and create their own networks. For example, viewers wishing to watch, say, the Paramount Network, could tap into the channel and be billed on a per-minute basis.

Others have been sceptical about whether VDT will achieve the desired goals, or even be implemented. Be that as it may, nothing in the position developed here commits us to either seeking a lighter regulatory burden or promoting the vastly expensive deployment of integrated broadband network services to the home. But the whole cable-telco convergence debate does oblige us to revisit the question of whether re-regulation or competition is the more appropriate method for restoring discipline to the delivery of television services to Canadians. Just before we outline the new regulatory issues emerging in the wake of convergence, we will comment briefly on two 1992 CRTC decisions that speak directly to the role of competition.

Dealing with competition after Unitel

Competition in communications is a scary concept for Canadians. It's associated with the American way of doing things, which has tended to mean the freedom to control our domestic markets for film, TV and other cultural products. It also conjures up the age-old problem of mass-market, ad-supported, over-the-air broadcasting: competition under those arrangements has always been demonstrated to *reduce* not enhance diversity. Either way, competition has been viewed with great suspicion, as likely to stifle Canadian creativity.

Until June 1992, it didn't look like the CRTC had a strategy for dealing with new competitive pressures within its jurisdiction. Then, after a century of having the telephone market to themselves, the CRTC told Bell Canada and its long-distance partners they would have to make room for Unitel, a common carrier owned jointly by Canadian Pacific and the ubiquitous Ted Rogers (whose company holds a 40% share). Although implementation of the widely publicized 1992 decision is being held up by a court challenge, Canadians can now in principle choose between two providers for long-distance and other related services.

The decision to open up competition to Unitel signalled an important change in the Commission's philosophy. This was a response to years of swirling change not only in the Canadian communications environment, but in the structure of communications services around the world. In the United States, Europe, Japan and elsewhere in the developed countries, these services have moved from a state-controlled PTT model to one of several forms of competitive or deregulatory model.

These changes have not been without their critics. Consumer advocates like Ralph Nader have denounced the historic breakup of AT&T and the creation of a competitive marketplace as being good for business and bad for regular folks. Back in Canada, telecommunications jurist Hudson Janisch has expressed public misgivings about C-62, finding it too conservative in its approach to new and emerging problems.

The Unitel decision has little in common with the AT&T divestiture (with which it is often compared) and might well have happened with or without the new legislation. What's important is that in arriving at its decision — after the most protracted and expensive public hearings process in its history — the Commission recognized it could no longer keep pace with technological change by administering the telecommunications infrastructure as a monopoly. Many issues are involved here besides the savings made possible by new technologies like fibre optic transmission. One of the major benefits of competition in this field, for example, is the incentive to invest in further technological research and development, in order to provide customers and end-users with innovative services and products.

The "MDS decision". Just days before it issued the order to allow long-distance competition, the Commission released another notice, which received virtually no public or press attention at all. This one — Decision CRTC 92-369, dated 18 June 1991 — demonstrates how long a road we have to travel in broadcasting to catch up with developments on the telecommunications side of the CRTC offices.

In this decision, the CRTC rejected applications from a number of firms, most of them established cable operators, seeking MDS licences, some of them intended to extend cable service to under-served areas. For what may be the first time, the Commission rejected the applications not on their individual merits but because of its expressed concern about the speed with which the associated technologies are changing:

> In the period since the call for applications, the broadcasting environment has continued to evolve at a rapid pace, characterized by significant developments in such new broadcasting technologies as digital video compression (DVC); direct broadcast satellite (DBS) transmission; high definition television (HDTV); digital signal processing, recording and transmission; and optical fibre.

In the two subsequent paragraphs of the decision, the Commission belies its ambivalence over the ramifications of letting loose a new distribution technology. In one breath it worries that the increased capacity afforded to MDS by digital compression "would increase the economic viability of MDS technology and, coincidentally, intensify its potential impact on existing components of the broadcasting system, notably conventional cable and conventional television services". And yet in the next breath, the Commission entertains the idea that "MDS technology, enhanced by DVC in this manner, may permit more than one subscription-based undertaking to operate in the same vicinity, perhaps in competition with each other or with existing cable undertakings". No resolution is offered in this decision:

> These, and many other issues now emerging as a consequence of recent advances in broadcasting technology, are matters that the Commission intends to pursue in the context of a structural hearing tentatively scheduled for the spring of 1993.

In this and other broadcasting decisions, the Commission seems to have interpreted the "public interest" as an orderly marketplace in which the business interests of incumbent licensees must be protected from new entrants. As we go to press, the industry is abuzz with speculation as to whether the structural hearing will finally be the forum in which the Commission reconsiders some of the basic regulatory assumptions that are now being overtaken by developments in technology and business.

From TV viewer to information consumer: the "protection" issues

As we said at the beginning of this chapter, convergence raises a number of new issues associated with consumer protection. Although these issues concern TV or video services, they owe their origins to the telecommunications model of a regulated, subscriber-based utility. Because of its central importance, the first of these — rate discipline — has already received extensive comment. The others include:

- → non-discriminatory access to distribution networks for service providers and end-users
- → service diversity and innovation
- → and a number of issues surrounding the protection of privacy

We are now seeing a growing concern among jurists, scientists, economists and others about the effects of the convergence of information technologies — TV, telephone, computers — on the public at large. What many of their comments share is a desire to redefine the public interest in a way that takes account of the new relationship between individual members of the public and the information technologies shaping their lives.

In a paper prepared for the Aspen Institute Conference on the Future of

Broadcasting held in February 1992, law professor Wilhelmina Reuben-Cooke suggests that the new technologies constitute "an essential, ubiquitous force in all aspects of the citizen's social, political and economic life [...]." As television becomes more and more transactional, she goes on to ask whether there is "something comparable to 'life-line' service that must be a basic entitlement to ensure individual well-being and an informed populace" (pp. 2, 24).

This line of thinking has spread beyond the ivory tower and reached as far as the executive offices of Kaleida Labs, the multimedia venture announced in 1991 by Apple and IBM — in itself an improbable example of how corporate convergence has brought the two arch-rivals of computerdom into a quiet partnership. Kaleida's mission is the creation of a software standard that will allow a range of multimedia technologies, from CD-ROM to interactive TV, to "interoperate" and be accessible to the average consumer. Kaleida's CEO is Nat Goldhaber, a self-made computer millionaire who shares the concern about how information technologies are controlled and applied (as reported by Weber in the *Los Angeles Times*):

> You have to believe that information about your world is empowering, or more accurately, that lack of information about your world is enslaving. [...] There is a very large segment of the population that is utterly disenfranchised with respect to information. They don't get it, it doesn't affect their lives and they are therefore unable to participate in the broader spectrum of social interaction.

These kinds of statements of principle take us far beyond the image of the passive TV viewer soaking up free broadcast entertainment. In fact, we can take some measure of the distance we've travelled if we return briefly to the viewer benefits with which we began several chapters ago — choice, control, quality and interactivity.

As video migrates from the boob tube to the smart-TV, Canadians are running a risk. The risk is we may settle for the superficial benefits of new TV technology while we overlook our rights as citizens of the information society.

Not that there's anything inherently wrong with the aforementioned benefits.

Overall viewer welfare is enhanced by a greater choice of program content, channels, services and exhibition times. So too is it enhanced by greater viewer control of the viewing experience — by the ability to program the TV set and other end-user devices, and thus to manipulate what ends up on the screen. Radical improvements in technical quality and the advent of genuinely two-way interactivity will also promote the welfare of at least some viewers — those with the interest and resources to take advantage of such improvements.

But these benefits will be illusory unless the regulator and the industry start to face up to the real issues of choice and control — those that affect people's pocketbooks, freedom of expression and of access to information, as well as their legitimate expectation of service diversity and personal privacy. We have to ask, for example, not only what new choices will technology bring to our screens, but who will bring them and who will control the prices?

Viewer welfare is not summed up by a wide choice of start times. And in a sense, the greater the number of channels and networks afforded by technology, and the closer we move to the convenience of video on demand, the more both end-users and service providers stand to lose...

The monopoly distribution of television services in Canada has enhanced the market power of cable companies, encouraged anti-competitive behaviour and raised doubts about whether third-party service providers with unconventional or unpopular views can expect non-discriminatory access. The regulatory framework has also allowed cable companies to ignore the content-carriage distinction.

"Freedom's just another word for much too much to choose"

After describing his frustration in trying to choose from among 300 varieties of socks, Steven Waldman suggests that "choice can be profoundly debilitating". Among the drawbacks of choice: it erodes commitment, takes up too much time, awakens us to our failings, leads to inept consumption, causes political alienation, erodes the self and reduces social bonding. (From a syndicated article published in The Globe and Mail, *January 25, 1992.)*

Does this enumeration sound familiar? It should: these are the leading reasons why the telephone companies are so closely regulated and not allowed to become information providers. Why does cable seem to be so different? Is sauce for the goose not sauce for the gander?

Everywhere we turn we stumble into this arbitrary division of rights and responsibilities. Take privacy. In the information age, transactions as varied as home banking and downloading an X-rated movie may all occur over a single, switched, broadband line. Vast amounts of personal information will end up on record at centralized computer banks. Yet even now, no clear enforceable right to privacy exists in the common law in Canada. Bill C-62 marks the first legislative reference to the "protection of the privacy of individuals" as an objective of Canadian telecommunications policy. The legislation addresses junk faxes and telemarketing in particular, and grants to the CRTC the power to regulate with respect to these issues.

It is all very well to promote in the telecommunications arena what privacy advocate David Flaherty terms (p.1) "informational self-determination". It is also reassuring to know that the phone company and third parties will have less opportunity to abuse the information contained in millions of calling and message records. But what about the pay-per-view provider? Can the record of adult movies purchased by individual subscribers be sold as part of a mailing list to marketing organizations? To credit bureaus? To insurance companies? The answer may be that the Charter of Rights and Freedoms has been relied upon by the Supreme Court to conclude that individuals have "a reasonable expectation of privacy".

That, however, is not the point. For in the big picture what's missing is a commitment in Canadian broadcasting policy to the needs of individuals — those who pay for TV through their taxes and subscriber fees. Instead, Canadian broadcasting policy is committed to the needs of licensees.

The historical reasons for this can be traced to the nation-building role shared by broadcasting and cable with the CBC and other public institutions. We've argued at length that the trade-off between nation-building and benefits to business is no longer justifiable. The licensed business interests have succeeded in winning concessions from the regulator that far outweigh any supposed cultural benefit. And meanwhile, the elaborate legal provisions created to protect the welfare of telephone customers are withheld from television customers as though this were still the heyday of the networks.

So far, we've been describing the effects of a convergence of communications technologies within our own national borders, effects over which regulators can begin to exercise some form of control. Beyond our borders, however, and largely beyond our control, another kind of convergence has been changing the media landscape. Though based ultimately on technological development, it manifests itself in the corporate merger, vertical integration and the consolidation of international market power. Welcome to the Time Warner beat.

The media multinationals & corporate convergence

Many reasons can be adduced as to why the large media multinationals are getting larger, concentrating their market power, crossing over into new lines of business and crossing national borders with unprecedented ease.

Technology has certainly played a role. It has created new distribution channels, like pay-per-view, over which the large media companies are determined to maintain control. Technology has also created both opportunities and problems in the spillover effects typified by direct broadcast satellite services. While national culture becomes an increasingly difficult basis on which to build coherent domestic policies for the new electronic media, national culture is also being moved aside by the forces of globalization. These developments are certain to cause disruptions. As we have noted previously, however, the vast increase in the sheer number of TV distribution channels in the developed world, combined with the ability to export program material effectively, may mean opportunities for enterprising Canadians.

At the same time, many of these international developments in TV and related media reflect classic business strategies. The media multinationals are trying to:

- → capture foreign markets;
- → reduce the risks associated with investing in new technologies;
- → realize economies of scale and scope;
- → and amortize their considerable investments in "software" — intellectual properties like movies and TV characters — across as many media and markets as possible.

By pursuing corporate convergence in the international business arena, companies like Time Warner are doing more than melding national cultures into a global entertainment culture. They are also shifting market power away from businesses like TV networks that have traditionally been subject to regulation. Both of these developments are important to the Canadian situation. To better understand the implications, let's take a closer look at the Time Warner example.

The Time Warner colossus

Time Warner is the largest entertainment company in the world, with annual revenues in the range of $13 billion. It was formed in 1989 when Time Inc. merged with Warner Communications. While Time Warner is unique in its holdings, diversity and market power, its overall strategy in the video and television business is a model for what is happening throughout the industry.

What Time Warner is doing can be described in two ways — horizontal consolidation and vertical integration. Horizontal consolidation has become important in the entertainment business because large capital expenditures are required to make use of new technologies. Smaller cable operators, for example, find it necessary to merge their operations in order to have the capital base to be able to implement fibre networks.

Vertical integration refers to the control of all phases of production and distribution of some commodity or product by one company or conglomerate. The TV business is usually considered to have three "vertical" components: these are the *production* of programs, by either independent producers or broadcasters; the *distribution* of programs, by physical delivery of tapes, satellite networks, broadcast transmission and other means; and the *exhibition* of programs to viewers, by means of off-air broadcast, cable, direct broadcast satellite, VCR playback and so on.

Industry players like Time Warner now find it to be essential to control an entertainment product's whole life cycle. Time Warner has holdings in all phases of the video and television business — production, distribution and exhibition — as well as in print and other media, like books and magazines.

Life with 150 channels

What do you get from Time Warner's 150-channel cable service? The first 90 channels include services such as Mind Extension University (28, 81), Comedy Central (40), American Movie Classics (48), Court TV (51), The Korean Channel (62), The Playboy Channel (67) and the NASA Channel (84).

Channels 94 to 150 are devoted to pay-per-view movies. New Hit releases start every half-hour and hour, Classic Hits, Kids, Art & Foreign, and Action films start every hour, and Adult films start every one and a half hours.

Quantum subscribers have a set-top box and remote control device that calls up menus on the screen, regardless of the age or type of TV. Your movie title choices and start times appear on menus and are chosen by pressing the appropriate numbers on the remote control keypad. If you change channels in the meantime, Quantum automatically retunes you to the right channel. And if you accidentally pick two movies at the same time, Quantum puts a message on the screen asking you, well, to make up your mind. All without having to touch the phone, let alone talk to an actual person...

By 1994, Quantum may have 500 channels.

T I M E W A R N E R

Time Warner's principal production company is Warner Bros, which holds one of the most extensive film libraries in Hollywood. Through Warner Bros, Warner Bros Television and Lorimar Television, Time Warner enjoys control of a large body of the most important asset in the filmed entertainment business — the software or intellectual property.

In TV distribution, Time Warner's premier company is Home Box Office (HBO), which began in December of 1975 and now has 17.3 million subscribers. Time Warner also has interests in other cable program networks, such as Cinemax (6 million subscribers), QVC Network Inc. (a shop-at-home network with 42 million subscribers) and CNN (with 59 million subscribers). Time Warner's grip on TV exhibition is even more extensive. With 6,718,000 cable subscribers, Time Warner Cable is now the second largest multiple cable systems operator (MSO) in the United States.

Time Warner's 150-channel cable system in New York makes extensive use of fibre-optic links, to within a few hundred feet of subscriber homes, and features a pay-movie system that implements near video on demand. Even this foray into new cable technologies may be only a stepping stone to far more advanced, computer-based cable systems.

In addition to this domestic strategy for its cable operations, Time Warner has been busy for some time buying minority interests in and forming strategic partnerships with media and entertainment companies in dozens of countries around the world. Time Warner described its strategy in its 1990 annual report (p.13):

> On its own, no global corporation can have [the] same advantage in every country where it does business. Nor can it avoid some degree of cultural or regulatory backlash if it tries to insert itself into another country as owner/manager... The answer lies in strategic partnerships that allow a company to use its subsidiaries to form international alliances that make it a French company in France or a Japanese company in Japan.

Time Warner has created division after division to ensure that the exploitation of its intellectual properties goes far beyond the traditional movie theatre. It owns Warner Home Video, which sells its movies on videocassettes and is the highest grossing company of its kind in the world. Despite its success with tape and the VCR platform, Time Warner is wasting no time to ensure that it's ready for the disc technologies.

Thus, Warner New Media is charged with both developing properties for the new electronic media and recycling existing copyrights, whether as whole entities like movies, or in the form of "out-takes", like reporters' files and photos that couldn't be fitted into scheduled magazine slots. As *Variety* reported (Fleming and Zimmerman) Time Warner encourages "synergies" among its various divisions:

> TW has led the league in cross-pollinization of media. A key example: They're producing "The Official Swimsuit Video," in part about the making of the mythic Sports Illustrated annual cover, via their HBO Video imprint. They're also developing a monthly music magazine for MTV, which of course also runs ads for Warner Bros. movies and has videos from Warner recording artists... That's synergytainment.

TV's new global village

Just as technology type — computing vs broadcasting vs telephony — no longer dictates relationships, so national borders no longer dictate market reach or strategic alliances.

The kind of convergence we're describing has become a model for the media multinationals.

→ Philips NV, the Dutch conglomerate which developed the CD standard, is through its Polygram division the world's largest distributor of prerecorded music. In the 1990s Philips is seeking to replicate the CD success story by introducing the CD-I (Compact Disc Interactive) format. It is backing up its huge investment in this new standard by becoming the largest producer of CD-I software through PIMA (Philips Interactive Media of America) and associated companies in Europe and Japan. And to make sure that its CD-I software gets adequate shelf space, Philips has purchased a 7.9% interest in Blockbuster Video, the largest American home video retailer (source: *Business Week*).

→ Until the late 1980s, it was unheard of for companies manufacturing consumer and computing hardware to take an active interest in controlling or developing entertainment "software", or distribution channels like cable TV. Yet in 1990, Sony, the largest consumer electronics company in the world, took control of one of Hollywood's oldest movie studios, Columbia Pictures (which it bought for $5 billion from Coca Cola), along with CBS records. Sony's strategy is to control the software that will be used with its consumer electronics. This strategy has been a good one — CBS records, for instance, has decided to no longer release LPs but only CDs in some instances, creating an increased demand for Sony's CD players.

→ Meanwhile, IBM, the largest computer company in the world, is negotiating a cable TV partnership with Time Warner, while at the same time is pursuing a joint venture with Apple to develop multimedia tools and standards.

The creation of regional and multinational "cultures" has even broader ramifications. The citizens of some EC countries are lamenting the end of their national cultures as business and technological pressures push them towards a single European trading bloc.

These international pressures provide important clues to the future of television in Canada and elsewhere.

"We fell in love with technology to the detriment of content. We prided ourselves on our cable grids, on our domestic satellite system, on feeding programmes to the Arctic. But we paid inadequate attention to content. We have built what is probably the most remarkable distribution system for pictures in the world — but discovered too late that wires and satellites do not constitute a national culture."

Mark Starowicz,
founding executive producer of
The Journal, *1986*

→ **Media are converging.** Control of creative assets will count more than ever, as these assets are recycled or cross-collateralized across theatres, pay-per-view, home video and other media. What this means for our purposes is that we can no longer look at the television industry in isolation — or expect to promote national cultural interests by continuing to protect and subsidize conventional broadcasters.

→ **Technologies are converging.** Home viewers will place less and less importance on the distinction between broadcast and non-broadcast TV. A digital signal from a direct broadcast satellite, from a coaxial cable and from a compact disc, all carrying the same program or movie, will all look pretty much the same, cost pretty much the same and feature a similar range of storage and special effects possibilities.

→ **Companies are converging.** This means concentration of ownership and continuing globalization of the media. The protection of certain aspects of national culture by means of regulation and non-tariff barriers will become more problematic.

Canada's national cultural goals for broadcasting are supposed to be achieved through a set of regulations that has staked everything on the prosperity of our distribution system. Our position is that this is no longer a sound basis for promoting national interests. Indeed, we go further: the current framework is focused on the wrong issues, is self-defeating and in many respects simply unnecessary. These weaknesses are reflected not only in the structure of our broadcasting system, but also, as we argued in Chapter 4, in the dissemination of Canadian films through theatres, rather than through the increasingly important and influential home entertainment media. Our story began in the living room and seems determined to stay there for some years to come.

We emphasize that this critical view is not a counsel of despair, nor is it tantamount to a call for deregulation. On the contrary, these are observations prompted by two encouraging developments. One of these, already discussed above, involves the new opportunities being created for enterprising Canadian producers by multichannel, transactional television. The other involves the hard-won acceptance of Canadian-produced material in the toughest and most important court of opinion — American television.

Leaders of the American television industry, like Jeff Sagansky of CBS, have declared that Canadian producers are now welcome in Hollywood on their own creative terms. This unanticipated Hollywood welcome mat bodes well for independent Canadian producers and the industrial policy goals of growth and job creation in film and television. Winning a slot in primetime American television is no mean feat. But the Canadian-produced programming that finally makes it into the big leagues is unlikely to be a substitute for home-grown drama and entertainment that truly reflects Canadian values.

All the evidence suggests that private broadcasters will play a diminishing role in the creation of such programming. That role will probably have to be reserved for Canada's public and educational broadcasters — above all, the CBC. One of these days, Canada's political leaders will have to decide whether they are willing and able to commit public funds commensurate with the lofty goals of the *Broadcasting Act*.

One final implication for Canada. That concerns the attempt to promote national interests through a narrowly defined policy framework which still owes much of its raison d'être to conventional broadcasting. If we accept even in part the premise that conventional television is rapidly becoming part of a much larger international information industry, then we would argue that this framework is no longer adequate.

If Canadians are to promote creative endeavour, to encourage the export of our cultural products and to keep abreast of technological change, then we must begin to reconsider how public policy affects television in a much wider context. That context must embrace not only cultural policy, but also economic and industrial policy, trade and export arrangements, as well as research and development in the many areas of technology that are changing the ways we create and communicate information.

That is my entire purpose: world domination, Canadian cultural imperialism.

Moses Znaimer, 1992

VOLUME

APPENDIX: SOME BROADCASTING BASICS

In a culture where much of life is mediated by electronics, we sometimes take the differences between electronic representations and the real thing a little too much for granted. Since the barriers of space and time stand in the way of our attending moon landings and countless other events, we've invented TV and other forms of electronic media as substitutes. The substitutes lack the vividness of being there in person, but they have a lot of other advantages. (On the cutting edge of new electronic technologies is a system of representation known as Virtual Reality or VR, whose goal is to give you the best of both worlds: take you electronically wherever you want to go, without sacrificing the real-life vividness.)

Let's start by thinking of what it is we do with consumer and business electronic products like radios, TVs, computers, telephones, cameras, faxes, modems, photocopiers, printers, cellular phones, etc. To see what they have in common, we have to stop thinking of broadcasting as so many programs, stories, voices, faces, emotions. Instead, think only of *information*. And of the task of representing information electronically.

Electronic media allow us to represent information of two general kinds: static and time-based. The first includes text and numbers, graphics, photos and other still images. The second includes sounds like the human voice and music, and moving images, like animation and movies. We can classify the information we get from these media in another way: for example, in visual terms such as shapes, colours, light and dark, and in auditory terms such as pitch, intensity, duration and so on. What concerns us is the idea that, electronically speaking, the actors in a TV show are just shapes, colours and noises that sometimes move around. This reductionist way of looking at art, business data and communication of all sorts as varieties of electronic information is of course what prompted the coinage "Information Society".

Electronic media represent all this information so that we can do certain things with those representations. One is to send them across the space barrier: the Greek for "distant" is what gave us telegraph, telephone, television and telecommunications. Another is to send representations across the time barrier, which is why people record texts, sounds and images for later use.

Broadcasting as an analog technology

Conventional over-the-air broadcasting has a major built-in limitation — its dependence on analog signal processing.

The visual and auditory information typical of television is carried as a series of modulations or pulses flowing through circuits of various kinds, or else, in the case of over-the-air transmission, as modulations imposed on electromagnetic waves radiating from a transmitter or broadcast antenna. The modulations — in the form of greater or lesser amounts of electrons, changes in voltage or magnetic field — act on a device or energy field further down the chain.

Light strikes a cell in a camera and its intensity is approximated by a charge of electrons. Fluctuations in an electrical current induce electromagnetic waves in a transmitting antenna, which approximate the original information by means of slight changes to their amplitude and carry it through the air, invisibly and at the speed of light. Then at the receiving end, the process is reversed, until the beam of electrons in the cathode ray tube fires on the light-sensitive phosphors and recreates the images being captured at the studio.

Or rather approximates them. Because at each and every stage as the original information — the light reflecting off actors and stage sets — is translated into yet another form of coded energy, something is lost in the translation.

This is precisely where "analog" signal processing gets its name. An analog or analogy is by definition not a perfect copy or reproduction of an original; it is only an approximation. Analog signal processing means information is moved in coded form through a series of devices like cameras, switchers, antennas, amplifiers, cables and so on, each of which changes the signal from one form of energy into another. The more changes or modulations the signal has to go through, the more likely it is to be degraded.

Consider a visual analogy. Like a switching or transmission circuit in a broadcasting studio, a photocopier takes information from a source feed and transfers it to a copy. Even with a good quality photocopier, we all know what happens when a first copy is made into a second copy and that into a third and so on. After several copying generations, we end up with something which is barely legible and on which any imperfections have become unsightly smudges.

Over the years broadcast engineers have developed many ingenious techniques to mitigate the tendency of analog circuits to degrade quality as information is "copied" or processed repeatedly. While modulations in an electric current are easier to control, several sensitive processing points remain, principally those at which one kind of energy is changed into another. In broadcasting, electricity is changed into electromagnetic energy, and vice versa, at four crucial points:

→ Light changes into electric current in studio cameras.

→ Current induces electromagnetic radiation at the transmitter.

→ These electromagnetic waves induce an electric current in the receiving antenna.

→ The display apparatus or TV set changes this current back into light, i.e. visible images.

All of these transformations of energy create special problems for engineers (and often require a family of devices known as "transducers": familiar home entertainment components of this nature include loudspeakers and the stylus in record turntables). But in conventional broadcasting the greatest limitations and problems are created in the actual transmission phase, as TV and radio signals are sent from an antenna to a receiver some distance away.

A couple of definitions might be helpful at this point.

First, the term "radio" comes from the same Latin root as "radiate" and "radiant" and means to emit beams or rays, and by implication to emit them in all directions. Broadcasting was originally based on the idea of a signal radiating from a terrestrial source in all directions for free capture by the general public. Although this was for many years the only way radio and TV were transmitted to homes, this technique is more and more becoming the exception.

Second, TV signals all depend on various forms of electrical energy at every stage, from image capture by a studio camera or editing equipment, to display on the home screen. Even the electromagnetic waves that radiate from a TV transmitter are actually generated by changes in the flow of current through the transmitter. The particular kinds of circuits used in TV sets and other audio-video appliances are referred to as "electronic" — hence the name "consumer electronics" to refer to TV sets, video games, home computers and so on (see accompanying box).

"Electronic" vs "Electrical"

Both electronic and basic electrical devices depend on flows of electrons to make applications possible such as the playback of a CD or operation of a motor. The difference lies in the medium through which they travel. Electronic circuits or devices incorporate special media for controlling the flow of electrons and use them to encode information or perform specialized functions. These media include both old-fashioned vacuum- or gas-filled glass tubes and newer, solid-state devices like silicon microchips. (These are referred to as "semi-conductors", because substances like silicon do not behave exactly like either an insulator or a conductor of electricity: they only "semi-conduct".)

Compare these with a simple, highly conductive copper wire carrying current to a light bulb, heater or motor. Without the refinements made possible by electronic components like transistors, all these appliances can do is convert electrical energy into light, heat and motive power respectively.

That's not to say there aren't important differences between vacuum tubes and the silicon chips that have become synonymous with the age of information and computing power. On the contrary, many devices we

The screen display

To the viewer, the most obvious and important TV function is the screen display, the reproduction of signals fed by an antenna, coaxial cable or device like a VCR.

TV display technology is over half a century old, having first been engineered by Vladimir Zworykin, who developed the iconoscope camera tube in 1923 and the kinescope (receiving tube) in 1926. Key components of the television were also developed by Philo Farnsworth between 1926 and 1928. By 1926, John Baird was demonstrating actual live TV in Britain. Three factors are of particular interest here:

→ the linear nature of the TV display;

→ the use of analog signal processing as the forerunner of digital processing;

→ the need to impose technical standards across the North American broadcasting industry, which differ from those used in other territories, such as Europe and Asia.

now take for granted, such as powerful desktop computers, programmable thermostats, camcorders and others, would have been impossible without the staggering advances made in chip technology in the last two decades. The one type of tube that remains nearly ubiquitous in TV sets and computer monitors is the cathode ray tube that displays the image on the screen. (These CRT displays are gradually being displaced by two other screen technologies for TVs, — projection systems and flat-screen liquid-crystal displays, or LCDs.)

The most significant advance in electronics was the reduction of scale permitted by microchips and the corresponding miniaturization of components and consumer devices like the Walkman or personal, portable stereo. Microchip development has evolved through a series of steps known as scale of integration: large-scale integration (LSI), very large-scale integration (VLSI), etc. Here the most telling and popular benchmark for progress in miniaturization and efficient operating power is undoubtedly the desktop computer.

Television images differ from film images in several respects. Conventional film is projected one whole image or frame at a time; each of these images or frames is like a finished photograph or slide, and can of course be seen directly with the naked eye. A film projector moves these self-contained images through the apparatus at a standard rate of 24 frames per second.

TV, by contrast, builds up each and every image dot by dot, on the fly, at the rate of 30 frames per second. The dots on a TV screen are known as picture elements or pixels for short. Think of a typical screen like a page of extremely fine graph paper. The number of little squares or pixels is determined by the number of horizontal lines that form the picture, known as the lines of scanning, multiplied by the number of vertical lines, known as the lines of resolution.

While the two types of lines together determine the overall amount of detail in the picture (one measure of picture quality), there's an important difference between the two. The number of lines of scanning is fixed as part of the North American standard for TV broadcasting. The standard is known as NTSC (for National Television System Committee, the American body that wrote the engineering standards). Under the NTSC standard, all TV sets in Canada and the United States operate with 525 horizontal lines of scanning. (The other two main standards in use elsewhere in the world, the PAL and SECAM systems, operate with different protocols and are incompatible with NTSC, which is why a TV bought in the U.K. will not work in the U.S.)

The FCC adopted the NTSC standard on April 30, 1941. The reason the Commission adopted this standard instead of any others proposed at the time was that NTSC was closest to being ready for the market .

The number of vertical lines of resolution (actually a measure of the number of vertical lines turned on their side and measured horizontally) is not fixed by international standard. Instead, it's partly a function of design decisions made by the firms that manufacture TV sets. As engineers have developed higher and higher quality TV components, the resolution standards in the marketplace have been rising. Only a few years ago sets were being marketed with as few as 200 lines of resolution; now the best sets offer as many as 600 or more. In a side-by-side comparison, the quality differences between sets of, say, 200 and 400 lines will be obvious to any observer: the picture is sharper, more true to life, better able to render shapes, textures and even colours.

In domestic TV sets, however, neither the theoretical number of lines of scanning, nor the advertised number of lines of horizontal resolution is ever fully utilized in displaying images on the screen. The number of picture elements or pixels actually visible and in use is always smaller, because some of the lines in the broadcast signal are used for technical control purposes rather than for picture display (this is known as the vertical blanking interval or VBI). These and other limitations concerning the maximum number of usable lines of resolution mean that even the best current NTSC TV receivers may actually reproduce as few as 340 scan lines and 330 lines of resolution.

The potential level of detail in the screen image is also limited by the quality of the signal being fed into the set. A side-by-side comparison on a high-resolution set between the picture rendered from a cable feed and that from a more controlled and high quality source, particularly a laserdisc, will show how little of a set's potential can be utilized by the broadcast signals coming into most of our homes via cable.

We can now better understand why TV images are described as linear. Each image is formed in much the way that our eye reads a page of printed text: by scanning back and forth in a linear fashion, from side to side and from top to bottom, then over again on the next page, and so on. What does this scanning inside the picture tube is an electron "gun", a device that fires a stream of electrons at light-sensitive phosphors on the inside of the screen.

These phosphors respond to brightness and colour information carried by the streams of electrons emanating from this gun, or cathode ray. To get some idea of just how complex this process is, consider that a high-resolution set operating on the NTSC standard displays over 100,000 pixels on its screen. (As a point of comparison, the monitors used with desktop computers, which operate on a different standard from TV sets, may display six or eight times as many pixels as a regular TV set.)

Each of these pixels is excited by an electron "hit" 30 times a second. During that fraction of a second the pixel must respond to potential changes in both brightness and colour, known technically as luminance and chrominance. The screen must capture this information in a way that renders even rapid motion realistically. Other features of the technology must correct for distortion caused by the curvature of the screen and a myriad of other problems, such as interference from other stations or electrical appliances. (In fact, for reasons we don't need to go into, NTSC receivers actually make two half-scans 30 times a second and then "interlace" them to get the desired picture display.)

Theoretically, a TV screen comprising 100,000 pixels that are scanned 30 times a second is conveying three million items of information each and every second. Practically speaking, not all of this information changes from frame to frame or even from second to second, simply because many images remain relatively static for longer periods of time. It is this redundancy of information from frame to frame that has allowed the breakthrough known as digital video compression.

The first and most important conclusion to be drawn from this description is that conventional TV images must represent very large amounts of information in order to convey detailed, full motion, colour pictures. This is true even under the somewhat compromised display conditions described above, whereby the full potential of the NTSC standard can't be utilized.

Hollywood has devoted a lot of money and energy to pleasing spectators by manipulating the size and proportions of the movie screen. For the first half century or so of its existence, however, the movie industry produced theatrical features using a standard aspect ratio of 1.33-to-1. Then, in the early 1950s, just as television was getting popular enough in the United States to get Hollywood worried, the moviemakers introduced the first of what were to be many different widescreen formats. A limited experiment with Cinerama, a multi-camera process, began in 1952, but quickly gave way to the less costly and more long-lived CinemaScope format. The first CinemaScope production was *The Robe*, released in 1953. For the last four decades, Hollywood has been experimenting with other widescreen formats, ranging from Todd-AO and VistaVision to 70-millimetre and the Canadian-developed IMAX systems.

The evolution of the movie screen has, of course, affected more than merely aspect ratios. Screens have also become much bigger in absolute terms, and been enhanced by more recent technological developments such as multi-track, multi-speaker sound installations employing noise reduction systems like Dolby.

Over this same 40-year period, by contrast, North American TV sets have stuck firmly with tradition and an aspect ratio of about 4-to-3. For almost as long as we've had theatrical movies on TV, viewers have been frustrated by the spectacle of seeing characters close to the edge of the frame disappear in whole or part from their TV screens. Eventually some stop-gap measures were introduced, notably the use of the so-called letter-box format, which reduces the size of a widescreen film image on TV sets, so that the width can be accommodated while the top and bottom of the screen remain blacked out.

Spectrum & bandwidth

It should be understood that the potential for a high-quality TV image is not somehow contained in the broadcast signal arriving at the set, which then compromises the standard because of limitations in the design of the receiving equipment. On the contrary, limitations are built into the NTSC standard itself as the result of policy decisions made decades ago by American regulators (whose position Canada was obliged to adhere to by the realities of geopolitics).

The limitations involve the assignment by government of parts of the natural electromagnetic spectrum for applications like over-the-air broadcasting, mobile and military communications, satellite links and so forth. The natural spectrum ranges from portions having extremely short wavelengths and high frequencies, like gamma and X-rays, to those comprising long waves and low frequencies. All portions of the electromagnetic spectrum share a property with visible light, which is that the product of any wavelength and the corresponding frequency equals 300 million metres per second, the speed at which light, and all these other waves or rays, travel through space.

Where do the limitations come in? First of all, only certain portions of the spectrum are suitable for broadcasting purposes.

Second, the spectrum is "natural" in the sense that once a certain frequency is assigned to a user in a certain geographical area for over-the-air communications, it cannot be assigned for any competing use. Like land, spectrum is finite and can't be duplicated. That is the basis for the all-important concept of spectrum scarcity, the fundamental legal rationale for the regulation of spectrum use. That of course is also the basis for assigning radio and TV stations to non-overlapping frequencies, in order to minimize interference of various kinds (not that this is always successful in practice).

Radio waves act as a kind of neutral medium on which codes can be written, a little like a blank page or canvas accepting the marks of pen or brush. Engineers have perfected two ways of modulating waves to signify content. One involves making slight changes to the amplitude or wave height and goes by the name amplitude modulation or AM. The other involves slight changes to the frequency (rate of oscillation) of a signal and is called frequency modulation or FM. These are the same familiar AM and FM bands from radio, i.e. sound broadcasting.

To capture and carry all the information involved, the transmitting apparatus must use a predetermined amount of spectrum, known as "bandwidth". Conventional TV broadcasting falls into the so-called Very High Frequency band, which may be familiar from the VHF connection for antennas and VCRs on the back panels of most TV receivers.

VHF TV broadcasting occurs in the frequency range lying between 30 MHz and 300 MHz. "MHz" stands for "megaHertz", the measure of frequency meaning one million cycles per second: a one MHz wave oscillates a million times a second and by definition is 300 metres from crest to crest, because one million cycles per second times 300 metres equals the speed of light. (Please refer to Units in the Glossary.)

What really counts here is how much bandwidth from this part of the spectrum needs to be set aside for each over-the-air television station. The amount of information that radio waves can carry is determined by their frequency: high information signals like TV need high frequencies, i.e. a lot of bandwidth, in order to achieve acceptable levels of quality. Channel assignments must also be carefully separated so as to minimize interference.

So the system we ended up with was, not surprisingly, a compromise. North American TV channels (and related non-broadcast video applications) are assigned about 6 MHz of bandwidth according to our established standards. More bandwidth could have been assigned by the regulators. The advantage to more bandwidth: more information carrying potential, meaning higher quality. The disadvantage, however, would have been room for fewer TV channels: fewer business opportunities, fewer advertising outlets, fewer choices for viewers. The laws of physics did not determine — except within general limits — either the number of lines in the NTSC picture or the 12 VHF channels (numbered 2 to 13) that we North Americans have always taken for granted.

Another way to look at this is that there's a fixed relationship between the standard bandwidth assignment for TV and the potential number of lines of resolution in the TV image — given the fixed number of lines of scanning used in the NTSC system. Spectrum was regarded as a scarce resource as television developed and many technical and regulatory assumptions were made with that in mind — including just how much quality was enough.

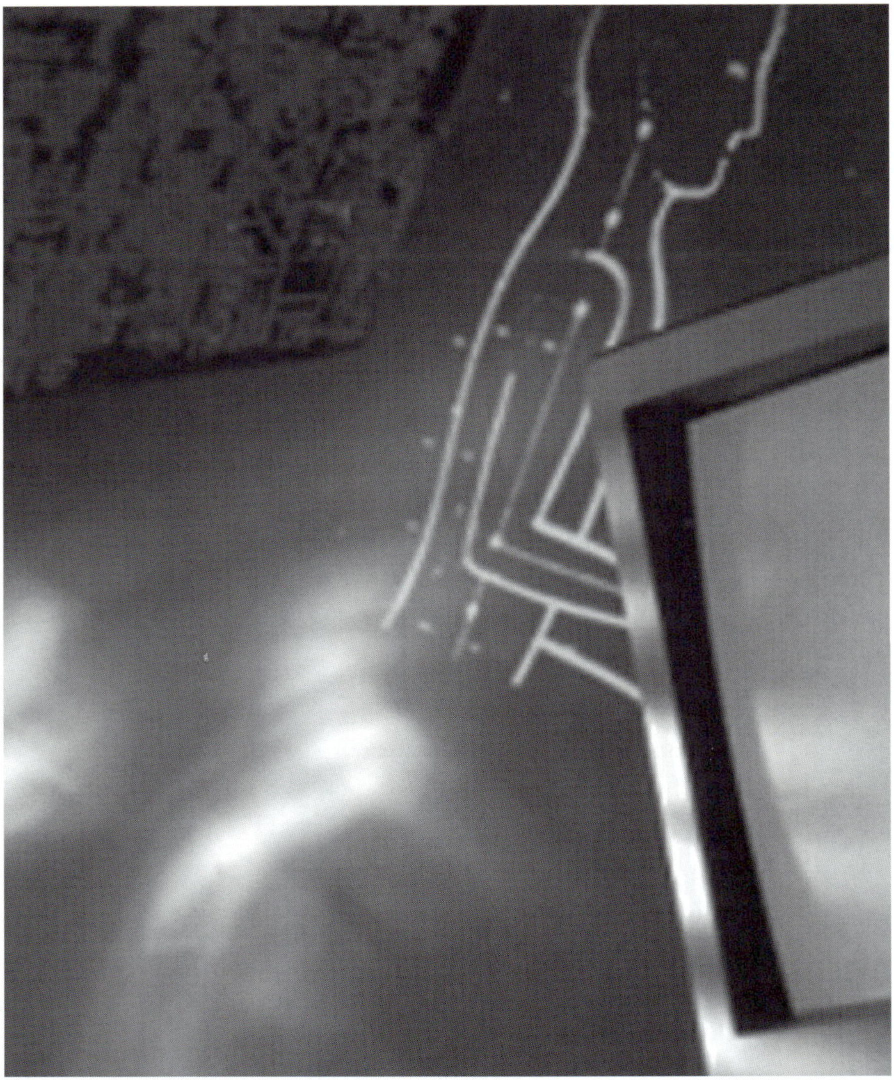

Bells, Whistles & Black Boxes

A Glossary for the Modern Viewer

ABSOC

→ Advanced Broadcasting Systems of Canada. Founded in 1990, the organization's declared purpose is to "prepare for the introduction of advanced broadcasting systems into the Canadian broadcasting system and the associated changes affecting the Canadian broadcasting, cable and satellite industries". ABSOC is made up of committees whose members are employees of private firms, and government agencies with a stake in the electronic media.

Addressability

→ A technology that allows cable operators to send ("address") programs or data to individual subscriber homes. The set-top boxes that permit this are known as "addressable descramblers". They give the cable operator a means of telling descramblers in authorized homes to unscramble a pay or pay-per-view service.

Advanced Television (ATV)

→ See HDTV.

Affiliate

→ A television station having a contractual agreement with a network, like CTV or ABC, to air a substantial amount of that network's programming, especially primetime entertainment programming, which would be too expensive for individual affiliates to produce on their own initiative. Most conventional networks own some stations and have affiliation agreements with others which are independently owned. The decline of network TV in the United States, and chaotic developments in the program selling market, have undermined the traditional loyalty of many of the Big Three affiliates (ABC, CBS, NBC).

In the cable industry, "affiliate" refers not to a broadcast station but to a cable operation which agrees to purchase a particular satellite-delivered specialty or pay service, like TSN or First Choice.

Algorithm

→ Mathematical formulas or procedures that work a little like recipes or sewing patterns. For example, they may tell an electronic signal how to change consistently from one form into another. One of their most important applications in the new media is to provide an efficient way to compress video signals (see Compression). "Algorithm" is a corruption of the name of a pioneering ninth-century Arab mathematician, al-Khuwarizmi.

AM, FM

→ "AM" stands for "amplitude modulation"; "FM" stands for "frequency modulation". Although the two terms are used to refer to radio stations, they have a wider application in electronics, including the transmission of TV signals.

In a general sense, modulation is the technique that allows audio or video information from an input source to be superimposed on a carrier wave to carry out some task, such as transmission of the information over the air to receiving sets (radios and TVs). Every licensed radio and TV station is assigned a channel allocation that corresponds to a certain frequency on the electromagnetic spectrum. Broadcast transmitters emit a carrier wave at this frequency, which has some nominal value on the receiver dial. This wave always covers a wider frequency band, from a point just below the nominal value to a point just above it (the actual points are set by regulation).

The carrier wave is varied by a modulating signal fed from sources like cameras and microphones. The modulating signal is what carries the desired information, while the carrier wave is the vehicle used to deliver the information to receivers, which can be adjusted to the frequency of each carrier wave — i.e. each available radio or TV station.

Electromagnetic waves are measured in terms of both frequency, the rate at which they oscillate back and forth (measured in Hertz: see Units), and amplitude, the peak "height" or displacement of a wave (measured in metres). AM is the process whereby the *amplitude* of the carrier wave is continuously modulated by the input signal. FM is the process whereby the *frequency* of the carrier wave is continuously modulated by the input signal.

In their application to radio broadcasting, AM and FM refer to particular frequency bands, i.e. parts of the electromagnetic spectrum. In North America, AM stations are located between 540 kiloHertz and 1600 kiloHertz (see Units) on the radio dial. FM stations are located between 88 megaHertz and 108 megaHertz (see Units) on receiver dials.

Amplitude

→ The height or displacement of a carrier wave. This corresponds to the signal's strength.

Analog

→ Along with digital, analog is one of two major types of signal processing used in television and other areas of electronics. In analog signal processing, some property of the signal, such as its voltage, magnetic field or frequency, varies *continuously* such that the output is "analogous" to the input.

Take, for example, a vinyl LP playing on a stereo system. The needle in the pickup head (tone arm) moves back and forth as it follows the wavy grooves in the record surface. That movement is translated into a continuously varying magnetic field in the pickup head, which in turn creates variations in the electrical signal flowing into the amplifier. These variations are filtered and amplified, then sent to the loudspeakers. Just as the stylus turned the mechanical energy of the back-and-forth movement into magnetic and electrical energy, so the loudspeakers change that back into mechanical energy, in the form of movements in the speaker elements that recreate audible signals. At each stage, analog circuits recreate continuous analogies or approximations of the information that is carried by the electrical signal.

→ *Digital* signal processing differs from analog in several important respects. First, whereas analog signals are continuous, like waves, digital signals are discrete, like numbers. In fact they *are* numbers, in the sense that they encode and process information in binary digits or bits, the ones and zeroes comprising the language of desktop and other binary computers.

Second, the discrete and unambiguous quality of digital signals means that when digitally encoded audio or video information is amplified, copied or otherwise processed, the output is identical to the input. This means a vast increase in the quality of digitized products compared to their analog counterparts. Digital signals convey information exactly as originally recorded or transmitted — at least within certain general limits. One of these limits is imposed by what happens when a digital processor reads and samples an analog signal. It can't quite capture everything, since audible and visual information, like music and TV pictures, start and end as sound and light waves, which by definition are analog.

Third, analog signals are application-specific; digital signals are generic. The analog information represented by the wavy grooves in a vinyl LP can't be altered or enhanced in any way. It can only be played back, with a greater or lesser degree of fidelity, just as it was recorded in the vinyl. Digital signals, on the other hand, are not dependent for their existence on a particular physical medium, whether vinyl or anything else. Most importantly, they can be reprocessed and enhanced indefinitely with the aid of computers. That's because devices like a CD player and a desktop computer speak the language of binary digits and handle information in exactly the same logical way.

Aspect Ratio

→ The ratio of the width of a television screen to its height. The aspect ratio for standard television receivers is currently 4:3. One of the changes proposed for the new High Definition standard is an aspect ratio of 16:9, which will make TV sets more compatible with widescreen movie formats.

Audience Measurement

→ *Share:* A proportion of the total audience actually watching television at a given time. Program share is the percentage of viewers or viewing hours captured by program X in its time slot. A station's audience share is the percentage of viewers it has captured in a particular time period, like prime time.

→ *Rating:* The proportion of all television sets tuned to a certain program. Since some households sometimes don't have their TVs on, program ratings are always smaller than program shares. Program X may have a 15% share of the audience in its viewing period, but a rating of only 10 or 10% if only two-thirds of TV households have their sets turned on at that time.

→ *Reach:* The number of viewers that have tuned into a program or station group in a given period (often a week) for a certain minimum length of time (often 15 minutes). Does not imply that viewers have watched an entire program.

See also Diary Method and People Meters.

Bandwidth

→ This is a measure of electromagnetic frequency. It refers to a band of frequencies lying between two points on the electromagnetic spectrum. For example, the bandwidth from 8 MHz to 10 MHz is 2 MHz. The wider this "band", i.e. the more frequencies it comprises, the more information it can carry. A carrier wave or transmitting channel with a wide band or range is termed "broadband", and services like video on demand that require a lot of bandwidth are often referred to as broadband services. Video signals require large amounts of bandwidth for transmission because they carry much more information than, for example, voice messages carried over phone lines.

Barter

→ Compensation for the right to broadcast a program given to the program rights holder in advertising availabilities rather than cash. This is a common practice in the United States and Canada, where stations or networks will often pay program rights holders with a combination of the two.

Baud Rate

→ The speed at which computers send data from one device to another. One baud is roughly one bit (binary digit) of data per second.

Binary Digits

→ A binary digit — "bit" for short — is a "two-way" digit, i.e. a digit that can have only one of two values. In digital signal processing, including desktop computing and scores of other applications, bits have the values "one" or "zero". Highly complex information, including graphic, video and audio information is coded into these bits, which processors translate into a corresponding electrical form, such as "on" and "off" or "open" and "closed". These representations are achieved by combining bits into bytes.

Bits

→ See Binary Digits.

Broadband

→ See Bandwidth.

Broadcasting

→ In Canada, "broadcasting" is defined by section 2(1) of the 1991 *Broadcasting Act* as "any transmission of programs, whether or not encrypted, by radio waves or other means of telecommunication for reception by the public by means of broadcasting receiving apparatus, but does not include any such transmission of programs that is made solely for performance or display in a public place". The 1991 *Act* repeals and replaces the former *Broadcasting Act,* originally passed in 1968. The *Act* applies to all broadcasting undertakings carried on in whole or in part in Canada.

More generally, a broadcast channel is a section of the electromagnetic spectrum allocated to a station for over-the-air transmission, whether television or radio. A station that "broadcasts" in this manner is available to anyone with the proper receiving unit.

"Broadcasting" is also used to describe a program or channel with mass audience appeal, as opposed to one with more limited appeal, often referred to as "narrowcast".

Broadcasting Undertaking

→ In the meaning of section 2(1) of the 1991 *Broadcasting Act,* a broadcasting undertaking "includes a distribution undertaking, a programming undertaking and a network".

A *distribution undertaking* is defined as "any undertaking for the reception of broadcasting and the retransmission thereof by radio waves or other means of telecommunication to more than one permanent or temporary residence or dwelling unit or to another such undertaking".

A programming undertaking is defined as "any undertaking for the transmission of programs, either directly by radio waves or other means of telecommunication or indirectly through a distribution undertaking, for reception by the public by means of broadcasting receiving apparatus".

Finally, a *network* is defined as including "any operation where control over all or any part of the programs or program schedules of one or more broadcasting undertakings is delegated to another undertaking or person".

Byte

→ Binary digits or bits are the building blocks of a larger coding unit called a byte. This is a string of eight bits that signify something common sense can relate to, such as the letters of the alphabet, punctuation marks or whole numbers. Amounts of computerized information, as well as the capacity of hardware like drives and memories, are usually conveyed in multiples of bytes — a 400 kilobyte (400K) file, a 100 megabyte (100MB) hard drive and so on.

For example, the eight-digit binary code for "A" is 00110000 and for "1" is 00110001. These correspond to particular ASCII codes, i.e. "65" for "A" and "49" for "1". These codes for "A", i.e. uppercase "A", are not the same as those for "a", i.e. lowercase "a". These codes include not only letters and numbers, but other marks and symbols as well. The full ASCII set comprises 255 such codes. See Units.

Cable Television

→ Cable television is a method for distributing television signals to subscriber homes through coaxial cable links. Cable, which used to be referred to as CATV (Community Antenna Television), first appeared in Canada in the early 1950s. Its original purpose was to improve the reception of locally available over-the-air television signals. A marginal technology for its first three decades, it was not considered important enough to be one of the foundation concepts of the 1968 *Broadcasting Act.* The CRTC based its regulation of the cable industry on the provision that it formed part of the broadcasting system. By the time the new *Broadcasting Act* was enacted in 1991, almost three-quarters of Canadian TV households subscribed to cable.

Canadian Film Development Corporation

→ See Telefilm Canada.

Carrier Wave

→ Every licensed radio and TV station is assigned a channel allocation that corresponds to a certain frequency on the electromagnetic spectrum. Broadcast transmitters emit a carrier wave at this frequency, which has some nominal value on the receiver dial. The value is nominal because this wave always covers a wider frequency band, from a point just below the nominal value to a point just above it (the actual points are set by regulation). This same principle also applies to common carriers like satellite operators. Thus, the nominal 6 GHz uplink frequency of a C-band satellite actually covers the band from 5.925 to 6.425 GHz.

Cathode Ray Tube (CRT)

→ The display technology utilized in most television sets and computer monitors. The CRT is the picture tube, the inside of which is scanned by a stream of electrons fired from a cathode ray "gun" in the back of the tube. See also LCD.

C-Band

→ See Satellites.

CD-ROM

→ Stands for "compact disc read only memory". The rather inelegant name misses a couple of crucial points. This is a CD that is physically just like the familiar audio CD. It too is read in a digital device that uses optical technology, i.e. a laser. Like the audio CD, it is "read only" because it can only be read and not erased or written over like a floppy computer disk. But there's a big difference. A CD-ROM is encoded to enable it to store vast amounts of information, which may include audio, text, animation, graphics and video. How vast? These days (1992) a single 5-inch CD-ROM disc can hold nearly 700 megabytes (MB) of data. One MB is roughly equivalent to 175,000 words.

The CD-ROM has become the basis for a burgeoning industry for both multimedia and database applications. See also Storage Media.

Cellular Telephony

→ A mobile telephone system that allows subscribers to dial into the public switched telephone network (PSTN) while moving about freely in areas where coverage is provided.

The system takes its name from overlapping "cells" or geographical zones, each of which is served by specially designed transmitters that send and receive telephone messages over the air. Both user mobility and the potential volume of calls are greatly enhanced compared to older mobile telephone technologies by the fact that each cellular transmitter automatically hands off calls to adjacent transmitters as users move from one cell to another.

Channel Surfing

→ Also known as grazing. Skipping rapidly through a large number of TV channels, typically by means of a remote control and with a view to watching any particular channel only as long as it provides a sufficient peak of excitement or diversion. See also Zapping and Zipping.

Chip

→ A small crystal of semi-conducting material such as silicon, typically no larger than a fingernail (the size and material make it akin to a chip). They are usually cut from larger wafers containing the imprints of integrated circuits (ICs). ICs are complete electrical circuits produced on a microscopic scale, whose components are permanently wedded together. Chips containing ICs are probably best known as the essential working components of desktop computers and other similar devices.

Coaxial Cable

→ So named because it comprises a core of solid copper wire surrounded by metallic and other sheathing all of which share a common axis (hence "coaxial"). This makes it unlike the wire used, for example, by telephone companies for subscriber drops, usually known as "twisted copper pair".

Coaxial cable or "coax" is a "broadband" transmission device, meaning that it has a lot of bandwidth and thus the ability to carry large amounts of information, like video signals. One of the technical disadvantages of coax is that it requires the frequent use of line amplifiers to boost signals as they make their way to subscriber homes.

Compact Disc

→ The compact disc is an optical storage unit whose digitized information is read by a laser device. The audio CD revolutionized the recording industry by vastly improving the sound quality of recordings available to consumers. According to 1989 data from Statistics Canada, musical CDs had moved up to a recording industry market share of 26%, compared to a declining 19% for vinyl records. More than half the market (52%) was still held in that reporting year by audio cassette tapes.

Several factors contribute to the CD's reputation for quality. Since CDs are read by a beam of laser light which does not make direct mechanical contact with the disc surface, they are spared the wear and tear that plagues other recording media, particularly vinyl records and tape. One of the CD's least appreciated attributes, however, is the highly sophisticated error correction technology that is part of the basic CD design. In fact, a substantial proportion of the digitized information pressed onto the disc surface is part of the system for detecting and correcting tracking and other types of errors that would otherwise impair the listening experience.

Note that optical devices like CDs are spelt "disc", whereas the magnetic storage unit used in computers is spelt "disk". See Storage Media.

Compression

→ In the TV context, compression refers to a reduction of the amount of information in a video signal, a process usually referred to as digital video compression or DVC. The goal of the process is to reduce the amount of channel space or bandwidth required to transmit TV pictures. The more bandwidth taken up by a transmission the more it costs; therefore, reducing the amount of transmitted information generally leads to cost savings.

DVC uses special algorithms to achieve compression. Different algorithms result in different amounts of information saved, which are indicated as compression ratios. Most systems, however, work by eliminating the redundant information in a television picture. Digital video compression can be utilized for all video transmission vehicles — satellite, cable and off-air broadcasting.

Convergence

→ This refers to several different phenomena in the communications industries.

→ (1) In its narrowest sense, it refers to what used to be called "plant integration", the idea that the physical plant owned by the telephone companies should be integrated with the network plant owned by cable companies serving the same areas. The rationale for the idea was that it would be more efficient and economical to supply subscribers with their communications services by sending it through one drop line into subscriber homes, rather than through two — the cable company's coaxial cable and the telephone company's twisted copper pair.

This was, however, an idea whose time never seemed to come. Two obstacles have traditionally stood in the way. First of all, CRTC regulations require that cable companies own their own physical plant. The concern is that if they leased network facilities from a third party, such as a telecommunications carrier, then it would be more difficult to hold cable companies accountable for the broadcasting services they provide.

Second, plant integration aims at combining two different technologies: cable's high bandwidth network, which makes it possible to carry video signals like TV channels, with the "switchability" of the telephone network, which makes it possible for subscribers to interact with any other subscriber on the network simply by dialing them up. The combination is often referred to as switched broadband. Despite the potential advantages offered by switched broadband services, the costs of implementation, especially using fibre optic distribution technology, have until recently been regarded as prohibitively expensive. See also Fibre Optics and Video Dial Tone.

In 1991 the Department of Communications appointed an industry committee to study this whole question. As of this writing, the Local Networks Convergence Committee (LNCC) had not yet made its report public.

→ (2) Convergence now refers to a much more pervasive phenomenon, which includes some of the elements of plant integration just discussed. This phenomenon is the blurring of traditional distinctions between technologies, media and media businesses. In large measure because of digitization, broadcasting is beginning to converge with telecommunications, computing and consumer electronics.

Co-Production Treaties

→ Canada currently has 23 official co-production treaties with other sovereign nations. These treaties, administered by Telefilm Canada, are with Algeria, Argentina, Australia, Belgium, China, the Commonwealth of Independent States (CIS), Czechoslovakia, France, Germany, Hong Kong, Hungary, Ireland, Israel, Italy, Morocco, Mexico, the Netherlands, New Zealand, Romania, Spain, Switzerland, the United Kingdom and Yugoslavia.

In Canada, certified co-productions are able to reap the advantages of domestic productions (e.g. government funding and status as Canadian content) even though they are not "wholly" Canadian. Certification is based on financial contribution levels and creative participation rather than on content. Once a co-production has been certified, it is eligible for Telefilm funding, as well as tax shelter benefits. Telefilm notes that its "financial participation in official co-productions aims to promote the development of the Canadian film and television production industry and is generally limited to projects in which the involvement of Canadian creative and technical talent is clearly identifiable."

CRTC

→ "CRTC" originally stood for Canadian Radio-Television Commission. In 1968, the then CRTC replaced the Board of Broadcast Governors as the federal regulatory agency responsible for broadcasting. Six years later, the CRTC became the Canadian Radio-television and Telecommunications Commission, when it was given authority over telecommunications, in addition to broadcasting.

Deathstar

→ See Satellites.

Department of Communications (DOC)

→ The Department of Communications was established in 1969 by the *Department of Communications Act.* The Minister of Communications is responsible not only for certain aspects of broadcasting and telecommunications, but also for other cultural industries, such as film, publishing and sound recording. Canada's federal cultural agencies, including the CBC, report to Parliament through the Minister.

When it was originally created, the DOC had a technological rather than cultural orientation. It continues to operate the Communications Research Centre, where DOC scientists and engineers developed, among other things, both Telidon and Canada's original communications satellites.

The DOC shares responsibility for broadcasting with the CRTC. While the Commission is more concerned with licensing matters affecting program content and licensee financing, the DOC is more concerned with technical matters, such as spectrum management. Broadcasting undertakings cannot be licensed to operate by the CRTC until the DOC issues a technical construction and operating certificate (TCOC).

Diary Method

→ Audience measurement procedure that requires participating viewers to record their television viewing, usually for every quarter hour, in a diary provided by the measurement company.

Digital

→ See Analog.

Digital Video Compression

→ See Compression.

Dish Antenna

→ An antenna used for receiving satellite signals. So-called because, despite variations in size and fabrication, the structure resembles a large dish. The shape is, in fact, determined by the precise geometric requirements of reception. It is based on the parabola (hence the synonym "parabolic antenna"). The use of the parabolic shape allows weak satellite signals to bounce off the inside of the antenna dish and be concentrated at a single point for pick up by an electronic receiving device.

Distribution Undertaking

→ See Broadcasting Undertaking.

Early Adopter

→ A consumer who habitually purchases consumer durables or services soon after their introduction into the marketplace, while their price is still relatively high and utility to the consumer unproven.

Earth Station

→ The ground-based receiver for a satellite signal. The earth station comprises an antenna or dish and the receiver electronics. Receiving satellite stations are sometimes referred to as TVROs, for "television receive only".

Electromagnetic Spectrum

→ The spectrum of electromagnetic radiation comprising all frequencies from the highest, like gamma and X-rays, to the lowest, including radio waves. All portions of the electromagnetic spectrum share a property with visible light, itself part of the spectrum, which is that the product of any wavelength and the corresponding frequency equals approximately

300 million metres per second, the speed at which light, and all these other waves or rays, travel through space.

Like land, spectrum is natural, finite and can't be duplicated. That is the basis for the all-important concept of spectrum scarcity, the fundamental legal rationale for the regulation of spectrum use. That of course is also the basis for assigning radio and TV stations to non-overlapping frequencies, in order to minimize interference of various kinds. Only certain portions of the spectrum are suitable for broadcasting purposes.

Conventional TV broadcasting falls into the so-called Very High Frequency band, familiar from the VHF connection for antennas on the back panels of most TV receivers. VHF stations are those operating on the lower channels, from 2 to 13. VHF TV broadcasting occurs in the frequency range lying between 30 MHz and 300 MHz.

Electronic Publishing

→ The dissemination of information by means of a volatile electronic medium, rather than on the printed page. Common examples include making stock quotes and other data available to subscribers who call up the information from a desktop computer through a modem and phone lines.

Encryption

→ See Scrambling.

Fax Machine

→ Fax or facsimile machines allow transmission of documents over telephone lines exactly as they are written or printed on the page. The two essential components are a scanner which reads and digitizes the information on the page to be transmitted, and a modem, which converts the digital information into a signal transmitted over a phone line. A new generation of fax machines known as "G4" will gradually become the standard in the 1990s. They will be able to operate exclusively in digital mode, send at much higher speeds and handle colour as well.

Federal Communications Commission (FCC)

→ The Federal Communications Commission is the agency that regulates broadcasting and telecommunications in the United States. The FCC's mandate derives from the *Communications Act* of 1934, under which the agency licenses broadcasting stations, regulates interstate and international radio communication, and supervises telephone companies and other common carriers, like satellite operators.

Feed

→ TV term referring to a transmitted signal fed from one location to another, often by satellite. Feeds may be programming in finished form or rough material that needs to be edited and packaged for broadcast.

Fibre Optics

→ Fibre optic technology conveys information in the form of laser light along thin fibres or threads of glass. This technology allows for a huge increase in carrying capacity over conventional technologies like copper wire. The signals carried over fibre optics also require far less frequent amplification. A single fibre can carry the equivalent of 100,000 telephone conversations. Even greater carrying capacity can be achieved by bundling multiple fibres into larger cables. In many applications, these cables can replace traditional copper wire and coaxial cable.

Because of its remarkable technical properties, fibre optics has been touted in many quarters as the ideal medium for a nation-wide broadband network to carry data of all kinds, including video. For just as long, debate has raged over the costs of such a network, since fibre optic technology is still relatively expensive. One crucial factor in assessing its cost is determining just how close fibre optic lines should be brought to individual homes.

While both telephone and cable companies have deployed thousands of kilometres of fibre optic cable over the past several years, most of it has been used for main trunk lines or as part of field trials. In the United States, Time Warner's New York City Cable Group has built hybrid fibre and coaxial networks as part of its 150-channel systems in Queens. In Canada, Rogers Cablesystems has deployed a substantial amount of fibre in its Toronto-area networks. In June 1992, Rogers and IBM Canada began testing the highest capacity fibre optic connection in Canada, an experimental facility that can move data at the rate of one gigabit per second, i.e. one billion binary digits per second — the equivalent of moving over 62,000 pages of text every second. See Units.

Financial Interest and Syndication (FinSyn) Rules

→ Rules adopted by the FCC in 1970 (along with the primetime access rules) in response to the vast market power of the U.S. networks. Though applying only to entertainment (not news) programming, the rules essentially limited the number of program hours that a network can produce itself and prevented the networks from owning syndication interests in shows that they broadcast.

The current rules permit the networks to assume a financial interest in all their non-primetime programs. Furthermore, the networks are allowed full financial interest and syndication rights in 40% of their primetime lineup, but are required to meet certain conditions before they can take an interest in the remaining 60%.

Even these much diluted rules are being disputed in court. The networks argue that the rules should be rescinded completely on the grounds that they are unnecessary and unconstitutional, given the decline of the power of the networks during the eighties. The Hollywood majors and independent producers, whose livelihoods are at stake, want to see some form of restriction maintained. For successful shows, the stakes are high. The *Cosby* show, for example, has already earned over $800 million from worldwide syndication.

Footprint

→ The geographic area covered by the transmission from a communications satellite. The area involved is typically very large. The AsiaSat I satellite, for example, which broadcasts the Star Channel service based in Hong Kong, covers 38 countries from the Middle East to the Pacific Rim, an area containing about 50% of the world's population.

Fragmentation

→ The breakup of the available audience for television into smaller and smaller sub-audiences as the number of channels and services on offer expands. The greater the number of channels, the lower the potential audience for any one channel.

The growth in the number of channels and services available to Canadians has far outstripped the growth in population or total viewing hours devoted to television. Audience fragmentation poses serious financial problems for commercial broadcasters, whose revenues depend on the size of the audiences for their programs.

Frequency

→ The number of waves or oscillations per unit of time. For purposes of electronics, expressed in cycles per second or Hertz. See Units.

HDTV

→ High Definition Television. HDTV is one of a family of emerging TV systems known generically as Advanced Television (ATV). While most are still in the experimental or prototype stage, their essential purpose is to provide a far more detailed and accurate picture display than is possible with existing TV systems, including the current NTSC standard used in North America.

Two other important innovations will probably go hand-in-hand with the superior picture quality offered by HDTV. One involves the aspect ratio of the screen, i.e. the ratio of width to height. Whereas the current aspect ratio is 4-to-3, the proposed standard for HDTV is 16-to-9. The other involves the likely changeover from analog to digital processing. The widespread deployment of digital TV is the most significant feature that advanced television could introduce to the home. The digitization of many or all TV set functions in North America will bring the home receiver a giant step closer to "smart-TV" technology.

Headend

→ This is the installation where television signals are received by cable companies from outside sources like satellites and terrestrial transmitters.

Hertz

→ The basic unit of frequency is the Hertz, which equals one cycle per second (cps). The electrical current that comes out of a wall socket in Canada is 60Hz (it alternates at a rate of 60 times per second.) Hertz was the first researcher to identify electromagnetic radiation in the late 19th century.

One kilohertz (also written 1 kHz) equals 1,000 Hertz (or cps); one megahertz (1 MHz) equals 1 million Hertz; and one gigahertz (1 GHz) equals 1 billion or 109 Hertz. Thus, a one MHz wave oscillates a million times a second and is 300 metres from crest to crest (because one million Hertz times 300 metres equals the speed of light). See Units.

Integrated Circuits

→ See Chips.

Independents

→ Either local TV stations that are not affiliated with a network, or production companies that are not owned by a broadcaster or major film studio.

Interactivity

→ As it is commonly understood, interactivity denotes a service or system that allows the user to interact with the service provider by sending back messages, instructions or choices. In television, interactivity is usually a misnomer for "selectivity", since most so-called interactive services and channels do nothing more than provide the user a limited selection of options from which to choose. This limitation is partly a function of content: conventional material like entertainment programming doesn't lend itself well to interactivity. It's also a function of technology, since neither over-the-air broadcasting nor cable transmission is designed for two-way communications.

The interactive device par excellence is the telephone and truly interactive services have until recently been confined to videotex and other on-line services that combine the functions of a computer, a display or monitor and a telephone line, accessed through a modem.

In early 1992, the FCC set aside a portion of spectrum for use by providers of interactive video and data services (known as IVDS) and has called for applications from interested parties. See Multimedia.

ISDN

→ Integrated Services Digital Network. An international telecommunications standard that allows simultaneous transmission of voice, video and data at relatively high speed.

Ku-Band

→ See Satellites.

Laser

→ Acronym for **L**ight **A**mplification by **S**timulated **E**mission of **R**adiation. There are many different kinds of lasers. Lasers are beams of radiation with special properties created in a source material such as a crystal or gas, which is excited or stimulated by a process such as the injection of electrons. The source material emits waves or particles that are concentrated and amplified by feedback and other techniques. The resulting radiation is sometimes part of the visible light spectrum, but may also be infrared or ultraviolet light.

Many different applications have been developed for lasers. The best known of these in the field of home entertainment is the compact disc, in addition to other optical recording and playback technologies, which are optical by virtue of their use of laser beams to read the digital information encoded on the disc. The purity and coherence of the laser beam allow it to be focused over the microscopically small surface pits that encode CD information.

Liquid Crystal Display (LCD)

→ This is the display technology used on most digital watches, pocket calculators and now on portable computers. It is also the technology that will probably allow large flat screens to be developed for HDTV applications.

Magnetic, Magneto-Optical

→ See Storage Media.

Major (noun)

→ One of the large, well-established Hollywood film studios, most of which have their own production facilities, libraries of film titles, distribution arms and access to large pools of capital to allow them to underwrite the production of films and TV programs by "independents".

Membership and ownership of the group have both changed in recent years. As of late 1992, the Hollywood majors are seven in number: Disney/Buena Vista (owned by the Walt Disney Company); Columbia Pictures (purchased in 1989 by Japan's Sony Corp.); MGM/UA Communications; Paramount (owned by Paramount Communications, formerly by Gulf + Western); Twentieth-Century Fox (owned by Rupert Murdoch's News Corp.); Warner Bros (owned by Time Warner); and Universal-MCA (purchased in 1990 by Japan's Matsushita).

Microprocessor

→ A small, integrated circuit. A microprocessor forms the heart of desktop computers.

Microwave

→ Microwaves constitute part of the electromagnetic spectrum, ranging from the upper portion of the VHF (very high frequency) band, to the middle of the EHF (extremely high frequency) band. In numbers, microwaves cover 225 MHz to 100 GHz (see Units). These high frequency waves (whose wavelengths are correspondingly small, many measuring only centimetres) are suitable for the transmission of over-the-air TV signals and satellite signals, as well as being utilized by common carriers for the transmission of other types of data over terrestrial links. And yes, they also cook your TV dinners in those ovens.

Modem

→ Contraction of "*mo*dulator-*dem*odulator". While a modem is generally any device that modulates signals to adapt them for use in two different types of equipment, the term refers most commonly to the device that allows computers to communicate over telephone lines. What modems do, among other things, is translate the digital information fed to it by a computer into analog information that can be transmitted over ordinary telephone lines; at the receiving end, they reverse the process.

This device has enabled the spread of electronic mail, computer bulletin boards and many types of videotex services. Modems operate at different speeds, expressed as their baud rate. In 1992, the home and office standard is moving to 9600 baud. One great advantage of modems over fax machines is that data sent by modem is dumped directly into computer memory in digital form and can be manipulated without any intervening steps.

Modulation

→ The method by which information is superimposed or impressed on a carrier wave. In a general sense, modulation is the technique that allows audio or video information from an input source to be superimposed on a wave or signal to carry out some task, such as transmission of the information over the air to receiving sets (radios and TVs).

MS DOS

→ See Operating Systems.

Multimedia

→ "Multimedia" is a term with wide, rather vague applications. Generally it refers to the communication of messages or information through the combined use of text, graphics, animation, audio and motion video.

Of course all of these "media" can be utilized by ordinary TV sets. Rock concerts and boardroom presentations could also lay claim to providing a multimedia experience. In the narrower modern sense, multimedia goes hand in hand with another basic concept of the new technologies — interactivity.

That's where computers enter the picture. Multimedia has come to mean more than just the convergence of voice, music, alphanumeric text and so on. It also implies that the user has some degree of interactive control over these elements, instead of being merely a passive viewer, as with broadcast TV. The elements had all been in place for years, but not in *one* place.

What happened eventually was computer engineers began figuring out how to take advantage of the soaring increase in the power of desktop computers to process and reproduce the sights and sounds normally associated with home entertainment products. The most difficult hurdle to overcome was (and in 1992 still is) how to handle full-motion, full-screen, colour video, so that the image looks like what we're used to from TV.

The marriage, or at least engagement, of the computer and the TV has given rise to a whole new industry devoted to interactive multimedia. The devices involved range from systems that integrate established technologies, like computer, touchscreen TV and laserdisc, to entirely new products like Philips Compact Disc Interactive.

In a broader perspective, "multimedia" is a synonym for convergence. Thus, any product, system, venture, agreement or technology that brings together components of more than one previously distinct sector of the media industry — be it publishing and computers or television and computers or film, graphics and text — can be described as "multimedia". IBM and Time Warner are discussing a venture whereby Time Warner would utilize IBM's intelligent networking equipment to offer radically new multimedia services to its cable subscribers. This would be "multimedia" in the sense that it brings together the telephone, cable transmission, computer and television set.

Multiple Systems Operator (MSO)

→ A company that owns and operates more than one cable television system.

Multiplexing

→ Multiplexing is the combining of two or more distinct signals on one channel or frequency.

Multipoint Distribution System (MDS)

→ Sometimes referred to as MMDS, for "Multipoint *Multichannel* Distribution Sytem". This is a wireless distribution technology whose basic function is similar to that of cable distribution — to package a number of channels and services and distribute them to local subscribers for a fee, only using microwave transmission instead of cables.

A number of such systems are operating in the United States in competition with established cable systems. MDS has certain constraints, such as the need for proprietary antennas and receivers and line-of-sight transmission. But it has the corresponding advantage of doing away with the need to build a cable network linking subscriber homes to the operator's headend, a lengthy and expensive process.

Narrowcasting

→ A television service that differs from broadcasting in one or more ways having to do with content, audience or technology. The concept is associated with pay and specialty channels, which were introduced in the United States in the 1970s and in Canada in 1983.

Narrowcast or specialty channels usually provide only one type of programming, rather than the general interest programming offered by conventional broadcasters. Some, however, provide fairly general programming but for a specialized audience, as is the case with ethnic services such as Chinavision and Telelatino. Finally, all such services tend to be "narrow-cast" in the sense that they are not transmitted over the air, but rather made available for a fee to cable subscribers or some other sub-group of the general television audience.

Network

→ A group of television stations located in different geographic areas, either owned by or affiliated with the same company. The stations usually air the same programming at the same time, especially during prime time.

See also Affiliate and Broadcasting Undertakings.

NTSC Standard

→ Refers to National Television Systems Committee, the body which developed the transmission and reception standards for television broadcasting in the United States, a standard subsequently adopted in several other territories, including Canada. (Broadcast engineers will tell you NTSC stands for Never Twice the Same Colour.)

Two other major TV standards are in use in Europe and elsewhere. These are the PAL system (for "Phase Alternation Line") and SECAM (for SEquential Couleur À Mémoire). The three systems are incompatible, because they set different specifications for the number of lines of scanning to be used, how colour and brightness information is carried, how colour broadcasts are made receivable on black-and-white sets and so on.

Optical Media

→ See Storage Media.

PAL Standard

→ The PAL system (for "Phase Alternation Line") is the transmission and reception standard for television broadcasting in the United Kingdom. It mandates 625 lines of scanning. See NTSC.

Pay-per-view

→ Pay-per-view (PPV) services offer programs for viewing to subscribers — up till now, mostly cable subscribers — on a one-shot basis. Viewers can pay to watch a particular movie or event such as a prizefight or rock concert. In Eastern Canada, PPV selections are available on participating cable systems from Viewer's Choice Canada.

Pay-TV

→ Pay-TV is a channel or service that subscribers pay for by the month, which gives them the privilege of watching everything offered on the channel in question. These are typically movie channels, like First Choice, which are discretionary (purchased separately from basic cable) and scrambled.

People Meters

→ Electronic audience measurement devices, distinguished from the manual or diary method of recording TV viewing. Meters are installed in sample homes by audience measurement firms. They consist of a small processor that keeps track of what channel each set in the home is tuned to and for how long, as well as a modem that sends the accumulated data over the telephone line to a computer at a central collection point.

While they are far more accurate in terms of monitoring activity in the set itself, meters have always presented the problem of how to measure the people watching as well as the channels tuned. Over the last few years, various methods have been devised to do so. Some of these have depended on the initiative of the participating viewers, who were required to push their personal button on the meter at the start and end of a viewing session. More recent and sophisticated technologies, such as one developed by A.C. Nielsen in the United States, would use an infrared scanning device to identify who is in the room.

Peripheral

→ A device that attaches externally to a computer, like a printer or scanner. Home TV sets had no equivalent devices to attach to them until the advent of cable and VCRs in the 1970s. Many contemporary high-end TV sets are essentially just display monitors, sold with separate components like a tuner-receiver and speakers. If the set is being operated from a separate tuner or VCR, it could be argued that the TV display itself has become the peripheral.

Phosphors

→ The inside of a cathode ray or picture tube is coated with phosphors. When an electron beam hits the phosphor it glows, thereby creating the image on the screen.

Pixel

→ Short for picture element, the little dots of light that make up the picture on a television or computer screen. The greater the number of dots or pixels, the higher the resolution.

Prime Time

→ The peak evening TV viewing period. The CRTC's regulatory definition of prime time, for purposes of Canadian content requirements, is 6:00 pm to midnight. This definition allows private broadcasters to concentrate Canadian programming, especially news, in the fringe periods from 6:00 to 7:00 pm and 11:00 pm to midnight, when far fewer people are watching than in the 7:00 to 11:00 period. By doing so, broadcasters are able to concentrate the more profitable American entertainment programming in the periods of heaviest viewing.

Production Values

→ A loose category of attributes used to describe the creative and technical polish of a movie or TV program. These attributes include the calibre and drawing power of the actors, the novelty and complexity of special effects, the quality of the cinematography and music or sound track, the use of stunts and so on. High or good production values need talent. But they are even more dependent on money. Movies made by Hollywood's major studios tend to have the highest budgets and the highest production values. Production values are mostly about execution and don't necessarily have anything to do with the quality of writing for the screen.

Programming Undertaking

→ See Broadcasting Undertaking.

Public Switched Telephone Network

→ Often referred to as the PSTN. The network that provides POTS, or plain old telephone service, as well as more and more intelligent functions, like voice mail, caller recognition and so on. The two key concepts here are "public" and "switched". The PSTN is public because regulation requires that any member of the public can become a telephone subscriber at published rates and send messages without interference from the carrier. The PSTN is switched, meaning that any subscriber can reach any other subscriber simply by dialing. Compare this capability with cable networks, which even in interactive systems are only designed to carry messages between individual subscribers and the cable operator's headend.

RAM

→ Acronym for Random Access Memory. This is the area in a computer where programs and data are stored temporarily while they are in use. RAM is known as "volatile" memory since all data stored in it vanishes the instant it loses power.

Rating

→ See Audience Measurement.

Reach

→ See Audience Measurement.

Real Time

→ A computer-related term, used of an event or process that takes place "on the fly" and at random, rather than in a preprogrammed fashion. For example, a computer that can digitize a video signal in real time will produce the digital output on the screen as quickly as the analog signal is fed in for processing.

ROM

→ Acronym for Read Only Memory. This is an area of computer processors which provide storage that is permanent and cannot be altered by the end-user, unlike RAM, hard drives and floppy disks. ROM is used to store basic instructions needed by the processor for handling applications.

Satellites

→ Most communications satellites in commercial use are of the geostationary type, meaning they appear to be in a fixed location about 36,000 km above the equator. Their purpose is to receive transmitted signals from an uplink site, which may be telephone calls or TV feeds, and retransmit them to a downlink site in some other location. Satellites perform these functions using a transponder, which is a combination receiver-transmitter.

Different types of satellites are designed to operate in different frequency ranges. The two most common types in use in North America are those operating in the C band, which is the 6/4 GHz frequency and those operating in the Ku band, which is the 14/12 GHz frequency. The C band is still the most common type of satellite in use for TV broadcasting in North America. The "6 GHz" in the "6/4" designation refers to the carrier frequency used to uplink signals; "4 GHz" refers to the downlink frequency. They have to be different so the two signals don't interfere with each other.

Satellites were not originally designed to send their signals directly to private homes, and for many years Canadian law prohibited the operation of private satellite reception by individuals. More recently, however, satellite technology and services have been conceived to provide programming not just to cable headends or broadcasters, but directly to viewer homes. Those that do so are known generically as direct-to-home (DTH) satellites.

Direct broadcast satellites (DBS) will offer service packages directly to paying subscribers. They are often distinguished from DTH satellites by the fact that they operate with a higher power rating, which allows for smaller receiving dishes.

Satellite Master Antenna Television (SMATV)

→ A privately operated cable system whereby signals are taken down from satellites by a large dish antenna, then distributed to a limited number of subscribers. The most typical application is in large apartment blocks.

Scrambling

→ The practice of making an electronic signal carrying TV programming unintelligible, except to viewers equipped with suitable descrambling equipment, by means of a secret electronic "key". The purpose is to protect distributor revenue by ensuring that anyone who gets a clear signal has paid for the privilege. Also known as encryption.

SECAM Standard

→ SECAM (for Sequential Couleur À Mémoire) is the standard for television transmission in France. See NTSC.

Share

→ See Audience Measurement.

Signal Processing

→ Signal processing refers to changes effected to electrical signals by devices such as amplifiers, TV sets and the like, in order to convey information or execute some task.

Smart-TV

→ A reference to the increasing ability of domestic TV receivers to perform functions beyond the passive reproduction of sounds and images. These more advanced functions almost all depend on the introduction of digital circuitry into modern receivers. These functions include the ability to suppress picture noise and correct other errors or interference automatically. Another involves the ability to process special effects like picture in a picture, frame storage, and programmable features like channel selection and clock functions.

Software

→ In its original usage, software referred to the programs written for computers, including both software packages (like word processors) and data (like text and graphics files). In a more recent coinage, "software" has become a generic term for entertainment properties — the content of movies, TV shows, video games, sound recordings and so on.

Specialty Channel

→ A special interest channel usually available only by cable. See Narrowcasting.

Spectrum, Spectrum Scarcity

→ See Electromagnetic Spectrum.

Storage Media

→ Two principal kinds of storage media are in use in the consumer electronics and computer industries: magnetic and optical. Their purpose is to provide a convenient method for recording and retrieving both entertainment program material like music and data processing material of the kind used in computers. The distinction between these two types of information is becoming more and more blurred. Moreover, both magnetic and optical systems are capable of storing information in either analog or digital form.

Magnetic storage media include audio and video tape on the one hand, and computer disks on the other. Optical storage media include compact discs, the larger discs known as laserdiscs used for movies and a host of other disc-based technologies that use laser light to retrieve and reproduce information. A hybrid technology known as magneto-optical has been developed by several manufacturers to allow end-users to re-record on discs, a feature previously unattainable with CD technology.

Superstation

→ A conventional broadcast television station (normally one operating in the UHF range) that is distributed by satellite and made available to a national or international audience through participating cable systems.

This was a concept invented by Ted Turner, whose superstation, WTBS, based in Atlanta, reaches the largest audience of its kind — some 58 million American TV homes. Several other American stations are currently distributed on this basis, including some, like WGN Chicago, which are available to Canadian cable subscribers.

Syndication

→ Sale of a television series, movie or individual entertainment program to different broadcasters. This applies to shows that have been aired on a network in a first and sometimes second run, before being made available at much lower cost to independent stations or network affiliates. Producers of TV programming do not usually begin to recoup their full production costs until a show is in syndication.

A series that lasts more then three seasons on a network will have significant value for the syndication market. Local television stations and cable systems will be able to obtain enough episodes to "strip" the program into scheduled daily runs over a period of at least several months.

Some programs, such as game shows, are produced specifically for syndication. This is known as first run syndication.

Telefilm Canada

→ A Crown Corporation whose mandate is to develop and promote Canada's film, television and video industries. Originally called The Canadian Film Development Corporation, Telefilm provides financial assistance through various Funds: the Canadian Broadcast Program Development Fund, created in 1983 to promote the production by independent Canadian producers of television programs; the Feature Film Fund, created in 1986 to stimulate investment in the production and distribution of feature films; the Feature Film Distribution Fund, established in 1988 to promote the Canadian distribution sector and the Special Production Fund, established in 1991 to assist Canadian television programs and films.

Telefilm also administers Canada's co-production treaties.

Teletext

→ In its basic form, teletext is a one-way data retrieval system in which pages of alphanumeric information are sent from a host computer to a TV receiver as part of a broadcast signal, normally using the vertical blanking interval or

VBI. A special decoder is required to capture and store particular pages of information.

Canadian researchers pioneered the development of a system known as Telidon, first announced in 1978, which incorporated a special coding scheme known as NAPLPS (North American Presentation Level Protocol Syntax).

Tiering

→ The marketing of cable television in service packages comprising one or more channels each. Cable tiers are often differentiated by whether or not subscribers are charged for access to individual channels in the tiers. Thus, so-called basic tiers usually include a number of conventional off-air broadcast signals, while so-called discretionary tiers offer specialty and pay services.

In both Canada and the United States, cable tiering has a major impact on both how cable is regulated and how much subscribers pay for the television services they consume. In the 1990s, we are witnessing a trend towards "tiering up" — the push by cable operators to position their services on more and more selective tiers.

Time Shifting

→ Recording a broadcast program on a VCR in order to play it back at a later time.

Transponder

→ The part of a satellite that receives a signal, amplifies it, changes its frequency and transmits it back to earth.

Twisted Copper Pair

→ The transmission medium utilized by telephone companies. Consists of two insulated wires twisted together. Twisted copper pair has a much lower carrying capacity than coaxial cable, the transmission medium utilized by cable companies.

Ultra High Frequency (UHF)

→ A band of the electromagnetic spectrum over which television signals are transmitted.

Units

→ In broadcasting, and electronics generally, a host of units are used to measure the properties of electrical current and electromagnetic radiation, the intensity of light, as well as the more mundane concepts of mass, length and time.

One of the most common yet potentially confusing usages concerns the prefixes kilo-, mega- and giga-. They are applied to the frequencies and frequency bands that make up the electromagnetic spectrum. "Kilo" means thousand, "mega" means million and "giga" means billion (i.e. a thousand million). The basic unit of frequency is the Hertz, which equals one cycle or oscillation per second.

One kilohertz (also written 1 kHz) equals 1,000 Hertz (or cps); one megahertz (1 MHz) equals 1,000,000 Hertz; and one gigahertz (1 GHz) equals 1,000,000,000 or 10^9 Hertz. Thus, a one MHz wave oscillates a million times a second and by definition is 300 metres from crest to crest (because one million Hertz times 300 metres equals the speed of light).

These same Greek prefixes are also applied to the units used in computing. The numbering scheme used above is decimal, i.e. based on "10". But the system used for binary computers is based on "2". Whereas 1 kHz can be expressed as 10^3, the computing unit for

1,000 bytes is equivalent to 2^{10}, which is 1,024 bytes. The same idea applies to higher units, namely mega- and giga-, as well as to bits. Strictly speaking, then, one megabyte (1 MB) does not equal one million bytes but 2^{20} or 1,048,576 bytes. The use of the binary system or 2-base also explains why so many computer specifications are given in multiples of 2: 8, 16, 32, 64, etc.

Vertical Blanking Interval (VBI)

→ A portion of the broadcast television signal during which TV receivers "blank" the electron stream that creates the image on the screen. Under the NTSC broadcast system, a predetermined number of lines of scanning (21) go blank so that the electron stream from the cathode ray gun does not interfere with the formation of the image on the screen as it returns from the bottom to the top of the screen to begin another scan.

The VBI has uses above and beyond the transmission of the TV picture. Like a spare compartment or holding tank, it can carry coded information of various kinds, such as teletext, closed captioning and other alphanumeric data.

Very High Frequency (VHF)

→ A band of the electromagnetic spectrum over which television signals are transmitted.

Video Dial Tone

→ The provision of video services over the public switched telephone network. Actual implementation will require the combining of large amounts of system carrying capacity (i.e. enough bandwidth to handle video), with the switched network employed by the telephone system, which would allow dial-up access for individual subscribers to the video services in question.

The concept of video dial tone was first popularized in 1991 by the Federal Communications Commission, when it issued a notice of proposed rule-making that would allow American telephone companies to provide video services in competition with the cable industry. In July 1992, the FCC decided unanimously to call for the development of VDT proposals from American telephone companies.

Video On Demand (VOD)

→ Video on Demand is an entertainment service to the home that is still on the drawing board. Such a service would allow viewers to dial up or place an electronic order for a particular movie or event directly from home through a cable or telephone network. A central repository would then transmit, or download, the movie or event immediately.

Some North American cable systems currently offer approximations of VOD, often referred to as "near video on demand". This includes PPV services. The idea behind pay-per-view services is to allow cable subscribers some freedom of choice in selecting the start time for movies or programs in which they are interested. On Viewer's Choice Canada (VCC), movies are made available on four different dedicated cable channels. On any given day, a particular movie may be available for viewing from two to six different times. As cable systems increase their channel capacity and two-way interactivity becomes technically feasible, services such as VCC will offer more and more start times, getting the system nearer and nearer to true video on demand.

Videotex

→ Videotex services have a number of things in common with teletext services. Both allow users to call up information on a TV screen sent by some communications link from a distant source.

Videotex systems make use of two-way links such as telephone circuits. This facility allows users to send individualized information back to the data source and thus to engage in interactive tasks such as banking.

One of the most widely deployed videotex systems is France's Minitel. Many other videotex systems have been launched, with varying degrees of commercial success, in England, the United States and Canada. Widespread consumer acceptance of these systems has been seriously hampered over the years by hardware and operating costs; the difficulties in finding attractive third party services; and perhaps most of all, by issues of user-friendliness.

Virtual Reality (VR)

→ A set of technologies that simulates environments or sensory experiences. Its two most distinctive features are the ability of a simulated VR environment to change in real time in response to the gestures of the participant (like turning the head); and the vividness and believability of the audio and video constructs that make up the environment. A forerunner of VR was the flight simulator, which drew on high-powered computers to have instruments, movements and perspectives in a training cockpit change in response to the actions of the operator-pilot.

Window

→ A colloquialism used in the entertainment industry to refer to the various distribution or release outlets for movies. In North America, movies get released in a hierarchical way in order to maximize revenues. The various windows in question include theatrical (i.e. movie houses), home video, pay-per-view, pay-TV and broadcast TV. The marketplace will be further shaken up in the 1990s as relatively recent windows, like pay-per-view, continue to encroach on both theatrical and broadcast distribution.

Zapping

→ The use of a remote control to skip from program to program usually to avoid commercials and other unwanted program material.

Zipping

→ The use of a remote control to fast-forward through the commercial messages in a broadcast program recorded on a VCR.

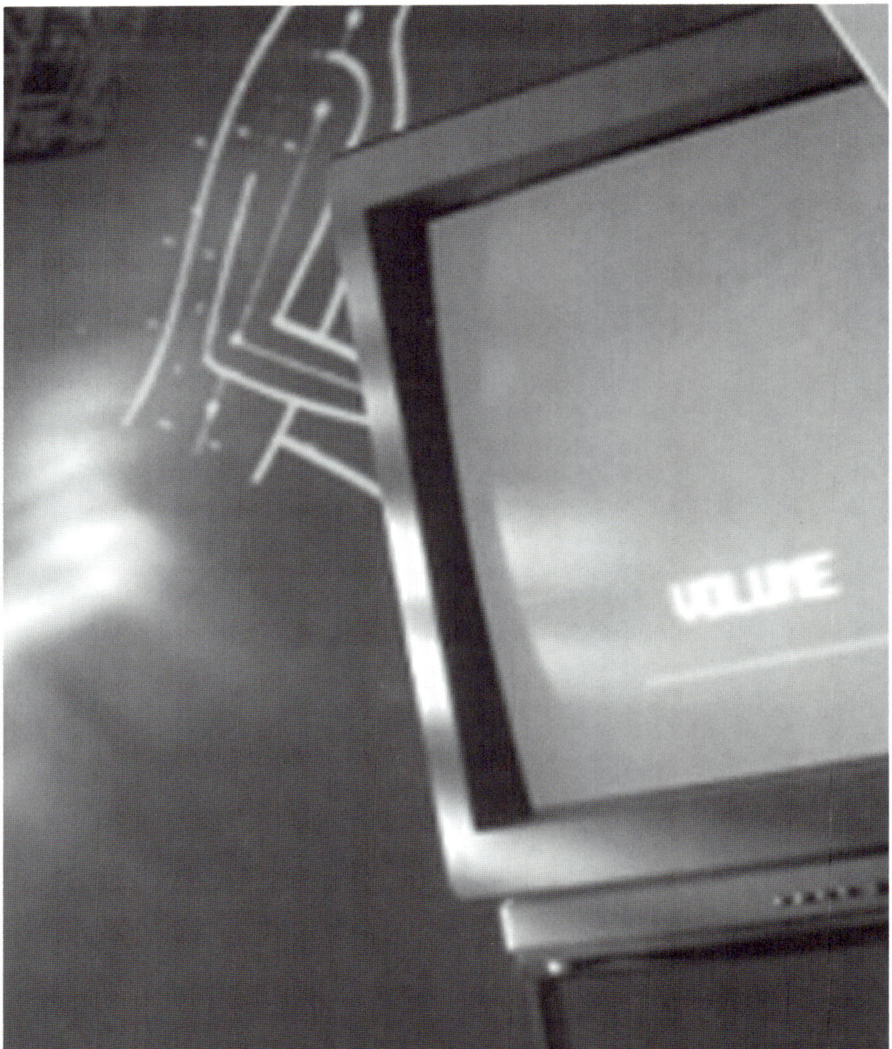
VOLUME

Bibliography

Books

Auletta, Ken. *Three Blind Mice: How the TV Networks Lost Their Way.* New York: Random House, 1991.

Babe, Robert E. *Telecommunications in Canada.* Toronto: University of Toronto Press, 1990.

Balio, Tino, ed. *Hollywood in the Age of Television.* Boston: Unwin Hyman, 1990.

Barwise, Patrick and Andrew Ehrenberg. *Television and its Audience.* London: Sage Publications, 1988.

Bird, Roger, ed. *Documents of Canadian Broadcasting.* Ottawa: Carleton University Press, 1988.

Broadcasting Research Unit. *Quality in Television: Programmes, Programme-makers, Systems.* London: John Libbey, 1989.

Caron, André H. and Pierre Juneau, eds. *Le défi des télévisions nationales à l'ère de la mondialisation.* Montréal: Les Presses de l'Université de Montréal, 1992.

de Sola Pool, Ithiel. *Technologies of Freedom.* Cambridge: Harvard University Press, 1983.

Ellis, David. *Networking: How Are Canada's English TV Networks Performing?* Toronto: Friends of Canadian Broadcasting, 1991.

Gilder, George. *Microcosm.* New York: Touchstone, 1989.

Grant, Peter S. *The Annotated 1991 Broadcasting Act.* Toronto: McCarthy Tétrault, 1991.

Hardin, Herschel. *Closed Circuits: The Sellout of Canadian Television.* Toronto: Douglas & McIntyre, 1985.

Hilmes, Michele. *Hollywood and Broadcasting: From Radio to Cable.* Chicago: University of Illinois Press, 1990.

Hoskins, Colin and Stuart McFadyen. *Canadian Broadcasting: The Challenge of Change.* Edmonton: University of Alberta Press, 1975.

Keirstead, Phillip, O. and Sonia-Kay Keirstead. *The World of Telecommunication: Introduction to Broadcasting, Cable, and New Technologies.* Boston: Focal Press, 1990.

Kubey, Robert and Mihaly Csikszentmihalyi. *Television and the Quality of Life: How Viewing Shapes Everyday Experience.* Hillsdale, NJ: Lawrence Erlbaum Associates, 1990.

Levy, Mark, ed. *The VCR Age: Home Video and Mass Communication.* Newbury Park, CA: Sage Publications, 1989.

MacDonald, J. Fred. *One Nation Under Television.* Toronto: Random House, 1990.

Mirabito, Michael M. and Barbara L. Morgenstern. *The New Communications Technologies.* Boston: Focal Press, 1990.

Pendakur, Manjunath. *Canadian Dreams & American Control: The Political Economy of the Canadian Film Industry.* Toronto: Garamond Press, 1990.

Vogel, Harold L. *Entertainment Industry Economics: A Guide for Financial Analysis.* 2nd ed. New York: Cambridge University Press, 1990.

Wilson, Kevin G. *Technologies of Control: The New Interactive Media for the Home.* Madison, WI: University of Wisconsin Press, 1988.

Young, E.C. *The New Penguin Dictionary of Electronics.* 2nd ed. Markham, Ont.: Penguin Books, 1988.

Reports and Unpublished Papers

Canada. Canadian Radio-television and Telecommunications Commission. [Therrien] Committee on Extension of Service to Northern and Remote Communities. *The 1980s: A Decade of Diversity: Broadcasting, Satellites and Pay-TV,* July 1980.

——— Department of Communications. *Report of the Task Force on Broadcasting Policy* [Caplan-Sauvageau]. Ottawa: Minister of Supply and Services, September 1986.

——— Department of Communications. *Report of the Film Industry Task Force* [Roth]. Ottawa: Minister of Supply and Services, November 1985.

——— Department of Communications. *Report of the Federal Cultural Policy Review Committee* [Applebaum-Hébert]. Ottawa: Minister of Supply and Services, November 1982.

——— Department of Communications. *Report of the Consultative Committee on the Implications of Telecommunications for Canadian Sovereignty* [Clyne]. Ottawa: Minister of Supply and Services, March 1979.

——— Statistics Canada. *Household Facilities and Equipment*. Catalogue 64-202, 1991.

Canadian Cable Television Association. *A Clear Vision*, 1992.

Caron, André et al. *A Study on the Uses of a New Interactive Technology: the Videoway System*. Montreal: New Technologies Research Laboratory, University of Montreal, June 1992.

CBC Research. *How People Use Television: A Review of TV Viewing Habits*. December 1991.

Grant, Peter S. "CRTC jurisdiction over the activities of Skypix, Aladdin and their agents or associates in Canada". Unpublished opinion, October 4, 1991.

Groupe Secor. *Evaluation of Telefilm Canada Feature Film Fund*. Prepared for Telefilm Canada, May 31, 1991.

Houle, Michel and Paul Audley & Associates. *Study of the Revenues Earned by Canadian Productions — Feature Films*. Prepared for Telefilm Canada, September 1990.

National Cable Television Association. *Cable Television Developments*. Washington: May 1992.

Neuman, W. Russell. "The Technological Convergence: Television Networks and Telephone Networks." Prepared for The Aspen Institute Program on Communications and Society. *Television for the 21st Century: The Next Wave*, January, 1992.

NGL Consulting. *Evaluation of the Feature Film Distribution Fund*. Prepared for Telefilm Canada. March 1992.

——— *Potential Market for U.S. DBS in Canada*. Prepared for the Canadian Association of Broadcasters, June 1992.

Pepper, Robert M. *Through the Looking Glass: Integrated Broadband Networks, Regulatory Policy and Institutional Change*. OPP Working Paper Series, 24. Federal Communications Commission, Washington: November 1988.

Reuben-Cooke, Wilhelmina. "Television in the 21st Century: Rethinking Legal and Policy Paradigms." Prepared for The Aspen Institute Program on Communications and Society. *Television for the 21st Century: The Next Wave*, January, 1992.

Roman, Andrew J. "Comments on Paper by C. Christopher Johnston Re: CRTC Regulation of Foreign Direct-to-Home Programming Services." Paper prepared for *New Developments in Canadian Communications Law and Policy: A National Symposium*. Toronto: April 1992.

Setzer, Florence and Jonathan Levy. *Broadcast Television in a Multichannel Marketplace.* OPP Working Paper Series, 26. Federal Communications Commission, Washington: June 1991.

ARTICLES

Alpert, Mark. "CD-ROM: The Next PC Revolution." *Fortune*, June 29, 1992.

Anson-Cartwright, Sarah. "So Many Good Projects." *Playback*, June 22, 1992.

Austin, Bruce A. "Home Video: The Second-Run 'Theater' of the 1990s." In Balio 1990.

Ayscough, Suzan. "Astral, WB Pact to Satisfy Quotas." *Variety*, July 13, 1992.

"Cable bill looks less relevant than ever as veto backers hit stride." *The Cable-Telco Report*, August 1992.

Caruso, Denise. "New Consumer Devices are Coming." *Digital Media*, July 22, 1992.

Chilton, D.P. "Newell Blasts Diary Method." *Strategy*, April 20, 1992.

" 'Consumer' HDTV Displays Appear." *Video Technology News*, April 1, 1991.

Dempsey, John. "Rookie Webs Ante Up in Cable Space Race." *Variety*, August 17, 1992.

Flaherty, David. *Consumer Insight*. April 1992.

Fleming, Charles and Kevin Zimmerman. "Cross-Media Megadeals Stoke the Synergists." *Variety*, February 10, 1992.

Flint, Joe. "HDTV: Too Close for Comfort?" *Broadcasting*. April 13, 1992.

"Frox Introduces Interactive Home Theater." *Multimedia & Videodisc Monitor*, October, 1991.

Gilder, George. "Now or Never." *Forbes*, October 14, 1991.

"Guide to the Gear." *Consumer Reports*, March 1992.

Hendren, Gord. "Event Marketing Research." *Strategy*, October 19, 1992.

Janisch, Hudson. "Bora Laskin and Administrative Law: An Unfinished Journey." (1985) 35 *University of Toronto Law Journal 557*.

Larson, Erik. "Watching Americans Watch TV." *The Atlantic*, March 1992.

Mazurkewich, Karen. "Many Films Find Home on Video." *Playback*, September 16, 1991.

Morgan, Joanne. "Forum: Cancon debate." *Playback*, October 12, 1992.

Partridge, John. "Zapping the Messenger." *The Globe and Mail*, December 17, 1991.

Roberts, Johnnie et al. "Age of Interactive TV May be Nearing as IBM and Warner Talk Deal." *The Wall Street Journal*, May 21, 1992.

Spence, Michael and Bruce Owen. "Television Programming, Monopolistic Competition, and Welfare." *Quarterly Journal of Economics*, February 1977.

"Television's Future, a Space Odyssey." *The Globe and Mail*, November 18, 1991.

Time Warner, *Annual Report*, 1990.

Video Innovations, June 1992.

Waldman, Steven. "Freedom's just another word for much too much to choose." *The Globe and Mail*, January 25, 1992.

Weber, Jonathan. "In Search of Computing's Holy Grail." *Los Angeles Times*, September 27, 1992.

Wharton, Dennis. "Telcos Admitted into Cable Club." *Variety*, July 20, 1992.

"Zapping concerns downplayed." *Playback Strategy*, April 8, 1991.

Endnotes

1. This is not a new problem. As far back as 1965, researchers using a device called the Dynascope — a stop-action camera that photographed the viewer and the screen every 15 seconds — revealed that "19% of the time the TV played to an empty room. For another 21% of the time, someone was present but so involved in something else that he or she didn't see the screen" (Larson, p.68). One can imagine what a problem this poses for both advertisers and audience research firms, whose people meters cannot yet distinguish whether a viewer is watching a program or sound asleep.

2. At the November 1992 convention of the Canadian Association of Broadcasters, pollster Angus Reid presented preliminary survey results suggesting that Canadians don't want more choice, but more quality. Reid carried out the national survey of Canadian cable subscribers on behalf of the CAB. In the event of a hypothetical increase in basic cable rates of 15 to 20%, respondents were asked what they would prefer to see done with the extra revenue. Some 62% said they would prefer to see improvements in the quality of existing channels — almost three times as many (23%) as said they would prefer more new channels.

3. The U.S. service, called "The Family Channel", is owned independently of the similar-sounding Canadian service, called simply, "Family Channel".

4. Some confusion exists over the use of the terms "DTH", for "direct-to-home" satellite services, versus "DBS", for "direct broadcast satellite" services. Even though they have somewhat different technical meanings, we use them interchangeably in this text. The important feature they have in common is transmission directly to viewers in the home, rather than to a redistribution source such as a cable headend.

5. The Hollywood majors and other rights holders still give preference to home video release over pay-per-view release in most markets (one exception is hotels). Yet *Variety* suggests (March 23, 1992) a significant shift may be in the offing:

> PPV funnels between 45¢ and 50¢ of every subscriber dollar into the pockets of the studios, compared

with only 20¢ of every videocassette dollar and 15¢ of every paycable dollar, according to a March 2 Goldman Sachs report.

6. Working within the context of commercial marketing research, the Yankee Group of Boston, Mass. has undertaken a number of studies around the concept of what they have dubbed "TAFs" or Technologically Advanced Families. These are families most inclined to be early adopters of new technologies for the home. The Yankee Group has found that only 15.7% of American families fall within their definition of TAFs.

7. The new definition of broadcasting is based on Recommendations 8, 9 and 10 of the *Sixth Report of the Standing Committee on Communications and Culture*, issued May 6, 1987. These in turn were based on recommendations made the previous year by the Caplan-Sauvageau Task Force on Broadcasting Policy. See Grant 1991.

8. The effects of importing American signals in the 1970s were offset somewhat by the introduction of two other policy measures: a 1975 tax measure known as Bill C-58, which disallows the deduction of advertising expenditures placed with foreign media like the U.S. border stations; and the 1976 simultaneous substitution regulations, which require that cable operators substitute a local TV signal for a distant one when they are more or less identical.

9. The unintended consequence of letting cable companies respond to perceived demand was not merely making more U.S. distant signals available to more Canadians. It was also ensuring that some viewers would be lost to Canadian programs and stations in favour of American ones. The Report of the Caplan-Sauvageau Task Force confirmed in 1986 (p.103) that households with cable watched more American programs than households without cable:

> The research data show among the effects of cable, that cable households watch far less CBC television than non-cable households [...] on the English side, roughly 19% as opposed to 31%, and on the French side, 32% versus 39%. Viewing of CTV and TVA also drops sharply in cable households.

The CBC's 1991 study, *How People Use Television*, drew similar conclusions. The CBC gets a disproportionate amount of its viewership from non-cabled households. Although non-cabled households (including non-television households) comprise 29% of total households, 36% of viewing time devoted to CBC English television is from non-cabled households (Anglophones 18+, 1990/91 Season, 6:00am – 2:00am).

This finding suggests that when presented with more American options, Canadian viewers will choose more of them. Audience research has also shown that when more Canadian options are made available, as has been the case since the mid-1980s, viewers will choose more of them.

10. Current laserdisc penetration in the United States is estimated at about 1%, a level it has stood at for several years (source: Electronic Industries Association, as of January 1992). Paradoxically, sales of laserdiscs have been on the rise in the past year. In 1990 total units sold were estimated at between five and six million. In 1991, this level jumped to between nine and ten million (source: Laserdisc Association).

11. This study appears to suffer from a number of methodological weaknesses. The most serious of these is the fact that the sample of respondents interviewed included only subscribers to the Videoway service.

12. This is not to suggest that digital processing or conversion can provide a perfect replication of reality. Despite their many real advantages, digitized music and pictures are only representations of reality, not the real thing.

13. It is this latter property that makes computers not only remarkably accurate and consistent, but also rigid and uncreative. Even if we never have computers that "think", we should be grateful in the meantime for their remarkable feats of number-crunching, memory work and other productivity enhancing features. The features we're talking about have moved far beyond the bounds of the desktop computer. Where once we used to turn a simple dial to adjust the household thermostat, we can now use a "programmable" thermostat to turn the heat on and off at predetermined times in our absence. And so too with telephones and cameras and a host of other common devices that now contain the equivalent of a little computer processor.

14. Professor Russell Neuman of the Massachusetts Institute of Technology has paid particular attention in his research to digital intelligence in communications — the ability of a digital device to "know" what is going on as it processes information. In an essay prepared for the Aspen Institute, Neuman has argued that the convergence of several once distinct technologies, particularly television and the telephone, will be hastened by a set of nine properties unique to digital signal processing: declining cost; declining distance sensitivity; increasing speed; increasing volume; increasing channel diversity; increasing two-way flow; increasing flexibility; increasing extensibility; and increasing interconnectivity.

15. In a large-screen TV, the display device or picture tube alone represents some three-quarters (75%) of the cost of manufacturing the set.

16. According to data from Market Facts, more than half of all the one million or so colour sets purchased each year from 1987 to 1991 were replacement purchases. Thus, in that five-year period, some two and a half million replacement sets were purchased by Canadians. Almost all the other purchases were for additional sets: in 1991, only 6% of purchases were for first-time colour sets.

17. The FCC timetable for the introduction of HDTV or Advanced Television is as follows:

1993:	announce standards
1996:	licence applications
1999:	licensees complete construction
2004:	full simulcast of NTSC and HDTV signals
2008:	surrender of NTSC allocations by broadcasters.

18. In March of 1988, the CBC broadcast the 14-hour series over its network in the usual NTSC format.

19. In order to keep as much spectrum free as possible, the FCC would like to see the HDTV transmission standard compressed to 6 MHz, the standard bandwidth of an NTSC signal. A digitized but uncompressed studio quality NTSC video signal has to move the binary digits or bits that carry the picture information at a rate of 166 Mb/s, i.e. 166 million bits per second. In contrast, a digitized but uncompressed HDTV signal must process information at a rate anywhere from four to six times faster — 600 Mb/s to as much as 1 Gb/s, i.e. from 600 million to 1 billion bits per second.

20. Not all of the monies expended by broadcasters for conversion to HDTV or other forms of Advanced Television should be considered a poor investment. Even without the standards conversion, broadcasters normally recycle or update NTSC production and post-production facilities every five to seven years anyway. Items like VTRs are replaced even more frequently — about every three to five years.

21. Section 1.1, Objectives, *Draft Revised Memorandum of Understanding between Telefilm and the Government of Canada*, Feb. 14, 1991.

22. We should note that most feature films eventually reach a much larger audience on free TV than in theatres — including most American films. At the same time, the revenue per viewer to the studios from theatrical release is much higher than from network licensing. Part of the logic of supporting theatrical release is to help boost the success of a film title in all subsequent windows, through expenditures on theatrical marketing. It remains to be seen whether this strategy will survive through the 1990s, as in-home entertainment accounts for an increasingly large share of the time and money expended by Canadians.

23. Tapp made these and other comments quoted here when he appeared as part of an industry panel at the 1992 Toronto Festival of Festivals Symposium. Other Symposium participants are quoted elsewhere in the text.

24. R.B. Bennett, "Speech in support of Bill 94, respecting radio broadcasting", 18 May 1932, *Debates*, 3035–3036.

25. NBC v. United States, 319 U.S.192 (1943), 226–227.

26. FCC v. Pacifica Foundation, 438 U.S. 726 (1978).

27. Telecommunications Research and Action Center v. FCC, 801 F.2d. 501 (D.C. Cir 1986).

28. In a 1977 study, Michael Spence and Bruce Owen demonstrated that both advertiser support and viewer fees lead to an under-supply of programs with high value to a small number of viewers. They conclude, however, that this under-supply is larger in the case of advertiser-supported programming than user-pays programming. See "Television Programming, Monopolistic Competition, and Welfare", *Quarterly Journal of Economics* 91 (February 1977): 103–126; quoted in Setzer and Levy, p.7.

29. These remarks were part of a speech delivered by Robert Lantos to a conference organized by the Canadian Film and Television Production Association and held in Ottawa during November 1991.

30. Janisch was commenting on *Canadian Radio-television and Telecommunications Commission v. CTV Television Network Limited*, [1982] 1 SCR 530.

31. Our assessment of the value of cable service is not shared by other observers — including one of Canada's most distinguished cable and broadcast engineers, Israel (Sruki) Switzer, who started in the cable business in 1954. In a private communication with the author (November 8, 1992), here is what he had to say about the value added by cable:

> Cable systems don't charge for reception of broadcast stations. They rent you a superior antenna. [In 1954] you could build your own 70' antenna and get mediocre TV reception, or you could rent our 200' foot antenna and get good reception. TV sets need an antenna of some kind. There is a lingering idea that $5 rabbit-ears are sufficient. They aren't — even in the shadow of the CN Tower. The cable system isn't selling you the TV broadcasts. It charges you the same whether you watch one minute or all-day every day. Its costs are not in the least bit related to whether it carries TV stations or not. It doesn't pay for the broadcasts it receives, it doesn't charge for passing them on to subscribers. The exception (properly) is "distant reception" involving use of microwave, satellite, etc. Most cable systems would now rather not carry TV broadcast stations. Removing them would leave more channels for PAY-TV services of various kinds. Dropping TV broadcast stations would ruin the UHF broadcasters — Global, TVOntario, CITY-TV [...]. Without cable as a "reception equalizer" they'd be dead!

32. "Statement on Federal Communications Commission Cable Television Policies, Recommendations and Initiatives": Subcommittee on Communications, Committee on Commerce, Science and Transportation, U.S. Senate, 17 Nov. 1989, p.8.

33. The quoted remarks were taken from a written transcript of the proceedings supplied by Financial Post Conferences.

34. A product announcement from Brack Electronics of Toronto, distributed in October 1992, indicates that Canadians can now purchase the AT&T VideoPhone — "the first full colour videophone that works over existing phone lines".

35. In 1991 the Department of Communications appointed an industry committee to study this whole question. As of this writing, the Local Networks Convergence Committee (LNCC) had not yet made its report public.

36. See, for example, the historical critique provided in Robert Babe's *Telecommunications in Canada.*

Graphic Design:
→ Hambly & Woolley Inc.

Typesetting and Production Assistance:
→ Kathy Dyer

Cover Photography:
→ Rob Davidson and Associates

Stock Photography:
→ Masterfile
→ Canapress

Printing:
→ Somerset Graphics Co. Ltd.